SUPERCHARGED LIVING

JANE O. PIEROTTI

CREATION HOUSE

SUPERCHARGED LIVING by Jane O. Pierotti
Published by Creation House
A part of Strang Communications Company
600 Rinehart Road
Lake Mary, Florida 32746
www.creationhouse.com

Unless otherwise noted, all Scripture quotations are from the King James Version of the Bible.

Scripture quotations marked AMP are from the Amplified Bible. Old Testament copyright © 1965, 1987 by the Zondervan Corporation. The Amplified New Testament copyright © 1954, 1958, 1987 by the Lockman Foundation. Used by permission.

Scripture quotations marked NIV are from the Holy Bible, New International Version. Copyright © 1973, 1978, 1984, International Bible Society. Used by permission.

Scripture quotations marked NKJV are from the New King James Version of the Bible. Copyright © 1979, 1980, 1982 by Thomas Nelson, Inc., publishers. Used by permission.

Scripture quotations marked NAS are from the New American Standard Bible. Copyright © 1960, 1962, 1963, 1968, 1971, 1972, 1973, 1975, 1977 by the Lockman Foundation. Used by permission.

Scripture quotations marked RSV are from the Revised Standard Version of the Bible. Copyright © 1946, 1952, 1971 by the Division of Christian Education of the National Council of the Churches of Christ in the USA. Used by permission.

Library of Congress Cataloging-in-Publication Data:
Pierotti, Jane O.
  Supercharged living / Jane O. Pierotti.
    p. cm.
  ISBN 0-88419-600-3
  1. Christian women—Religious life. I. Title.
BV4527.P54 1999   99–24531
248.8'49—dc21   CIP

0 1 2 3 4 5 BBG 8 7 6 5 4 3 2
Printed in the United States of America

To Donna Kay and Dino, the first people with whom I first risked removing my mask—and who loved me anyway.

To Joanie, my weathervane, who points me back to the Word and reminds me that I am in Christ when I forget.

I would like to express my appreciation to the many ministries and Christian organizations that have touched my life, including:
- *Joyce Meyer Ministries*
- *John Avanzini Ministries*
- *Kenneth Copeland Ministries*
- *Kenneth Hagin Ministries*
- *Creflo Dollar Ministries*
- *CBN and Pat Robertson Ministries*
- *Jerry Savelle Ministries*
- *Marilyn Hickey Ministries*

…and to my church, New Life Fellowship, and our pastor, Robert E. Crews, who preaches the uncompromised integrity of the Word of God.

CONTENTS

Foreword . . . . *vii*

Introduction . . . . *viii*

1   Outside In or Inside Out? 1

2   Garbage In, Garbage Out 5

3   Garbage In, Garbage Out (the sequel) 9

4   Molten Metal, Plaster Casts 13

      PROGRESS CHECK 17

5   Wrong Moves 19

6   The Tie That Binds 22

7   Magnetic Force 26

8   Microwave Faith 31

9   Keyhole Vision 34

10   False Gods 38

11   What You Say Is What You Get 42

12   What You Say Is What You Get (the sequel) 47

13   The Good News Is the Bad News Is Wrong 50

14   Three Strikes and You're Out 55

15   Breaking Out 62

16   Beyond Slim-Fast 65

17   Better Than Wall Street 69

18   A Backward Kingdom 73

      PROGRESS CHECK 81

19   Less Is More 83

20   Uncle 90

21   Black Belts and Hockey Players 97

22   Through a Glass Darkly 101

23   Hair Shirt, Size Medium 107

24   Promise Made, Promise Kept 113

25   What, Me Worry? 120

26   The Enforcer 126

27   Which Water Are You In? 130

28   Mountains Out of Molehills 135

29   And the Horse You Rode In On 140

30   I Did It My Way 144

31   Feet, Don't Fail Me Now! 148

32   Feet, Don't Fail Me Now! (the sequel) 153

33   Lights, Camera, Action 157

34   Bull's-eye! 161

35   Room Temperature IQ 164

     PROGRESS CHECK 168

36   Ain't No Big Thing 170

37   Too Cute by Half 175

38   Got Ya Last! 181

39   No Place to Hide 187

40   Kiss Me, I'm Irish 193

41   Labeled 198

42   Sharkproof 204

43   Wing Tip Torte 209

44   Why Gallup Is Wrong 213

45   The Great Rip-Off 217

46   Name Tag ID 222

47   Making Yourself Immortal 228

48   Everybody Gets an A 232

49   The Great Enabler 236

50   The Return of the Great Enabler 241

51   Bob Dylan or Ricky Nelson? 245

52   Is It Soup Yet? 250

     Notes 253

FOREWORD

God has a plan for you, and we want to help you fulfill it. That is why the leaders of *SpiritLed Woman* magazine and Creation House are launching a new line of books created to challenge you to grow spiritually and address practical life issues with spiritual insight.

We are excited to present *Supercharged Living* by Jane Pierotti as one of our first offerings. We believe you will find Jane Pierotti's humor and candor refreshing. With disarming wit, Jane gets real with women about overcoming guilt, fear and condemnation.

Filled with self-tests, this book will help you to identify patterns of failure and defeat in your life. Knowing what your problems are is not enough. Jane Pierotti also provides a proven, biblically based road map for change.

We trust you will enjoy the refreshing insights in this book and will be encouraged to be Spirit-led in every area of your life.

—JOY STRANG, PUBLISHER
SPIRITLED WOMAN MAGAZINE

INTRODUCTION

You know her—the voice that says you'll never be thin again. Your thighs should have U.S. Prime stamped on them. Get used to that crepe-paper skin on your arms. Can't you do anything right? You don't fit in anywhere. You're not smart enough.

You know her. She's been talking to you since you were a child. She has told you for years that you're not as pretty as your friends. You're trapped in your current situation. You'll never have a healthy relationship with a man. Your kids will all end up drug addicts and malcontents. You're a bust as a mother anyway. You don't spend enough time with your children. Your house is a wreck. And you might as well get ready for the flu this winter, because you get it every year.

That voice in your head never shuts up. Even when you do something right, the voice says it's wrong—or at least it could have been better. The voice answers every sentence with *Yes, but...* or an *Oh, yeah?* or *But you could have done it better...*

To whom does that voice belong? It's the voice of the High Priestess of Guilt and Condemnation. She set up a campsite in your head when you were a kid, pitched a tent and brought in all her tacky relatives—Fear, Doubt and Unbelief. And she'll control your life if you let her. Why? Because there's a direct link connecting thoughts, words, actions and results. The thoughts you think and the words you say control your actions, and if the High Priestess is in charge, your actions will produce disappointing results. What you think is what you get, and you'll get one failure right after another.

But there is another way. Evict the High Priestess of Guilt and Condemnation and tell her to take a hike. Learn how to break the patterns she has established, how to repair the damage she has done and how to challenge old assumptions, create new ones and develop new, successful patterns.

HOW DO YOU KNOW THIS BOOK IS FOR YOU?

Answer these questions. (No, you don't need a number two pencil. Use your worn down lipstick if you have to. There aren't any wrong answers. Isn't that a relief?)

1. Are there areas of your life with which you are unhappy, such as finances, relationships, work, family and appearance?

    ❏ Yes   ❏ No

2. Have you repeatedly tried to improve these areas, but to no avail?

    ❏ Yes   ❏ No

3. Have you tried so many ways to solve these problems that you're frustrated to the point of hopelessness?

    ❏ Yes   ❏ No

4. Do you look out the window hoping to see Ed McMahon as the one-in-a-million solution?

    ❏ Yes   ❏ No

5. Are you in danger of being crushed under the weight of your self-help books and audiotapes?

    ❏ Yes   ❏ No

6. Do you think that if only you could just change your husband, boyfriend, child, boss, friends or body, then your life could be better?

    ❏ Yes   ❏ No

7. Is your life like a remake of *Beat the Clock,* with never enough time

to do everything that you are supposed to do?

❑ Yes   ❑ No

8. Do you live in constant fear of lack—not enough money, friends, support, time, pantyhose, you name it?

❑ Yes   ❑ No

9. Do you see God as being the Wizard of Oz—maybe He will and maybe He won't, but either way you don't deserve it?

❑ Yes   ❑ No

10. Do you feel you're destined for failure because you were born the wrong gender or into the wrong ethnic group, economic status or family?

❑ Yes   ❑ No

11. Are you sick and tired of being sick and tired?

❑ Yes   ❑ No

12. Do you feel powerless to make your life better?

❑ Yes   ❑ No

SCORING

Two or fewer *yes* answers: You're bulletproof, in denial or on drugs. Get a grip. Go look in the mirror and take the test again.

Three to five *yes* answers: You're worn out. Part of your life is apparently working. Other parts are running on empty. If your life feels like the plate-spinning act at the circus and it's taking every drop of energy to keep the plates from crashing, this book will help even out your life.

Six to twelve *yes* answers: You're broken. Admit it. (There—doesn't that feel better?) Your way isn't working, and there is a way out. You don't have to live in defeat. You've tried to live life under your own power. How about trading in your power for God's power and your ways for His ways?

If you're willing to do a chapter of this book a week, as well as the suggested steps, you can position yourself to change your circumstances on a permanent basis. This book provides truth in time-released capsules. Read on.

1

OUTSIDE IN OR INSIDE OUT?

I just want to be happy." That was the response of a young woman at her graduation when friends asked about her goals. Ten years later she wailed, "I just wanted to be happy. He told me if I married him, he'd make me happy for the rest of my life. This marriage is making me miserable. My life isn't working!"

Happiness is the goal of everyone: "Don't worry; be happy." That's a familiar phrase, and it's a favorite of the High Priestess, the hag that lives in your head and nags at you all day long. She's the mother lode of guilt and condemnation. She loves to tell you that if only you'd get promoted, you'd be happy. If your kids could get straight A's, then you'd be happy. If you lost fifteen pounds or could get a new dress or a better apartment or a newer car, then you'd be happy for sure.

On particularly stressful days, the High Priestess informs you that you'd be happier if only that last pair of on-sale pantyhose you bought didn't fit you so poorly that you had to tie them in a neat knot over your head. Or if your hair looked shinier—not as if someone had combed mayonnaise through it. You know the drill.

But here's the truth: Happiness is *external*. It's lip gloss. It's ice cream. It's a compliment or a bargain or an experience. Happiness is nice and it feels good, but it's not permanent. Happiness is only superficial; it tries to create internal peace by using external fixes. Happiness is like a fickle lover. The fickle lover sticks around as long as he's on the receiving end. But as soon as your usefulness to him runs out, he'll take a powder and go find another sucker, someone who can provide a lifestyle for him to which he'd like to become accustomed.

Fickle lovers are takers, not givers. The constant pursuit of happiness puts the supreme taker, your flesh, in charge of contentment, and the flesh is never satisfied. It will steal time, energy and faith from you until there's nothing left to give. Pursuing happiness is like going after a continual high.

Consider this. I can be *really* happy in ninety-five-degree heat floating around in a swimming pool, sipping a large lemonade from Chick-Fil-A... We're talking major happy! But after the ice melts and my skin puckers, then what?

We're told to pursue happiness. Stretch and achieve—then you'll be happy. Conquer the impossible—then you'll be happy. Develop pride in yourself—then you'll be happy. We've been sold a bill of goods. Happiness isn't the goal; joy is. You mean there's a difference? You bet. Let's start with the basics.

DICTIONARY DEFINITION

Webster's dictionary defines *happy* as "favored by luck or fortune; enjoying or characterized by well-being and contentment; characterized by a dazed, irresponsible state."

Notice two things. First, happy is external, as indicated by the words *luck* and *fortune*; it's outside in. Second, being in a "dazed, irresponsible state" means you've temporarily checked out. You've indulged your flesh. Sure it feels good—you've momentarily run away from reality.

But let's look at Webster's definition of *joy*—"a source or cause of delight; bliss." Get it? Joy is internal, a source causing bliss. What could the source be? Let's look at the truth.

SCRIPTURAL MEANING

The Bible suggests that happiness is external as well, indicating that *happiness* is "to beautify; to be fortunate, secure or successful; to be in safety." *Joy,* as determined in the Bible, is "a state of exceeding gladness, fullness, mirth, glory, rejoicing, delight; the divine influence upon the heart and its reflection of life, including gratitude." Now be honest. Doesn't this sound better than Sara Lee cheesecake?

Notice that the Bible also implies that while happiness is external, joy is internal.

Let's cut to the chase. You'll never make yourself happy outside in. The pursuit of happiness is an endless race, because your flesh has an un-quenchable appetite—it's never content. Yet true gladness and delight are produced inside out, because they stem from joy.

THE REAL TRUTH

Nehemiah 8:10 says that "the joy of the LORD is your strength" (NIV). Take another look at these other verses about joy:

> But let all those that put their trust in thee rejoice. Let them ever shout for joy, because thou defendest them; let them also that love thy name be joyful in thee.
>
> —PSALM 5:11

> In thy presence is fulness of joy; at thy right hand there are pleasures for evermore.
>
> —PSALM 16:11

> We also joy in God through our Lord Jesus Christ, by whom we have now received the atonement.
>
> —ROMANS 5:11

The pull of the world is so strong. I tried so hard to get smart enough, pretty enough, thin enough and powerful enough to feel good about myself. I never could get there. There was a hole inside me I couldn't fill up with jewelry, clothes, praise or possessions. God knows I tried. At any point in time, you could have figured out my net worth—I was living in it, driving it or wearing it.

Why wasn't I happy? Because I was trying to change the condition of my inside by controlling things on my outside. It wasn't until I submitted to Someone with much greater power that things began to change for me—on the inside where it counts. Hey, it was a good deal—I traded in *my* power for *His*.

Submitting my will to the Lord and developing a relationship with Him has filled me with such joy that everything on the outside has become icing on the cake. That decision to submit also gave me a jump-start on shutting up the High Priestess of Guilt and Condemnation.

WHAT TO DO

1. Spend time with the Lord. Get to know His character. Bask in how much He loves you. Set aside at least fifteen minutes a day to spend with Him. Look up the preceding four scriptures. Write them down. Close your eyes and think of Him as you meditate on the power of His Word.

2. Meditate by repeating His words—these promises—over and over until they get down in your heart. The more time you spend with the Lord, the less time you'll have to listen to the voice of the High Priestess. She'll always condemn you and encourage you to seek another external Band-Aid.

If you're operating in the joy of the Lord, your peace is coming from the inside. That frees you up to tackle life with gusto. You'll not be operating out of lack but out of abundance. So which will it be? Will you live inside out filled with joy, or outside in struggling for happiness? Your choice—your move!

2

GARBAGE IN, GARBAGE OUT

The computer made a mistake." We used to say that frequently, with disgust. After all, those answers couldn't *possibly* be right! Ultimately we had to admit the truth. The computer didn't make the mistake—we did.

Then, as now, entering bad data into a computer produces bad output. Faulty assumptions deliver flawed conclusions. Garbage in, garbage out.

Well, guess what? Our minds are exactly like computers. The quality of what we feed our minds produces the quality of the results we achieve. Input controls choice. Choice drives actions. Actions determine results. Garbage in, garbage out.

Your mind is a storehouse of facts, figures, images, beliefs and opinions. The supply in your storehouse has been collected since childhood, added to by parents, siblings, teachers, neighbors, friends and acquaintances. Your storehouse is further supplied by what you read, what you watch and what you experience.

What you have stored in your mind creates the assumptions that drive the decisions you make—and the actions you take.

So how do you know you have the right stuff in the storehouse? How do you know the right data has been entered? If thoughts produce results, how do you know you have the right thoughts to create the right results?

SUPERCHARGED LIVING

Let's Do a Garbage Check

Do you have areas of repeated failure in your life? Are you:

- Always broke, merely existing from paycheck to paycheck?
- Constantly entering into or coming out of a painful relationship?
- Continually worried over your inability to gain weight or frustrated over not being able to lose weight?
- Far too dependent on alcohol, food, cigarettes, work or drugs to give you momentary relief from that gnawing feeling inside?

If the answer is *yes* to any or all of those, then the High Priestess of Guilt and Condemnation has set up a neighborhood in your head and populated it with thugs assigned to enforce wrong assumptions. The High Priestess and her little friends work tirelessly to focus your energy on taking actions, knowing that focusing on actions produces certain defeat. The answer isn't in the actions. (That's the end of the pipeline.) The answer is in the assumptions that create the actions. (That's the beginning of the pipeline.)

I Needed Drano...

I spent most of my life convinced that I was "less than"—not smart enough to really shine. Any minute they would find out what I really was, a fraud. I was convinced that my body needed to be spray-painted black from the waist down; I thought wearing any color but black made me look like an orca. I feverishly worked sixty hours a week, convinced that work gave me my identity. I smoked cigarettes until my office looked as if it were inhabited by a dragon. I was overdrawn at the bank and in debt up to my ears. You get the picture.

I always thought the next promotion would be the answer. The next diet would be the ticket. The next raise would catapult me out of debt. The next cigarette carton would be my last. Yeah, and the tooth fairy pays off in hundred-dollar bills.

My life was filled with promises to myself, different sets of actions to drive different behavior, which always resulted in failure—followed by shame, frustration and a solemn promise to try again. Oh well, God was probably putting me through this to teach me something, to build my character.

6

Here is a news flash: God is a good God. He wants only the best for us. He promises that in His Word. He doesn't put us through turmoil to teach us something. Would you give one of your children cancer to teach them something? God says in His Word that He loves us more than we love even our own children. (See Luke 11:11–13.) His Word is a manual for life. The problem is that most of us were never given the owner's manual. It sure missed my mailbox.

James 1:13 says, "Let no man say when he is tempted, I am tempted of God: for God cannot be tempted with evil, neither tempteth he any man." God doesn't create an obstacle course for us to see how well we perform. Want some proof? Look in James 1:17: "Every good gift and every perfect gift is from above, and cometh down from the Father of lights, with whom is no variableness, neither shadow of turning."

Does that sound like somebody who's putting you through trials to teach you something? No way. The Word clearly states that the good stuff comes from the Father. So where does the bad stuff come from? Simple—check out John 10:10. How do we enter into error? Why do we suffer because of our circumstances? We simply do not do what has been provided for us by our Maker in His owner's manual.

HERE'S THE DEAL

Do not be conformed to this world (this age), [fashioned after and adapted to its external, superficial customs], but be transformed (changed) by the [entire] renewal of your mind [by its new ideals and its new attitude], so that you may prove [for yourselves] what is the good and acceptable and perfect will of God, even the thing which is good and acceptable and perfect [in His sight for you].
—ROMANS 12:2, AMP

That's the bottom line. The patterns of this world are driven and reinforced by you-know-who in your head. The accuser. The nagger. And she'll relentlessly point you to the world for answers. But the Bible clearly states that the world doesn't have the answers. In fact, it tells us not to be conformed to the patterns of this world. Instead, we must be transformed through the renewing of our minds by the Word of God.

We have a choice—we can follow the wisdom of the world or the wisdom of the Word. One produces failure, the other success. Easy choice. I was born at night, but not *last* night...I can figure out which one I want! But wanting it and having it are two different things. I had to want God's wisdom enough to pursue it—and to study it—to find out what was mine.

It wasn't until I stopped resigning myself to a life of consuming carrot sticks and lettuce leaves, a life of working sixty-hour weeks and being overdrawn, that it occurred to me that I had a head full of misinformation—misinformation that was driving me to overeat, overwork and overspend. Only then did I see the necessity of calling in the Roto-Rooter man to flush the garbage out of my head and replace it with truth.

WHAT TO DO

1. Take out a sheet of paper and list your areas of failure.

2. Create two columns. Label the column on the left "The Lie." Label the column on the right "The Truth."

3. Under each failure area, write down all the lies that the High Priestess tells you on a daily basis.

4. Run, don't walk, to a Christian bookstore. Invest some money in a concordance, a rich storehouse of truth that will help you understand the Bible. Look up words in your concordance that pertain to your area of weakness (such as *lack, bondage* and *discipline*) and write down the scriptural truth about that weakness.

5. Select a few scriptures (the truth) to write opposite each lie.

6. Confess the truth daily. Over time, the truth will transform your mind and push out the lies.

I promise, it works. I'm out of debt, with a savings program under way. My weight is stabilized at size ten. The cigarettes are gone. And, oh yes, I work forty—count them—only forty hours a week. You see, I finally figured out how to use the owner's manual. OK, so I'm a late bloomer. How about you?

3

GARBAGE IN, GARBAGE OUT (THE SEQUEL)

Have you learned yet that your thoughts frame your results? If not, keep going.

On the previous pages, we focused on how to root out the garbage that frames our thoughts, develops assumptions and creates results; we also learned how to replace garbage with truth. (I'm not nagging, I'm not your mother and I promise not to bug you about your hair. *But*—did you buy the concordance yet?) Now let's talk about how to create the right pipeline and avoid pouring in more garbage.

WHAT'S YOUR SOURCE?

To what things are you giving your attention? Where do you get information? If you're like most people, information about life comes from TV, magazines, movies, radio and celebrity advice. But wait, do Tom Brokaw and LaToya Jackson really have your best interests at heart? If you believe that, you need to go to the bank, take out some money and buy a big clue.

Most of us give our attention—far too much of it—to the television set, the boob tube that pumps out bad news twenty-four hours a day. The morning local news is a festival of fires, stabbings, drug busts and city council scams. The evening national news is a nightly celebration of Ebola virus outbreaks, terrorism threats, economic deficits and the whining of special-interest groups. It's enough to make you want to lock yourself in a room filled with nothing but Archie and Jughead comic books.

The daily mail arrives, featuring fistfuls of overdue bills and three magazines filled with Cindy Crawford-looking creatures in size four dresses. The High Priestess of Guilt and Condemnation reminds you that you look like the son of Flubber. Your friends at the office are predicting another corporate bloodletting. Your children's babysitter is sick with the flu. And your mother calls, wondering why you haven't written or called her.

WHAT'S REALITY?

Well, like it or not, we all define reality based on those things to which we give our attention. Recent research indicates that the average American watches 6.5 hours of TV a day, a truly horrifying thought. Think what's on the television these days.

Talk shows cram the air, allegedly giving us a slice of life. Here is a sampling of daily talk shows pulled from *USA Today*:

- Jerry Springer: "Gay and Lesbian Weddings"
- Ricki Lake: "Teens Paid for Sex"
- Jenny Jones: "Teen Marries Seventy-Year-Old"
- Sally Jessy Raphael: "Older Women, Younger Men"
- Montel Williams: "Freeloading Sisters"

Are you looking for the barf bag yet? If not, this should do it....

Children watch thousands of hours of television by the time they enter the first grade. By the time these same youngsters become teenagers, they will have witnessed thousands of murders and even more acts of violence.

SO WHAT?

What's wrong with this stuff? We believe it. Faith comes by hearing. Hitler knew it. "Quotes From Thinkers" on the worldwide web credits his minister of "disinformation," Joseph Goebbels, with saying: "If you tell a lie big enough and keep repeating it, people will eventually come to believe it." At the other end of the spectrum, the Bible says, "Faith comes from hearing" (Rom. 10:17, NIV).

If you define happiness based on input from friends, coworkers and the entertainment industry, you'll live your entire life feeling trapped and hopeless. I know. I took every test in *Cosmopolitan* for a decade. I flunked every one. I never could get the hang of decorating rooms that looked like the ones in *Better Homes and Gardens*, dinners that tasted as if Martha Stewart prepared them or closets that didn't look like a habitat for small animals.

My friends told me things would never change. Television told me things would never change. And my own experience, aided and abetted by the High Priestess, cemented the pattern. But when I got sick and tired of being sick and tired, I was ready to do anything to break the mold.

WHAT TO DO

1. *Turn off the TV.* Ask yourself, "Is what I'm watching building me up spiritually, mentally, emotionally or physically?" If not, pull the plug.

2. *Read.* Thousands of new books are published every year, books on every conceivable subject. In our age of ever-increasing knowledge, performance experts tell us that if we're not deliberately choosing to read two books a week, we're deliberately choosing to fall behind.

3. *Listen.* Most of us spend more time in the car than we'd like. Why not turn your car into a traveling library? Audiotapes are available everywhere, on every subject. For several hours a day, you can put lots of good stuff into your head if you're willing to turn off the traffic report. Isn't it worth it?

4. *Make a list.* Write down the names of the four people with whom you spend the greatest amount of time. Then ask yourself this question: "Do these people support me, nurture me and encourage my creativity and ideas?" If the answer is *no,* get rid of those people. OK, so they're your family. You can't blow *them* away. But if the four people with whom you spend the most time drain you, you *must* augment your list with other people. It's a matter of life or death—it's that important.

With whom you spend your time frames your world and influences your decision-making capability. If you're surrounded by the Bad News

Bears, give yourself a break and make yourself some new friends. More importantly, forge a relationship with the One who loves you best. The Lord Jesus Christ paid a price for you. He laid down His life so you could live. He paid the price for your bondage so you could be free from it. Spend time in His presence. Find out who He is through His Word.

"In thy presence is fulness of joy; at thy right hand there are pleasures for evermore" (Ps. 16:11). Who needs TV when you can have this?

4

MOLTEN METAL, PLASTER CASTS

L ook at that hamster go! Round and round that wheel, getting no-where. I remember as a kid looking at one of those hamsters on the treadmill and thinking, *Doesn't he get bored with this game?*

Little did I know my life would turn out like that treadmill. Do you feel the same? It's not that you're not trying. You've tried plenty—and failed plenty. Maybe next time.

Do you know my definition of insanity? It's doing the same thing over and over and over again, hoping for a different result. Continuous failure in your life means you're locked into a failure pattern that will continue to replicate itself unless you take drastic steps to change. Half the time we're stuck in patterns and don't even know it. Or we're in denial about the need to break them.

Webster's definitions of *pattern* include:

- A form or model proposed for imitation.
- Something designed or used as a model for making things.
- A model for making a mold into which molten metal is poured to form a casting.
- The flight path prescribed for an airplane coming in for a landing.
- A prescribed route to be followed by a pass receiver in football.

Think about it. "A model proposed for imitation" means that what you're getting will be repeated again and again and again. If it's not what you want, you're stuck in a pattern. Failure will continue to dog you.

But it doesn't have to be that way. Patterns that continually deliver a successful result can be established. But you have to screw up enough courage to break the mold and start over (and silence the voice of condemnation in your head).

A Bad Mold

I was convinced for years that I couldn't perform well in groups. The High Priestess of Guilt and Condemnation had set up a reign of terror in my mind to focus my attention entirely on what people might think of me. If I couldn't open my mouth and sound like Einstein (which she informed me I never would), I'd better not talk at all. After all, I was only marginally intelligent and would open myself up to ridicule. I used to sit in meetings in a cold sweat, knowing that at some time I had to open my mouth and make a contribution but fearful that I wouldn't say the right thing or that I wouldn't sound smart enough. When I did communicate, the High Priestess would begin talking the minute my mouth closed, saying things like, "Boy, that was really stupid! Now they know you're an idiot."

Paradoxically, I knew I could knock 'em dead whenever I delivered a prepared speech in front of an audience. That was something I was good at, and I was willing to practice. I had confidence in that role but not in speaking up as part of a group.

Have you ever listened to some of the celebrities being interviewed by Jay Leno on *The Tonight Show* and thought they sounded as if their IQs were one point above that of a houseplant? Did you then wonder how they could possibly sound so good on film? Does it ever make you feel any better that they bomb on *The David Letterman Show?* It never did for me, either.

A Bad Result

Well, look what I was doing to myself. Look at the third definition under Webster's description of *pattern,* the one about making a mold and pouring molten metal into it. The mold is the assumption through which you view the circumstance. The mold in my head (my assumption) about my participation in meetings was one of not measuring up. The molten metal that I poured into my mold was my effort. In other words, my effort to perform in meetings was being poured into a mold of failure. As a result, guess what my casting was. You've got it—failure. Even though I held a senior position in a major corporation, meetings were torture for me.

Can you see how my effort wasn't the problem? It was the assumption driving the effort that was flawed.

Think of it this way. An airplane coming in for a landing follows a pre-selected flight path. The flight plan is filed before the plane ever takes off from its origination point. A travel blueprint from Cincinnati (the origination point) to New Orleans (the destination point) will not vary unless an emergency arises. You don't take off in Cincinnati and end up in St. Louis. If the flight plan says New Orleans, that's where you're going.

What I didn't know was that I wanted to go to St. Louis but filed a flight plan for New Orleans every time. My flight plans were created by wrong assumptions, and they established failure patterns for me. And I kept repeating them. Time and time again my results were unsuccessful. I finally realized it wasn't my participation that fell short—it was how I viewed my participation. Fortunately, the mold that created my casting has been crushed. I broke the sucker and started again.

How? When I stopped trying to control my world and submitted to the Lord Jesus, asking Him into my life, my world changed. After a lifetime of shopping around for better advice, I acknowledged that all the advice I had obtained wasn't working. My knowledge had created defective molds in my head, and misfiled flight plans were making it impossible for me to arrive at my destination. The High Priestess may have been having a big time with all of it, but I sure wasn't. I had to be willing to break the mold, walk away from what I knew and reach for what I didn't. What was it?

BREAKING THE MOLD

I turned away from focusing on who I was and riveted my attention on *whose* I was. After all, I'm a child of the King. I'm His blood-bought child. I found in His Word what He thinks of me, *not* what the High Priestess of Guilt and Condemnation thinks of me (Eph. 2:4, 6).

I joined a church that teaches the reality of Jesus Christ and the power of the Holy Spirit. Oh yes, that was another broken mold. This church is not the one I knew from my childhood, one of those nice, formal churches where everybody looked nice but nobody was ever healed or set free from drugs and where God's power was not demonstrated. (Why would I want to hang out at a church like that anyhow?)

I made God the top priority in my life. Part of that process meant dedicating my work to Him. When my focus became dedicating my work to His glory, suddenly it didn't matter what "they" thought—only what He thought was important. It was about that time, by the way, that I suddenly became creative and bold, and yes, began to make tremendous contributions in meetings. (Amazing how that works.) I made a commitment to get up at six o'clock in the morning to study the Word and pray for an hour before my day gets going. And if you think this is easy, you're nuts. You're talking to the original night owl. But since I'm operating on a direct power plug to God, I have to plug into Him daily to recharge my faith.

For months, I gritted my teeth and spit bullets as I clawed out of bed. Hey, come to think of it, that's another mold I've smashed. I've been at it for three years now. Not only does plugging into God on a daily basis yield results, but it makes my days go so much better.

THE PUNCH LINE

What has all this produced? A series of success patterns that replicate themselves. Today I walk into meetings expecting to make contributions, expecting to be a blessing to the people who are there, expecting to enjoy the process. And I do. But that's just part of it.

Walking away from the Church of the Frozen Chosen and hooking up with a pastor who teaches the uncompromised truth—which results in seeing the demonstration of the power of the Holy Spirit—has set up a whole series of new molds in my head, ones that say He's God and I'm not. Ones that say He promises me abundance and if He says it, He'll do it (Mark 11:22–25). I now pour my efforts into new molds that work.

Finding the right church also placed me among believers who nurture me, demonstrate the power of God working in their lives and pray for me. The end result is so good you have to wonder why I didn't get to it sooner.

And oh yes, that extra hour of prayer and study in the morning? It's just like my American Express card...I don't leave home without it.

Progress Check

1. Are you examining the assumptions upon which you've based your life?

   _____

   _____

2. Are you ready to do what it takes to put a muzzle on the High Priestess and her gofers?

   _____

   _____

3. Have you honed in on some failure patterns that you'd like to change?

   _____

   _____

4. Are you willing to change your behavior to get better results?

   _____

   _____

5. Are you willing to change your belief system to receive victory?

   _____

   _____

6. Are you willing to step out of your comfort zone and experience the uncomfortable in order to improve?

   _____

   _____

7. Have you begun to question where you get your information?

   _____

   _____

8. Are you still hanging on by your fingernails trying to control your circumstances, or are you more flexible about submitting to the One who can make a difference?

_____

_____

_____

_____

9. Are you willing to set aside some time to work on changing your life?

_____

_____

_____

_____

10. Are you willing to let go of the old order to embrace the new?

_____

_____

_____

_____

5

WRONG MOVES

I t was my worst nightmare. It's bad enough to look stupid in front of one other person, but embarrassment before a whole roomful? That's heavy. That's when you want to go look for a pistol.

I was having lunch with a potential client. Things were going unusually well as I was describing to him how he could get his message across to his employees. I must have been feeling good that day, because I had on a white suit—something I seldom wear. White suits are meant only for picket fences and stick people.

As I looked across the restaurant, I noticed a waiter coming toward me with a tray filled with food. Have you ever known what's going to happen before it does? Well, this was one of those times. As I saw the waiter coming at me, another diner seated in the waiter's path abruptly stood and pushed back his chair.

SLO-MO

Scenes like this frequently unfold in slow motion. I opened my mouth to say something, but nothing came out. Blindsided, the waiter tripped. The tray he was carrying shot through the air. Flying directly toward me was one of the dishes on the tray.

It was then that I made the mistake—I leaned forward instead of backward.

19

As I did, the item coming at me flip-flopped and landed upside down on my head. It was a bowl of clam chowder. It fit just about perfectly, like a helmet. (I know—you want to know whether it was white or red clam chowder. It was white.)

It's pretty tough to look cool when you're wearing a bowl of clam chowder on your head, surrounded by waiters picking pieces of potato off your shoulders. (Naturally, the entire restaurant burst into laughter.) It's also virtually impossible to finish a business lunch with white gook in your hair. So I beat feet to the closest beauty shop. By the way, don't think I was having an esteem-building moment as I rode down in the elevator with several other people, all of whom were looking at my head and inching away from me.

WHY ME?

Maybe some of you have been the butt of jokes or have unintentionally done things that caused you embarrassment. That's when the High Priestess of Guilt and Condemnation cranks into high gear, reminding you that you're a fool and everyone thinks you're a dork.

But wrong moves aren't the end of the world. I've made plenty of them. When the clam caper happened to me, I didn't know the Lord. I had no clue how much He loves me, so for weeks I was eaten up with shame over the incident. How did I try to deal with the problem? I made another wrong move—one I had been practicing for years. I tried to eat the pain away and then compulsively exercise and starve myself to get rid of the calories. It didn't decrease my discomfort; it only increased the width of my backside.

But now—thanks to a real relationship with the Lord and friends at church who nourish me—I have a new picture of who I am. And *whose* I am. When embarrassing things happen now, I can just shrug them off. Being able to do that is one of the most liberating realities of my life. Now, rather than eating, I make a better move and turn to the real source of comfort, the Lord.

If you're beating yourself up over wrong moves, wrong decisions, wrong relationships, wrong business partnerships, wrong responses to problems, stop and get a grip. Tell the High Priestess to zip it! Then turn to the One who can provide relief and ask Him to help you make different decisions, today and in the future. Then turn loose of the past and leave it there.

WHAT TO DO

1. Take out your trusty paper and pencil (I know I sound like a broken record, but writing it down makes an enormous difference). Write down the major decisions you've blown.

2. Make another list of your responses to pain and embarrassment. Ask yourself whether those responses brought relief or created more problems.

3. Hold your paper up to the Lord and say, "Father, I repent for bad decisions and wrong moves and bad responses. I ask for Your forgiveness. I receive Your forgiveness, and I forgive myself."

4. Wad your paper into a ball, toss it against the wall and say, "I cast the care of all of these problems and responses onto You, for Your Word says to 'cast all your anxiety upon Him because He cares for you'" (1 Pet. 5:7, NIV).

5. Turn loose of all of it and don't let the High Priestess harass you. God says in His Word that once you repent, He throws your transgressions into the sea of forgetfulness (Col. 2:8–14; Isa. 38:17). He's forgotten it. Why should you remember it?

6. Ask Him to show you different responses to handling mistakes. Practice them. Remember—your goal is progress, not perfection.

7. Look up the following scriptures and meditate on them: Psalm 147:3; Isaiah 61:3; Jeremiah 31:13.

6

THE TIE THAT BINDS

Don't get mad; just get even. It's a cute line. It makes good copy. It trips easily off the tongue. When we read a story in a newspaper or magazine about someone who got theirs, our reflex response is, "Yes!!! It's what they deserved!"

Getting revenge may be emotionally pleasurable, but it destroys the soul.

"But you don't know what he did to me!" my friend wailed. "I'll never forgive him for this as long as I live." And she never did. She lost her job, her children, her self-respect and her health by nursing that grudge. It ate her up from the inside out. Besides losing her family and possessions, she ended up with a horrendous case of arthritis—and you'll never convince me that bitterness didn't bring on that physiological condition.

Several people encouraged her to let go of her bitterness and to forgive and forget. "Oh no," she said. "I'll never forgive, and I'll never forget." She didn't, and she paid the price for it.

The High Priestess loves unforgiveness. It's one of her favorites. As long as she can keep you focused on real or perceived offenses by other people, she can keep tied up in granny knots. And make no mistake— anger over an injustice (real or imagined) by another person can feel good because it produces an emotional high. Our adrenaline pumps. Our color deepens. We feel morally justified in doing everything from gossiping to setting the offender's hair on fire.

The mother of another friend of mine (and a grandmother of four) was so enraged over her daughter's divorce that she actually slashed the tires on the car of her soon-to-be ex-son-in-law. This is a woman who is a pillar of the community. *Please.*

GOTCHA!

It's a basic human instinct to want to be loved, to be accepted, to be valued by other human beings. People choose various strategies for achieving all that, but the drive is the same. When people don't accept us, we're wounded. We feel our basic value has been challenged. We want to strike back. But think about it—does striking back change the other person's opinion? Does it change their behavior? No. If anything, it justifies their original offense against you. They now feel vindicated.

Are you nursing a grudge? Perhaps against your parents, who didn't treat you right? Or your siblings, who may have violently abused you? Or your ex-husband or ex-boyfriend? Or current or ex-employer? If so, you're not alone. All you have to do is listen to other people's conversations to determine that. I sat in a restaurant recently and listened to two women at the next table laughingly describe how they had retaliated against some guy who had dumped one of them. These were middle-aged women. Nice snapshot of adult behavior, isn't it?

Well, here's the real scoop: Unforgiveness prohibits the power of God from working in your life. Want some proof? Look at Mark 11:25.

Those of you who are familiar with the Bible probably groove on Mark 11:23–24, which says that if we believe and don't doubt when we pray, we can have what we pray for. Sounds pretty good so far. Just one little problem—check out verse 25. It says that if we hold an offense against anyone, all bets are off. (My translation, not the King James.) Scripture does say, though, that if we hold an offense against anyone, it stops our prayers.

ROADBLOCKS

Unforgiveness not only prevents the Father from answering your prayers, but it also keeps you in bondage. The offender keeps right on truckin' while you eat yourself up on the inside.

I used to be a walking litany of offenses. I could chronicle every offense by every person who had ever done me wrong. I blamed my parents for not being what I wanted them to be, my coworkers and superiors for not treating me right and my friends for not being as supportive as I wanted them to be. And that was just a partial list. I could nurse a grudge for years. Oh sure—I never let people see it on the outside, but inside I was seething. It was also one of the principal causes of my eating disorder. I turned to food to soothe the anger. Food, of course, never worked.

When I became a member of my current church and began to study God's Word on a regular basis, His Word revealed to me the reasons I'm to turn offenses loose. Jesus' way is to turn the other cheek. I know that doesn't make any sense in the natural realm, but it does in the spiritual. By refusing to take offense and by making a conscious decision to forgive the person or persons who have wronged you, you free up God's ability to work in your life—and in theirs! Hey, this isn't just talk—I've learned it the hard way.

OUCH!

Let me give you a concrete example. The girl who had prayed for me for years and had prayed me into God's kingdom fell into deception and tried to destroy my business. This was another *Christian!* I was devastated. I thought she was my best friend, and yet, being deceived by greed, she tried to destroy me (and almost did).

You know what I wanted to do? Yanking her hair and leaving her bald-headed would have been my opening move. I also hoped that she'd wake up instantly fat, covered with cellulite and with a face full of zits.

Fortunately, one of my mature sisters in Christ saved me from myself. She told me I'd have to repent and ask God to forgive me for taking offense, and then I'd have to forgive my friend and begin to pray for her.

You've got an accurate picture of how much I wanted to do that, don't you? About as much as I wanted to eat dirt. But I decided to follow the advice, because I knew it was valid.

I said, "OK, God, I repent for taking offense, and I ask for You to forgive me. I receive Your forgiveness, and I forgive myself. And now, Lord, with *Your* forgiveness, I forgive her. And with *Your* love, I love her. And with *Your* power, I will pray for her. None of this is on my own steam because, God, You know what I want to do to her. But with Your love,

Your forgiveness and Your strength, I will follow Your Word." (Where is that bullet to bite on?)

The High Priestess of Guilt and Condemnation (true to her name) assaulted me, at least five to six dozen times a day, telling me that I hadn't forgiven my friend and that I had every right to be angry. But every time I had to say, "No, I've repented and been forgiven. I've forgiven this person, and with God's love, I love her." And then I'd pray for her.

Was it easy? Of course not. Did I want to do it? As much as I wanted to swim the English Channel. Sometimes I'd have to repeat those phrases seventy times a day. But after about six months, as the High Priestess assaulted me one day with how I hadn't forgiven my friend, I responded with, "That's wrong. I've forgiven her, and with God's love, I love her." I realized astoundingly that it was true. Being obedient to God's Word had brought about the miraculous. I actually felt no animosity toward her. And in the meantime, God had restored my business and brought back every dollar that I'd lost and then some. You see, He's faithful to perform His Word (Jer. 1:12).

WHAT TO DO

Here's the deal. If you want to break free of the tie that binds, here's your prescription:

1. Ask God to reveal to you anyone against whom you are holding an offense.

2. Repent for taking offense and ask for His forgiveness. Then receive His forgiveness and forgive yourself.

3. Confess that with His forgiveness, you forgive the offender or offenders. Confess that with His love, you love them and pray for them. (That's the tough part.)

4. Confess these phrases every day and pray for the person or persons every day. Then watch God show Himself.

Walking in unforgiveness or forgiveness is a choice. One works in your favor; the other destroys. But consider this—forgiveness is a gift you give yourself.

7

MAGNETIC FORCE

Circumstances don't happen to us randomly. We bring them about by what we believe and what we say.

What are you afraid of? Are you afraid of going out at night because of the increasing crime rates? Are you afraid to take a walk for fear of dogs? Are you afraid that your money won't last until the end of the month? Are you fearful of not being able to take care of yourself in your older years? Are you afraid of the aging process—and that you'll look less desirable as you age? Are you afraid of what might happen—or might not happen—to your children? Are you afraid of losing your spouse or someone else who is close to you? Are you afraid of trying new things, starting a new career, leaving your current job...all because of fear of failure?

More importantly, do you express these fears frequently? If you do, I can guarantee you something: Your fear will attract what you don't want just like a magnet.

I saw a newspaper story recently that described the kidnapping and murder of a young girl. After her body had been found, some of her friends were interviewed on TV. Several of them reported that the kidnapped girl had talked repeatedly about what she feared the most—being kidnapped. Ironic that it happened that way? No; her fear drew the kidnapping to her like a magnet.

If you're continually fearful, the High Priestess of Guilt and Condemnation has set up a fortress in your head. She's constantly bombarding you with images and words that create terrifying scenarios. She has hampered your decision-making ability and your belief system by forcing all your decisions and actions through a series of thoughts such as *What if...? I'd better not, because...I'd better watch out...remember what was on TV last night.*

The High Priestess will also tell you that you have to live with fear—"You know, it's a dangerous world out there." Or she'll indulge you by saying, "Oh, you pitiful little thing! You've suffered so much, you can't help but be afraid."

BUMP IT

Hogwash! God Himself said "fear not" more than sixty times in the Bible. He wouldn't have given us that command if He hadn't also given us the power to obey it. But how can we obey it?

Let me introduce you to another force in life—faith.

Faith is stronger than fear. And just as fear draws to you what you *don't* want, faith draws to you what you *do* want—if you're willing to base what you want on the Word of God and believe God to fulfill His promise.

Second Peter 1:3–4 tells us, "According as his divine power hath given unto us all things that pertain unto life and godliness, through the knowledge of him that hath called us to glory and virtue: Whereby are given unto us exceeding great and precious promises: that by these ye might be partakers of the divine nature, having escaped the corruption that is in the world through lust." He has given us all things that pertain to life and godliness! Does a car pertain to life? You bet. How about a decent income? Of course. How about plenty left over to take care of your family, your friends and emergencies? Does all of this pertain to life? It sure does.

So why are so many people operating without it? Most people don't even know that God has promised it to them already. Nor do they know how to appropriate those promises for themselves.

YOU HAVE A CHOICE

The decision to operate in fear or in faith is one that no one but you can make. And make no mistake, you're operating in one or the other. Or if you're as I was, you think you're parked in the middle, saying things like, "That won't happen to me; I'll just push that thought out of my mind." "I'll just make a quality decision to go in the morning instead of at night because...well, just because." Guess what? You may think you're parked in the middle, but you're really operating out of fear.

VELCRO WOMAN

Yep, that was me. Everything I feared the most and talked about incessantly happened to me. All the bad things I didn't want were stuck to me like Velcro. I believed I'd be on a diet my whole life, and I was. I always thought somebody was mad at me, and they usually were. I feared never being able to get ahead financially, and that's what happened. I was terrified that my stepchildren wouldn't like me, and they didn't. I was even anxious about split ends. You've got it—my hair resembled a Brillo pad.

Every time that I got what I was afraid of, it reinforced my fear. I spoke about it more often. I concentrated more on it, and I got more of what I didn't want.

WHAT YOU THINK ON GROWS

What you give your attention to, focus on, believe in your heart and say with your mouth delivers the results you experience—whether good or bad. I let the High Priestess con me into confessing the worst, and I usually got it. It never occurred to me that I could put somebody else in charge of my thought life.

When I became tired of living with my stomach knotted up in a wad, I realized that nothing would change until I changed. Since I had at that time just given my life to Jesus Christ, I thought I'd find out what He had to offer. I found out through Him that God makes available everything I could ever possibly need—every conceivable blessing through the promises in His Word. And if I would believe them, I would then activate the law of the Spirit of life, and those promises would manifest in my life (Rom. 8:2). But I had to change my schedule to go find out about Him, hear His promises and study His Word.

THE BAD GUY IS REAL

The elitists laugh, and the intellectuals scoff (and to be fair, so did I). But the simple fact is that the opposite of God's law of the Spirit of life is the law of sin and death perpetrated by Satan. Yeah, he's real all right. He's mentioned many times in God's Word, and he comes to kill, steal and destroy (John 10:10). While God's promises make available everything we could possibly ever need, the devil challenges those promises with fear. He brings us contrary circumstances to convince us God's promises can't ever come to pass. He and his hand puppet, the High Priestess, tell us lies.

So whom will you choose to believe? The apostle Paul writes in Romans 10:17 that faith comes by hearing and hearing by the Word of God. In the same way, fear comes by hearing and entertaining the threats of the devil—threats and accusations about your past, your present and your future.

WHAT TO DO

1. Read Hebrews 11. Hebrews 11:1 says, "Faith is the substance of things hoped for." As you meditate on that, think of how fear is the substance of things not hoped for or desired. Consider that faith reaches into the realm of the spirit and brings about the promises of God. On the other hand, fear reaches into the unseen realm and brings about the reality of the threats and taunts of the High Priestess.

2. In Hebrews 2:14–15 study how Jesus became flesh and blood: "That through death he might destroy him that had the power of death, that is, the devil; and deliver them who through fear of death were all their lifetime subject to bondage." There you have it—fear is bondage.

3. Learn about God's provisions for you. First John 4:18 says, "There is no fear in love; but perfect love casteth out fear." God's love is perfect love. He loves us as no man can. He looks through our faults and sees us as His perfected work. As we learn to develop a picture of that love, we know how important we are to Him. And when we know our importance to the Creator of the universe, we gradually can cut fear out of our lives just as this scripture promises.

Oh, by the way—tell the High Priestess to butt out. When you feel fear rising in you, say aloud, "No! God did not give me a spirit of fear, but of power and of love and of a sound mind." (See 2 Timothy1:7.) Say, "God loves me. And when God is for me, who can be against me?" (See Romans 8:31.)

If you're willing to follow these steps and hook up with a Word-teaching church that believes God heals, delivers and causes us to prosper today—it will change your life. Millions of people are living a victorious life. Why not you?

8

MICROWAVE FAITH

dd water and mix. Reheat and serve. One size fits all. We live in a quick-fix world, a world of fast food, drive-through banking transactions, eight-second sound bites and instant gratification.

So what? So we expect quick solutions to difficult problems. Instant resolution to foreign policy disputes. Overnight legislation to rectify wrongs. Mail-order answers to lifelong hurts. We have everything from instant potatoes to instant gravy, from fat pills to instant management answers.

There's even a drive-through funeral home in Detroit that stays open past midnight (for the bereaved but busy). You just drive in, sign a condolence card, pass the viewing window for a moment of silence and exit into traffic. Total elapsed time: thirty seconds. The deceased is displayed in a casket tilted at a forty-five-degree angle toward the viewing window. Two bodies can be displayed at the same time. Crass? Definitely. Convenient? Of course. Successful? They're in the process of franchising.

I WANT IT NOW!

Because of our fixation with the quick fix, most of us think that every problem in our lives can be resolved if we can just find the right product, the right resource or the right Band-Aid. But think about it...most of us have problems that have developed over decades. We have years of practice in doing the wrong thing. In every case, our problems were caused by ignorance, rebellion or deception. In every case, our problems were the result of the choices and decisions we made. In other words, those choices are a part of our behavior pattern. Why then would we think that a lick-'n'-stick solution would fix years of bum decisions?

Most of us don't like to admit it, but our predicaments are caused by the choices *we* make—no one else.

TRUTH SERUM

OK, I know I'm stepping on somebody's toes. You think the circumstances you find yourself in are because of someone else or maybe lots of someone elses. That may seem true. Not everybody treats us fairly or does us right. Often others can place us in unwanted positions.

But the choice of how to respond to those circumstances is yours. And the decision to stay in those circumstances is yours alone. If you're like me, the truth of that statement is a difficult bullet to bite.

For years, I blamed my parents, my ex-husband, my coworkers and the Ides of March for my poor self-image. The High Priestess carried on a constant dialogue in my head about those who had wronged me, through both real and imagined slights. She convinced me that overindulging in food like a Speed Queen garbage disposal and buying out department stores would make me feel better about myself. After all, I deserved it.

I ended up with a closet filled with clothes ranging from size six to size fourteen, and enough earrings and accessories to outfit a small Third World nation. Did any of it make me feel any better? Nope, or if so, only for a day or two.

After trying everything else on earth to ease the gnawing inside, I tried God. Of course, I went whining to Him, expecting Him to snap His fingers and fix it all for me. But I found out He's not an add-water-and-mix God.

Oh yes, He does perform miracles. Sometimes out of His great mercy you get answers immediately. (He healed me instantly from a lifelong struggle with hay fever, allergies and chronic sinus problems and headaches.) But I found out that many of my problems were behaviorally based, bad choices made over and over and over again. Unless I exchanged the falsehoods in my head for truth, I'd still be making the wrong decisions. And without truth, I'd need God to stand around every day to give me a miracle.

PUMP IT UP!

I found out that each of us is given the same measure of faith by God, but the development of that faith is our job (Rom. 12:3). It's not a microwave project. In fact, faith is like building up a muscle. You don't start on day one of weight training and expect to bench-press two hundred fifty pounds. It takes a while to build up those muscles in order to accomplish the feat.

So it is with faith. Faith is the muscle that moves mountains, delivers captives, heals bodies and solves problems. But we have to work at it. We have to take the same measure God gave to each of us and build on it. By the way, don't think I wasn't put out with the realization that God wasn't going to show up on my doorstep like a glorified butler with the answers to all my problems. (After all, I thought I had perfected the art of whining.) He did better than just show up; He showed me in His Word how to permanently unravel my problems so that they stay fixed.

<u>WHAT TO DO</u>

1. Romans 10:17 tells us that faith comes by hearing, so get out of that bed Sunday morning and go to a church where the Word is taught. If yours doesn't teach the power of the Word, find one that does. You'll never exercise that faith muscle unless you hear the Word taught.

2. Stop blaming others—and yourself—for your current circumstances. Make a quality decision to forgive those in your life who have hurt you. I know how tough that is. And forgive yourself too, which is sometimes even tougher. Wipe the slate clean and start over. Declare that this day is a new day. Proclaim this: "My future will not duplicate my past!"

3. Find one thing to do each day that reinforces your new behavior—no matter how tiny that thing is. Turn down one cookie. Study one more scripture. Repeat one less rumor. Say *no* just for today to a trip to the mall. These actions also build muscles.

The wonderful thing about life is that it's never over until it's over. It doesn't matter how many times you've failed; you don't have to fail anymore. The decision not to fail is up to you. Work the tools, and they'll work for you.

33

9

KEYHOLE VISION

Doors don't have see-through keyholes in them anymore. They come equipped with double and triple locks, deadbolts and chains. But when you were a kid, did you ever sneak up and look through a keyhole into the room beyond to find out what was going on? If you did, you remember that your vision was limited. You could see just a little bit of the room and what was inside.

I can remember as a child sneaking up the stairs to look in the keyhole of my parents' bedroom on Christmas Eve. I knew they were wrapping packages for me. The thing I wanted most was a pair of roller skates. As I peered through the keyhole, I could see my parents wrapping something. But it wasn't roller skates. Boy! Was I disappointed!

Yet Christmas morning, under the tree were my roller skates along with a couple of other special gifts. The roller skates were in my parents' bedroom all along. I just couldn't see them because of my limited view through that keyhole.

LIMITED SCOPE

How many of us view the world the same way? We have keyhole vision of our career opportunities, relationships, financial prosperity, fitness and health. How do our keyholes get constructed? By what we learned at

34

home, by our experiences, by the best-intentioned advice of friends, acquaintances and coworkers. Advice and experience can be wrapped up into one phrase—the traditions of man.

Of course, the High Priestess in your head is the commander general of the traditions of man. She is the Green Beret of rules. She constantly tells you, "That's the best you can do. Don't get your hopes up. That's not for you. You'll never be able to attain that." And anything that goes beyond the traditions of your upbringing, your church or your culture is automatically out of bounds.

Today schools are filled with students struggling to achieve something beyond what their parents accomplished. The workforce is teeming with people clawing to get to the next rung on the ladder, thinking it might be their last. Church pews are filled with people who gobble up crumbs of religion without having any idea what a relationship with the Creator of the universe is all about. Keyholes—looking through keyholes. What confines us to viewing life through them? Fear. Pride. Snobbishness. Thinking we have all the answers. The discomfort of stepping out of our comfort zones. All of it keeps us from living in abundance.

ABUNDANT LIFE

Let's see what God has to say about abundance. In Matthew 6:33, He says, "But seek ye first the kingdom of God, and his righteousness; and all these things shall be added unto you." All things? What things? How much?

Abundance means different things to different people. I've been told that some stars earn as much as $40 million in just one year—and some producers are worth more than $200 million. It's commonly known that the highest-paid executives can earn from $20 to $30 million annually.

Do those numbers make you nervous? Why? Is it because the stars and executives aren't really worth what they earn? Or is it because you think they're not worth it because you don't have it?

If you answered *yes* to either one or both of those questions (come on . . . be honest), you're looking through a keyhole instead of a picture window.

Webster defines *abundance* as "an ample quantity, profusion, affluence, wealth." What does God say about abundance?

Second Corinthians 9:8 says, "And God is able to make all grace (every favor and earthly blessing) come to you in abundance, so that you may always and under all circumstances and whatever the need, be self-sufficient [possessing enough to require no aid or support and furnished in abundance for every good work and charitable donation]" (AMP). See— He's a big God. He's got lots of everything. So why don't we have it? We don't think we deserve it, we never could picture ourselves with it or no one in our families had it. You're right. We're looking through a keyhole. We don't see ourselves as wealthy, because our experience clouds our picture.

Now, before you think the High Priestess has shorted out my circuit board, let me give you some examples of keyhole philosophies:

- "I've got to save some for a rainy day."
- "We live on a fixed income."
- "Wanting too much is selfish."
- "Be satisfied with what you've got."
- "Eat every bite on that plate. Don't forget the starving kids in Armenia (or China or whatever country your parents used)."
- "I'll shop around for a better deal. I never buy anything that's not on sale."

Do these sound like 2 Corinthians 9:8? No way. So how do you get through the keyhole?

WHAT TO DO

1. Dump the traditions of man (Mark 7:13). If man and his traditions knew everything, there'd be no disease, poverty or addiction.

2. Look up Acts 16:31. You thought *saved* meant spiritually, right? It does, but it means much, much more.

3. Look up *save* in your concordance. The word is *sozo*. Now take a look at all it means. It means "to save, deliver, protect, heal, preserve, do well, be made whole." It's the whole ball of wax!

4. Search out the scriptures that deal with health, prosperity, freedom from bondage—all the things you desire. You can find the words in your concordance. Then look up the scriptures. Write them down on

cards and carry them with you. (My purse is always bulging with cards that I pull out and look at when I have a few minutes.)

5.   Speak the Word instead of your circumstances. The Word of God has the power to bring about a change in your circumstances.

You may think I've gone around the bend—but I can tell you, this stuff works. Speaking the Word of God over my circumstances has delivered me from addiction, brought me out of debt, healed my family and guided my career. It's replaced my keyhole vision with a panoramic view of God's best for me.

Hey, come on. What have you got to lose? Nothing will change until you do. Give it a try. If you're not walking in abundance now, aren't you ready to make a change?

10

FALSE GODS

One by one they disappointed me—all the people that I held in high esteem, each one that I placed on a pedestal and revered. Sometimes they were teachers. More often, they were friends. In my teen years, it was the boys that I dated. Then my husband, bosses and coworkers. The ones that earned the right to be placed on a pedestal would remain there for some time—until they failed me. Sometimes what caused my heroes to fall from grace was a decision I didn't like, lack of support for me or behavior that hurt me. Each time it was painful.

Of course, my heroes were destined to fail. We all are, because we're only human. And here's a news flash: Humans fail because we're imperfect. We make bad decisions. Sometimes our ethics fail, and we're selfish and inconsiderate of others' feelings. It happens.

Can you relate to this? Have you placed people on pedestals, hoping they'll make you feel complete, that they'll endorse you, reinforce you, grant you value—only to be disappointed by the very ones you esteem?

Painful, isn't it? My mistake was that I never learned from the experience. I'd begin the search for the next person to make me feel whole. I was a brains-and-talent junkie, so the brighter and more talented they were—particularly if they had power—the more attractive I found them.

You may be the same. Or maybe you're attracted to other characteristics like wealth, a sense of humor or looks. Whatever your laundry list of desirable traits, if you're waiting for somebody else to make you whole, you've just stepped into the *Twilight Zone*.

STRIKEOUTS

I was sort of a lardo in grade school and junior high. In high school, my height caught up with my weight, so by the time I reached my junior year, the fact that the star of the basketball team was interested in me was pure heaven. He was good-looking all right, but as dumb as a stump—my first detour off the brains-and-talent route. When he dumped me in my senior year, I thought my life had ended. It wasn't until I dated a couple of guys who could actually put a noun and a verb in the same sentence that I began to see that basketball stars weren't everything.

In college, the *real* love of my life came along, I thought. He was a senior, and I was a sophomore. He had brains to the max and was gorgeous. I even transferred colleges to finish up while he went to grad school. Three weeks before the wedding, I found out he was a pathological liar. Where have all the heroes gone?

After college, when I married, I assumed that my husband was going to make me complete. Five years later, we were divorced. I'd like to blame him completely—but I know better. He probably thought he'd married the Wicked Witch of the West sent directly over from Central Casting.

My track record at this point had featured a series of work heroes—people I liked, admired and wanted to emulate. But they fell more quickly, like dominoes...each one a crushing disappointment.

Ten years to the day after I married my ex-husband, I married my current husband—causing my father to ask on my wedding day, "Are we going to be doing this every ten years until you get it right?" Husband number two, of course, was going to complete my circle. He didn't—but it wasn't his fault. I was emotionally needy going into the relationship. What I didn't learn until later was that he was, too.

My husband and I have been through some good times and some rough times. But I've had to come to terms with the reality that no human being can fulfill me, nor should I expect anyone to. Fulfillment comes *only* through a relationship with the Lord. Since that relationship has filled in my empty places, my relationship with my husband has become the frosting on the cake.

SUPERCHARGED LIVING

Fool's Gold

If your present sounds like my past, let me give it to you straight—you're worshiping false gods. You're worshiping the creation rather than the Creator. On top of that, your quest to find wholeness through another person means you're operating out of need. Needy relationships produce disaster because they place too much emphasis on the behavior of another person to sustain you. It's a disaster because you're trying to attain fulfillment *outside in* instead of *inside out*. Trying to create fulfillment outside in forces you to exist with part of you exposed, just ready to be hurt. That reminds me of an incident that happened to the sister of a friend.

Thanks for the Memories

My friend's sister works in the public relations department of a major automotive plant in Detroit. Although it wasn't part of her job, she agreed to conduct a facilities tour for a group of visiting Japanese businessmen. She thought she looked pretty spiffy that day in a nice, new silk shirtwaist dress. At the beginning of the tour, she asked the Japanese delegation to pause briefly while she used the restroom. When she came out, she led the parade of visitors through an hour-long walk-through of the factory. As the guests bowed and shuffled behind her, she heard workers snickering.

It wasn't until she got back to her office that she knew why. One of the administrative secretaries looked at her and yelped. That visit to the restroom had been a disaster. She had inadvertently tucked the back of her full skirt into her pantyhose. She had conducted the hour-long tour with her pantyhose exposed to the Japanese, the plant workers, the world. No one had told her. She felt embarrassed, betrayed and foolish.

That's the way we feel when we put our trust in someone, expecting to be made whole—only to have that person use us and walk away. We might as well pin a "Kick Me" sign on our back. It means we're operating out of need instead of abundance.

Real Gold

It's a fact of life that each of us has a God-sized hole on the inside. It cannot be filled by another person, work, possessions, power or fame (though

God knows I tried). When you make a conscious decision to fill that hole with the real God, not the false ones, you become complete. Instead of operating out of deficit, you're operating out of overflow.

Some of you may have been praying for mates, and you may be frustrated because you haven't found one. Maybe it's because you're still needy yourself. It isn't that God is holding out on you—He yearns for a relationship with you more than you yearn for a relationship with another person. Yield to Him. Draw close to Him. Talk to Him. Listen to Him. Study His love letter to you, the Bible.

When you're full and complete in Him, then and only then can you enter a relationship with another person as a whole person yourself. When you're whole, the people in your life become a bonus.

WHAT TO DO

1. Set aside some time each day to fellowship with the Lord. Get up thirty minutes earlier in the morning if you have to. (Don't tell me you don't have time—you always find time to do what you *want* to do.)

2. Make this time the top priority in your life. As you put God first, before obligations and desires, not only will you find that God works out your time schedule to make up for the time committed to Him, but He'll also fill that hole on the inside of you.

3. Meditate on John 3:16. Yes, I know we've heard it a million times. Guys wearing rainbow-colored wigs at golf tournaments hold it up on signs. But look at the words and think about them. "For God so loved the world, that he gave..." He so loves you that if you had been the only person on the planet, He would have sent His Son to die on the cross for you and then ascend into heaven in order to restore your relationship with Father God. He loves you so much He sent His best, His only Son. He loves you more than you can ever know. He loves you more than man ever can. His love is unconditional and everlasting, and you don't have to do anything to earn it.

Oh yes—the next time the High Priestess tries to condemn your actions or accuse your behavior, tell her to pound salt. You're a blood-bought child of the King.

11

WHAT YOU SAY IS
WHAT YOU GET

I t's an undeniable fact that you'll live your life based on words—either words of defeat or words of victory. It's your choice.

Your words are the building materials with which you construct your life and your future. You live within the confines of the boundary that you create with your own mouth. Circumstances and conditions that surround you are all subject to change, but the power of your words can change those circumstances or cement them in your life forever. Want some proof?

A 1991 article in *Reader's Digest* titled "Patient Knows Best" included the results of a study of more than twenty-eight hundred elderly men and women who were asked to rate their health. Those who rated their health poor were four to five times more likely to die in the following four years than those who considered their health to be excellent. In some cases, the health of the respondents was in fact comparable. Five other studies, involving a total of twenty-three thousand people, reached similar conclusions, according to the *Reader's Digest* article.

Think of it—people who have an image of themselves as being in poor health speak sickness into being even though they may be in good health. And they live out the reality of the image they have of themselves—an image of being sick.

Here's why: "Death and life are in the power of the tongue" (Prov. 18:21). Jesus put it this way: "A good man out of the good treasure of his heart bringeth forth that which is good; and an evil man out of the evil treasure of his heart bringeth forth that which is evil: for of the abundance of the heart his mouth speaketh" (Luke 6:45).

What you've got in your heart comes out of your mouth. What comes out of your mouth establishes your circumstances.

EXPLODING MYTHS

How many times have you said, "Oh well, I'll just make the best of it." Or, "I can't control it—I'll just endure it." Or worse, "I guess I'll just always be fat." Or, "I'm just a slob. Nothing will ever change that." Or, "I've always been lousy at math. It's just a curse I'll have to live with." Or any of those other lies the High Priestess has embedded in your brain cells.

These confessions establish passivity and continue to reinforce negative traditions. Is this what you want?

Well, let's kick over a sacred cow. Conventional wisdom says you take what comes and turn it over to God. You can do that if you want to, but it's not God's best. When you think you can't endure one more "let go and let God," why don't you move off the defense and go on the offense? Yes, you can—just listen up.

Throughout the Bible, God gave us building blocks to control our lives:

- "Thou shalt also decree a thing, and it shall be established unto thee: and the light shall shine upon thy ways" (Job 22:28).

- "A fool's mouth is his destruction, and his lips are the snare of his soul" (Prov. 18:7).

- "A man's belly shall be satisfied with the fruit of his mouth; and with the increase of his lips shall he be filled" (Prov. 18:20).

- "Whoso keepeth his mouth and his tongue keepeth his soul from troubles" (Prov. 21:23).

- "The mouth of the upright shall deliver them" (Prov. 12:6).

- "He that keepeth his mouth keepeth his life" (Prov. 13:3).

- "The lips of the wise shall preserve them" (Prov. 14:3).

- "A wholesome tongue is a tree of life: but perverseness therein is a breach in the spirit" (Prov. 15:4).

- "The heart of the wise teacheth his mouth, and addeth learning to his lips" (Prov. 6:23).

- "Pleasant words are as an honeycomb, sweet to the soul, and health to the bones" (Prov. 16:24).

Do I mean that you can control your circumstances by what you say? Yes, words have power!

Let's kick over another sacred cow. Remember that phrase from your childhood, "Sticks and stones may break my bones, but words will never hurt me"? Wrong…words *will* hurt you. Want some more proof?

CHECK IT OUT

Look at the first chapter of Genesis. Notice that every time God spoke, creation took place. Look in your own Bible and circle the word *spoke* every time it occurs. You see? He created the whole universe by speaking it forth. "The worlds were framed by the word of God" (Heb. 11:3). Without words, there wouldn't have been any creation.

By the same token, your words create images that you live out of. The images you've created define your reality.

Check out John 1:1: "In the beginning was the Word, and the Word was with God, and the Word was God." See—God is the Word. Jesus is the Word made flesh. No wonder God advised us, even before He sent Jesus, "My son, attend to my words; incline thine ear unto my sayings. Let them not depart from thine eyes; keep them in the midst of thine heart. For they are life unto those that find them, and health to all their flesh" (Prov. 4:20–22).

Here God is telling us that His Word is life. He is also telling us that His Word is health—it's medicine to our flesh. If that isn't power, I don't know what is.

Is It Soup Yet?

Have I made you mad yet? Are you saying, "Why have I never heard this before?" Or, "They never taught me that in my church." Or, "That sounds arrogant and controlling." I said all of that (and more). The High Priestess of Guilt and Condemnation did a war dance in my head, saying, "It can't be that easy. If it were, everybody would be doing it. You're not entitled to it. That's heresy"...and on and on.

But a friend of mine named Angel who lives in Hawaii said it all. She was sharing the Word one day with someone who wanted to argue with her. He said, "So what's your opinion of such-and-such?" She looked right at him and said, "You know what? I don't have an opinion. The only opinion I know is what God said in His Word. If He said it, He means it. If I believe it, He does it. It's as simple as that."

Over the last five years, I've had to let go of all my exalted opinions developed over the years through research, the wisdom of the world, experts and what I'd been taught—and turn instead to God's opinion in His Word. Then I've had to learn how to speak His Word—not my circumstances—to bring about different circumstances in my life.

Love Letter

To my amazement I have found that God's Word really is His love letter to me. It's an instruction manual for life. If I put His Word in my mouth and speak it, I can create change and bring about victory.

Jesus said, "If ye abide in me, and my words abide in you, ye shall ask what ye will, and it shall be done unto you" (John 15:7). When God's Word becomes infused into your spirit, it becomes a part of you and can't be separated from you. It's not just your thought and affirmation—it *is* you. So when God's Word concerning healing, prosperity, peace, joy or freedom from bondage takes root in your flesh, it becomes greater than your circumstances. That means victory is at hand. When you speak God's Word from your heart, faith gives substance to the promises of God.

My Personal Prescription

I've learned to speak the Word daily over my family, my business, my neighborhood, my property, my church, my city and my country. Hey, you may think I'm smoking something, but the results I get from the time I spend speaking the Word is a far greater return on my investment than chewing my cuticles and worrying. That never got me anything except bad-looking hands and a knotted-up stomach. The Word brings a continuous flow of peace in my household, clients into my business, freedom from bondage and health in my body. It works for me, and it will work for you.

WHAT TO DO

Don't just rely on my opinion. Study it for yourself.

1. Build your faith slowly by speaking the Word. Don't begin by believing for oil wells and Rolls Royces. I heard a Bible teacher once say, "You have to begin first by believing God for a pair of socks or a parking place." Then build your faith level from there.

2. Take the number one thing on the list of circumstances you want changed. Search the Word and write down the scriptures that pertain to your circumstance.

3. Shut up about your circumstance. Don't say one more word about it. Confess only the scriptures. Carry them around in your purse. Confess them every time you think of it.

4. Watch God go. (Remember, there's a period of time between the end of your prayer and the tangible result. During that time, confess the Word and close your eyes to the circumstances.)

OK, so this may not have been a humorous lesson, but you're not into this for humor—right? You're into this for a change in your life.

12

WHAT YOU SAY IS WHAT YOU GET (THE SEQUEL)

I f anybody had a gripe, it was Job. Sometimes I find myself moaning because I'm having a bad hair day or because on the way to work three of my toes burst through the end of my pantyhose, or I got a speeding ticket. Or it's because the computer system is down, someone snapped at me or the printer missed a shipment on my stationery.

That's nothing—harassment at best. Job lost everything. His servants were carried off and slain. His oxen were stolen. His sheep were burned up, his camels were carried off and his house fell on his sons and daughters and killed them all. That's a bad day.

I'm sure Job probably had the Old Testament male version of the High Priestess living in his head (maybe called the High Potentate of Shame and Rebuke). But Job never gave in to him.

He never rebuked God for his circumstances, and when he spoke about God he never spoke of anything but God's goodness. Oh yes—and Job also offers a powerful clue to how his horrendous circumstances came upon him.

Check out Job 3:25, where he says, "For the thing which I greatly feared is come upon me, and that which I was afraid of is come unto me." Remember what we've said before? Like a magnet, fear draws what you don't want right to you. And faith draws what you *do* want right to you.

COME AND GET IT

Job's fear opened the door for Satan to come in and take everything he had (Job 1:9–12). But that's the bad news. Do you know what the good news is?

Even against the recommendations of his so-called friends—who all told him he was nuts and that he should rebuke his God and turn from Him—because of Job's faithfulness God restored to him *twice* what he had before (Job 42:10).

Now why is that relevant to what we talked about in the last chapter? Some of you may have been wondering whether I was having peanut butter hallucinations when I told you that the power of the words you speak frames your circumstances. They do, and here's some more evidence.

Job 22:28 says, "Thou shalt also decree a thing, and it shall be established unto thee: and the light shall shine upon thy ways." We reviewed that scripture in the last chapter. God wasn't on a peanut butter high either when He included this in His Word.

"Thou shalt also decree a thing…" The promises of God, the sayings of God— all "shall be established unto thee." When we speak forth the Word of God, we're not just blowing smoke; we're declaring with our mouths what God has spoken. The power is not in our speaking; it's in the Lord who gives the message of our speech.

All those bumper-sticker philosophies people love to tell us when we're down—"Don't give up," "Hang in there, baby," "It's always darkest before the dawn"—may be given with the best of intentions, but none of them can change your circumstances. There's no power in bumper-sticker words or in the person who created them.

Let's take this one more step. In Webster's New Collegiate Dictionary, the word *decree* means "to command, to determine or order judicially; to ordain." So if your declaration is in line with the Word you have received from God, you can declare a thing and it will be established for you. Count on it.

Are you encouraged? Once again, don't take my word for it. Study it for yourself.

WHAT TO DO

Here's a bonus—no new assignment. School's out today. The only thing you need to do is follow the instructions in the last chapter. Go back and look again. Four steps, four actions that will change your life.

Now, just do it!

13

THE GOOD NEWS IS THE BAD NEWS IS WRONG

D id you ever notice how negative today's journalism is? The facts often seem lost in the negative spin, conflict and human misery.

I recently read a report by the Washington-based Media Research Center indicating that the average sound bite today lasts seven seconds. How is it possible for a political candidate to get his or her position across in seven seconds? The same report revealed that 72 percent of broadcast time is taken up by journalists negatively interpreting the news for us (presumably because we're too stupid to figure it out for ourselves).

When was the last time you saw an empowering human interest story on TV or in print? They're few and far between. I did hear a wonderful three-hour radio talk show that was devoted exclusively to calls from listeners, all of whom had been laid off in their forties and fifties. Each had been forced to start over again—and had made it. What a shot in the arm! Each individual or family had to regroup, sometimes selling all their possessions, taking some risks and moving across the country—in short, doing painful things to make a new start. But each individual had grown from it and prospered financially. Hearing so many positive examples was better than a B_{12} shot.

The thing that intrigued me most about this radio show was that I didn't hear any complaining from the callers, not one word of blame. None of them wallowed in the injustice of being put out of work, and none of them waited around for the government or somebody else to fix things for them.

LIFE AIN'T FAIR

Whoever said it was? The unexpected happens. It happens to all of us. And when it does, we have a choice. We can deal with it the way the world does, or we can lean upon our birthright.

What do I mean? If you have accepted Jesus Christ as your Lord and Savior, the deck is stacked for you. (That may not be fair either, but I like the odds. And besides, I didn't set up the rules. God did.) If you don't know the deck is stacked in your favor, then it may require some study on your part for you to be convinced. But hey, it's worth the effort to find out what's been purchased for you.

Can you imagine how you'd respond to reading about a homeless person—living on the streets for decades, scrimping and scratching, barely able to eat—who dies without knowing that twenty years earlier a wealthy relative left him an estate of five million dollars? Wouldn't that be the pits? And wouldn't your heart ache for all the anguish the poor homeless person endured not knowing that riches were available the whole time?

YOU HAVE A RICH RELATIVE, TOO

God Himself, the Creator of the universe, loves you enough that He sent His Son to die on the cross and take all your sin, sickness, poverty, distress and pain on Himself so that you don't have to bear it. Jesus purchased your freedom from lack, disease and bondage. He took your place. He took all your pain to His grave, then rose again to live in heaven and constantly make intercession for you to Father God (Heb. 7:25). All He needs is some faith from you to bring about the provisions that He already shed His blood for you to have. Bottom line—you have a covenant with almighty God in which He promises to provide for you. And God doesn't go back on His Word.

Philippians 4:19 says, "My God shall supply all your needs according to His riches in glory in Christ Jesus" (NAS). He knows your needs. He's already provided for them. He's paid the bill in full so you don't have to.

So you say, "OK, if that's true, then why am I strapped for cash, home

51

with sick kids, being put out of my house and closed out of my job?" Maybe it's because you don't know your rights—what God has provided for you—or what you have to do to obtain them. After all, if somebody demanded that you sit in the back of a bus or informed you that you couldn't eat at a lunch counter, you'd squeal like a stuck pig because you know your freedoms have been guaranteed by the Constitution of the United States.

You have something that's even better than the Constitution. Isn't it time you knew what your covenant with God is all about?

PRACTICAL APPLICATION

Your covenant works on obedience and faith. Being obedient to God's principles and using the currency of your faith bring God on the scene. For example, a couple of years ago my business was steaming along just fine, supported by several annual retainer contracts that had been renewed each year by a number of large corporations. I was in fat city. Then the unpredictable happened: corporate down-sizing, reorganizations, decisions to bring work in-house rather than contracting it out.

Every contract I had was jerked out from under me. The High Priestess of Guilt and Condemnation was euphoric, break-dancing in my head daily about how surely I must have brought it all on myself. My clients didn't like me. My work wasn't good enough. I'd never get any more contracts. And on and on and on—all lies.

I can't honestly say that it was a particularly fun time for me, anymore than getting a tooth drilled is fun. The procedure doesn't really hurt. You just think it does because it sounds so bad. The news was bad, but it provided an opportunity to test what I believe. The cancellations were facts, but I knew those facts weren't the truth. There is a difference. The truth is that financial lack is not part of my covenant with God.

As a tither, I am assured that God will keep me supplied. In Malachi 3:10, God says that if I tithe, then I have a right to challenge Him to prove His supply to me. I knew I had some studying to do.

Naturally, the last thing I want to do when I'm under pressure is set aside more time to study, pray and seek the Lord. The High Priestess screams, "You can't do that! You need to get out there and make sales calls. You're being lazy. If you don't kick up some dust, nothing will happen. You'll go under."

Putting aside all the unsolicited advice, here's what I did:

- I looked up scriptures on tithing, confidence, peace, prosperity, promise and deliverance.

- I wrote the Scriptures on three-by-five cards and carried them around with me.

- I spent time each morning reading and confessing the scriptures (the truth) over my business.

- I asked two of my prayer partners to agree with me in prayer, according to Matthew 18:19, for a successful conclusion.

- I played gospel music tapes in my car and drove around town singing praises to God and thanking Him for the answer, confessing that business prosperity is my birthright according to His Word.

- I refused to listen to reports or advice from anybody who said anything contrary to what I was confessing.

- I sowed seed. That means I gave extra gifts into God's kingdom. Now you're probably thinking, *She's gone off the air on this one.* But God's Word is all about sowing and reaping (notice it's not reaping and sowing). If you want love, you have to sow love. If you want time, you have to sow time. If you want money, you have to sow money. Money was what I needed, so money was what I sowed. And I believed God for the increase.

THE ENVELOPE, PLEASE...

The results? A whole new lineup of clients. People that I hadn't heard from in years called me. Business came from the most unexpected sources. God restored everything I had lost and then some.

Now just in case you think this was an easy process, it wasn't. Nothing of value ever is, is it? But in my heart I knew the bad news was wrong. And also in my heart I knew I needed to do whatever it would take to stake my claim as a child of the King.

Can you relate to any of this? Are there areas in your life in which you feel beaten down, where the light at the end of the tunnel is an oncoming train? Well, if you'll approach those areas in God's way, the only way you'll lose is if you quit. We've read the back of the book, and we win. Also, if He came through for me, He'll do it for you. He says in His Word that He's no respecter of persons (Acts 10:34).

WHAT TO DO

If you have a crisis in your life, follow the process above.

1. Write down the desired end result, what you're believing God for. Be specific.

2. Follow the same process I did. I've worked it in every area of my life. I've worked it for healing, for restoration of relationships, for solving contract disputes, you name it. I go to a church filled with people who are working the same process and have a list of victories a mile long.

3. Just remember who you are…you're God's child. He loves you. He's provided for you. He wants the best for you. All you have to do is find out what He left you in His last will and testament. Activate your faith for it.

The world's way doesn't work. His Way does. You choose. Choose His way—then go for it.

14

THREE STRIKES AND YOU'RE OUT

I won the argument. It was a heated debate that had gone on all day. My then-husband had tickets to a baseball game. I had tickets to the theater. You can see how the battle lines were drawn.

"But we've been to the baseball games twice already this week," I whined.

"But it's the play-offs," he reasoned.

"But I hate baseball—how much more do I have to endure?"

"Come on, be a sport," he said. And on we argued.

By five o'clock he'd heard enough. "Oh, all right!" he said. "I'll go to the theater. You know I hate the theater, and I'll despise every minute of it, but I'll go."

It was a Playhouse in the Park production, and the night was beautiful. I just knew the evening would be wonderful. What I didn't know was that the play was an obscure production with a twisted plot and definite Marxist overtones.

It was also one of those plays that nobody knows what's going on, but everybody pretends that they do so they look intelligent. Bill (my ex) grumbled, mumbled and swore under his breath throughout the first act. The madder he got, the more nervous I became.

The second act featured a mutiny on a Spanish frigate. The Spanish captain had been lashed to the mast of the ship while the crew mutinied, releasing the slaves from the hold. (None of us could be absolutely sure this was actually the story line—it was the best we could assume.) As the play and the evening wore on, my irritated husband became increasingly chapped—and increasingly vocal.

The ship's captain had his scepter snatched from his hand and was beaten. One of the released slaves picked up the ball and chain from his own ankle in one hand, held the scepter in his other and leaned into the captain's face, screaming, "Who am I? Who am I?"

Bill, who could not bear it not one minute longer, screamed, "Willie Mays!" It brought down the house, and we were thrown out.

I heard the next day that the only bright spot in the production had been my husband's outburst. It didn't do much to minimize my embarrassment, but it did teach me something.

STRONG-ARM TACTICS

I won the argument, but in reality I lost. I lost because I forced my husband into doing something he didn't want to do. As a result, not only was he miserable all evening, but I was, too.

How many times have I repeated that pattern, forcing people to behave the way I demanded? I would assume that if they *behaved* a certain way, they'd *believe* a certain way. Wrong! Getting people to do something doesn't mean they agree with you when they do it.

Action doesn't mean agreement. Acquiescence doesn't mean loyalty. Any bully can prevail for awhile. But bullying, nagging and lecturing doesn't create long-term obedience; it creates rebellion.

THE BEST-LAID PLAN

Can you relate? Do you think if you lay down the law one more time with your kids it will work? Do you think one more impassioned plea to your husband will make him quit smoking? Have you been thinking that one more threat to a family member, coworker or boss will change their actions? If you do, then you're the one who needs to be locked in the hold of a ship.

THE SEEDS OF REBELLION

I was reared with what my mother calls "smother love." She meant the best for me, but I interpreted her best as a nonstop stream of words—telling me what to do, what to think, what to wear, who to see, how to feel and so on. We argued about everything—my hair, my clothes, my appearance, my friends, my opinions.

The more she nagged, the more resentful I became. And I became more determined *not* to do what she demanded.

I knuckled under when I had to, but inside I boiled over with resentment, just waiting for an opportunity to defy her. The more she lectured the more contrary I became, whether I expressed it or not. I didn't know it at the time, but as a very young child I turned to food in rebellion to alleviate the anger. It served to comfort me momentarily, but it also fed my defiance. It was something I could do that my mother couldn't control. The defiance soon became a full-blown addiction. It took me thirty years to break out of it.

What You Hate, You Become

You'd think that I would have learned not to do what set my own teeth on edge. Right? Wrong. I hated "smother love." It made me feel incompetent and stupid. I felt it diminished me as a person since it didn't accept or value my opinions, views, thoughts or feelings. I chafed at its confinement.

And then I recreated it in my own life. The High Priestess of Guilt and Condemnation conned me into thinking that nothing would ever go right unless I muscled my circumstances into place. She convinced me that control was the key to happiness—if I could control the people around me and the circumstances that confronted me, I'd be happy.

It's a seductive strategy, and I went for it. But it never brought me the happiness I craved, and it drove everybody around me nuts.

Whom are you trying to control with your words? Your children, your spouse, your boss, your employees? Give it up. Your words won't make it happen.

A Better Way

It may surprise you to know that God left us an instruction manual for rearing children, for forming partnerships with our spouses, for living life. And His way doesn't require state-of-the-art nagging.

He doesn't say to let our children grow up without instruction or to go through life mute, not expressing our opinions. He does, however, speak of modeling behavior. He speaks about operating in the manifested power of His love toward our family and others, and confessing His Word over our spouses, family members and the rest of our household. Why? So He can bring about His perfect will in their lives. Imagine—they're in *His* job description!

Remember, His Word spoken and believed in our hearts is the power switch that brings about His best. When we speak His Word over our family members and believe Him for the end result, He goes to work wooing them gently into position, changing their hearts and developing in them a desire to behave and act appropriately. Isn't it better to operate in His power than in yours?

Unlike us, He doesn't muscle people into place. His love gently draws them and woos them into alignment. He doesn't lecture, scold or nag. What a relief!

Put Pressure on Your Covenant

Are you a born-again child of the living God? Is Jesus your Savior? Well, make Him your Lord, too. If He's not Lord of all, He's not Lord at all. Make Him Lord of your marriage. Make Him Lord of your children. Make Him Lord of your finances, your health, your home, your city, your country.

It doesn't matter what kind of mess your family is in; if you make God Lord of your family and believe and confess His Word, He'll unravel every problem you've got and make it right.

Listen to some of the things God has to say about our children:

- "The children of thy servants [that's you] shall continue, and their seed shall be established before thee" (Ps. 102:28). That means your children will be established before the Lord.

- "But the mercy of the LORD is from everlasting to everlasting upon them that fear him, and his righteousness unto children's children" (Ps. 103:17). That means God's righteousness flows through your children to your grandchildren.

- "The seed of the righteous shall be delivered" (Prov. 11:21). That means your children shall be delivered from sin, from bondage, from sickness, from lack, from addictions, from all the snares of the evil one.

- "I will pour my spirit upon thy seed, and my blessings upon thine offspring" (Isa. 44:3).

- "But thus saith the LORD, Even the captives of the mighty [He's talking about Satan here] shall be taken away, and the prey of the terrible shall be delivered: for I will contend with him that contendeth with thee, and I will save thy children" (Isa. 49:25). That means that God will take on whoever messes with you, and He will save your children. Is this good or what?

- "And all thy children shall be taught of the LORD; and great shall be the peace of thy children" (Isa. 54:13). Believe me, I confess this one a lot. We've had lots of junk in our family—alcoholism, drug addiction, codependency—you name it.

- "Who are kept by the power of God through faith unto salvation" (1 Pet. 1:5). God is keeping your children through your faith until the time they turn to Him in spirit and in truth. What a comfort!

What about your marriage?

- "For he is our peace, who hath made both one, and hath broken down the middle wall of partition between us" (Eph. 2:14).

- "Nevertheless let every one of you [husbands] in particular so love his wife even as himself; and the wife see that she reverence her husband" (Eph. 5:33). Doesn't that sound like a God-ordained partnership?

This is just a smattering of scriptures you can confess over your spouse and children. It doesn't matter how out of line with these scriptures your circumstances appear to be. Your circumstances are fact, but they're not the truth. The Word says circumstances are subject to change, but God's Word never changes.

DOES IT WORK?

Every time. My youngest stepson and husband never got along. I don't know what the problem was, but being with them was like observing a cat and a dog in a bag. The tension in the house was unbearable.

Being the duly elected "Junior Holy Ghost," I thought it was my job to "fix" both of them and solve the problem. So I'd talk to my husband about his behavior, then talk to my stepson about his. I was certain that if I just said the right words, they'd both see the light and fall into each other's arms. Right!

The more I nagged, the more hostile they were toward each other—and the more vexed I felt. Vexation then turned to anger. I was mad at *both* of them for ruining *my* parade.

One day in prayer, the Lord asked me why I didn't get out of the way.

"Huh?" I said, thinking I was hallucinating. But the gentle urging of the Holy Spirit was real. He showed me that I was the problem—not them. If I'd get out of the middle and pray for their hearts to be changed, He'd go to work on my behalf. What a concept! I began to confess Luke 4:18 over them daily. I confessed that the gospel had healed their broken hearts, had delivered them from captivity, had recovered their spiritual sight and had set them at liberty because they were bruised. I also refused any longer to engage in conversations regarding their negative relationship.

A friend of mine from church had experienced similar circumstances. He agreed with me in prayer regarding my stepson and husband. Then we consistently prayed for them. God began to change their hearts. Within a year they were talking on the phone regularly.

At the time my stepson was with us only summers and holidays. Not long after, they went on a fishing trip. Today they're extremely close, and it's as if there were never a breach.

It took me getting out of the way and using the power of God's Word to change the chemistry between them.

So how about you? Are you ready to quit trying to control those around you and let God do it?

WHAT TO DO

1. Admit to yourself and to the Lord that your own lecturing and nagging isn't getting the job done.

2. Admit to yourself and to the Lord that positive change in your loved ones must come inside out, not outside in (your words are outside in).

3. Ask God to do a work in your loved ones by changing them inside out.

4. Get in agreement with God's Word by choosing a scripture or two and continually confessing that scripture over your loved ones.

5. Get in agreement with a mature Christian. Pray Matthew 18:19 over the desired end result.

6. Make a decision to walk in love toward this person or persons. That doesn't mean you allow them to abuse or take advantage of you. It may mean, though, that you have to distance yourself for a while. It may mean you need to gently draw the line with them and quit enabling their destructive behavior. Do the spiritual work, and let God do the rest.

Oh yes! And don't forget to thank and praise God *every day* that it's already done. God says that He inhabits the praises of His people (Ps. 22:3). And your praise not only hurries the answer, but it also builds your hope.

15

BREAKING OUT

You know what happens at the beginning of every year—people make New Year's resolutions. And every year the television camera crews are out on the streets asking people about those resolutions. Many resolve to lose twenty pounds. Just about as many resolve to quit smoking. Other typical responses include exercising regularly, giving up red meat and getting up earlier in the morning.

I used to be the queen of New Year's resolutions. Every year I was going to quit smoking and lose weight. This year I made a new one—never to make another New Year's resolution. Why?

New Year's resolutions are earnest attempts to change. Unfortunately, most people don't realize they're setting themselves up for failure. A resolution promises gain but lacks the substance to produce it. A resolution tries to bring about change by fleshly effort rather than by the power of God. Fleshly effort has no substance.

A lasting victory in an area of our lives is never achieved by our own might or power. True change—total victory—only occurs when we exercise our faith in the transforming power of God.

Every weekend, the High Priestess of Guilt and Condemnation would bait her trap for me to begin a diet on Monday. And she usually succeeded. The High Priestess is probably working on you full time, too—to get you to give up this or start doing that or promise to do something else.

She knows that as long as she can keep you in the resolution arena, she can keep you frustrated... and failing.

I used to promise myself ten or twelve times a week that I was going to begin a regular exercise program—and I really had good intentions. But my idea of exercise had always been a brisk nap. I never seemed to get an exercise program off the drawing board. Every time I failed, I not only beat myself up, but also felt miserable because I had failed again.

IT SOUNDS GOOD

In theory, resolutions sound good. In practice, however, they're destined to fail. Desperate resolutions are simply carnal methods that play right into the High Priestess's deceptive strategy to keep us frustrated and failing until we lose all hope that we'll ever be free.

If the High Priestess of Guilt can keep you in the arena of the flesh, using carnal weapons to fight a spiritual war, you can be defeated, over and over again. *But* if you'll take the weapons of your warfare, which are not carnal but mighty through God—as Paul states in 2 Corinthians 10:4—you can defeat the enemy and overcome destructive habits in every area of your life.

WHO SAYS?

Jesus said that if we continue in His Word, we will know the truth, and the truth will make us free (John 8:32). *Knowing* the truth will set us free. So don't let the wench in your head lure you into another cycle of failure and disappointment with the temptation of a quick fix. There isn't one.

There is a way out, but you'll need more than a New Year's resolution to get there. You'll need to make a decision to put your hope and faith in God.

WHAT TO DO

1. Continue in His Word every day. (See John 8:31–32.)

2. Resolve not to make any more resolutions.

3. Look up the word *Christ* in your concordance and find out what it means. (Hint: It's not Jesus' last name.)

4. Study what the *anointing* means. When you pray in the name of Jesus, you're praying in the name of the Anointed One and His anointing.

5. Meditate on the burden-removing, yoke-destroying power of Jesus, the Anointed One, and His anointing; meditate on how it will set you free from your bondage.

16

BEYOND SLIM-FAST

F*asting.* Yuck! The very word makes me dizzy. Anyone like me who has ever had an eating disorder knows that fasting is a mechanism you use to try to make up for the food you binged on last night. And for any of you who have never been on a diet or don't understand what an eating disorder is all about, good for you.

For some of you, the word *fasting* may not carry the emotional weight that it does for many of us. But I'll bet it brings up the image of doing without. It's a picture of loss. And here's a real bummer—it's talked about a lot in the Bible.

Fasting does mean "doing without"—setting aside something you enjoy, establishing discipline over something you enjoy. I used to use it where food was concerned—in the wrong way and for all the wrong reasons.

I once fasted for fourteen days, drinking only water and choking down only two ounces a day of pre-digested liquid protein. (I know—you want to know who digested it first.) In fourteen days, I lost fourteen pounds. I was wearing skirts and pants that hadn't been out of the dark recesses of my closet in years. I was looking mighty fine—or so I thought. Unfortunately, two weeks later all the weight was back on again, and then some.

Living with me when I was fasting was like living with a terrorist. And that was when I was in a good mood. Fasting for me was what I imagined cloistered monks did when they donned hair shirts and flogged themselves.

SUPERCHARGED LIVING

IT'S GAIN, NOT LOSS

Amazingly, fasting is positive and not negative. Why? Because it puts down your flesh—you know, that thing that keeps screaming, "Entertain me, feed me, put cigarettes in me. Give me something to drink. Pet me, pamper me."

You know the voice of the flesh, right? It is the High Priestess herself, always telling you, "You poor little thing, you need to be pampered and petted. The next hour zoned out in a chair in front of the tube will do the trick for you. That bottle of wine will fix you. A drive-through McDonald's and a Big Mac and double fries will elevate your mood."

But she's a liar, and so is your flesh. Fasting is a positive for two reasons. First of all, God tells us to do it. Not because He's an old grump, but because it's good for us; His Word tells us why. Secondly, fasting is like training a muscle. Every time we fast (whether food, TV, CDs, novels—whatever we love), we're sowing seeds of self-control. That means each time we fast, it becomes easier.

WHAT IS GOD'S DEAL?

Isaiah 58 is the classic fasting chapter. Although fasting is encouraged throughout the Bible, God says it all in this chapter. The bottom line is this: By putting your flesh under, you can better hear direction from the Lord Himself. The advantages of fasting talked about in this chapter include:

- Loosing the bands of wickedness (v. 6).
- Undoing heavy burdens (v. 6).
- Breaking yokes (v. 6).
- Ministering to others (v. 7).
- Receiving your reward for fasting (v. 8).
- Restoration of your health (v. 8).
- The removal of all your yokes (v. 9).
- Guidance from the Lord (v. 11).
- Delighting yourself in the Lord (v. 14).

In addition, the glory of the Lord shall be your rear guard; when you call, the Lord shall answer you; and He'll cause you to ride upon the high places of the earth (vv. 8–9, 14).

How's that for a pretty good deal? All you have to do is tell your flesh to shut up. While you're denying it, spend some extra time in prayer. The Lord will reveal things to you.

What's My Deal?

You can fast anything—for a day, two days, three days, a week or a month. It just has to be something you love (no fair fasting Brussels sprouts.) As an example, I am very interested in politics. As a result, I read a lot and watch C-Span, plus a host of political programs on TV. So I decided one week to fast all of my political TV programming. After three days of not watching C-Span, I was ready to chew the leg off a table, but by the end of the week, I was OK about it.

The result of that fast was a loosening of the hold that the political scene had on me. It lasted for several months. (It occurs to me that I need to do this again. I'm up to my neck in politics again.)

I've also fasted food many times—one day, two days, three days. (I drink water and fruit juices only, although there are many different kinds of fasts.) It's always a struggle to get started, but the payoffs are enormous. God always honors your fast with increased knowledge of the Word, with the answers to your prayers and with incredible peace and joy.

So what is it that you love, that you're willing to put down in order to discipline your flesh? Think about it. What are the things you enjoy that take up your time and keep you from drawing nearer to God? It may be shopping, nights out with the girls, sewing or gossiping (you probably need to get rid of that one anyway).

Whatever it is, start small. Try giving up something you love for a day. As your flesh rises up in protest—and it will—tell it to shut up. You can get through it. God loves you so much that He would never tell you to do something and then not give you the power to follow through.

WHAT TO DO

1. Read Isaiah 58.

2. Make a list of the things you could fast.

3. Offer one of them up to the Lord, pray over it, sow it as a seed of discipline and self-control and tell the Lord that you believe you receive all of His promises in Isaiah 58.

4. While you're fasting, take some extra time to seek Him. As you pray, thank Him for the power to carry you through. After it's over, congratulate yourself—you did it! (See—it wasn't so bad, was it?)

17

BETTER THAN
WALL STREET

re you just getting by—running short on money, living from paycheck to paycheck or running short on time, possessions or
temper? Are you living in the Land of Not Enough and don't have a clue
about the Land of More Than Enough?

I used to have more than enough money. I made a huge salary, but I
spent it all. Then I was in debt, so I had less than enough. I never had
enough love or respect. (Maybe that's why I tried to buy it with dollars.) I
never had enough peace—I never knew what that was. Of course, it's
tough to recognize peace when you live your life tied up in knots, fearful
of being discovered as a fraud, waiting for the next unexpected negative
thing to happen. Abundance was never a concept I could get my mind to
grasp.

BREAKING OUT

When I left my nice, cushy corporate job and started my own business,
the phrase *not enough* again had new meaning. Working for a corporation, I had taken a lot for granted. The literature drawers were always full.
The paycheck always came. The benefits package was covered. The
postage meters always had plenty of postage. The coffee machines were
never empty. Suddenly I discovered what cash flow was all about.

Then my business began to prosper, but it seemed as if I was always just one jump ahead of lack. Every time I'd get ahead, taxes would go up or a new expenditure would be on the horizon or something would break or my car would need replacing. You know the drill.

At one point I thought, *Is there no end to this? If I work hard enough to get abundance in the bank account, then I have so little time that I can't enjoy it. And no matter how hard I work, the federal government gets hungrier to extort more money from me. How do I put Washington on a diet?*

THE TRAP DOOR

Living in the world guarantees you will never get ahead. Is there an answer? Is there an escape hatch? You bet. Knowing God's biblical economics, economics that pertain to everything—including money, time, love, children, relationships, talent—everything. It all has to do with sowing, with planting seed. Seed is a biggie in God's Word. Planting seed is featured in forty-three books of the Bible.

God's kingdom is based on sowing and reaping. Have you ever heard anybody say, "Boy! When my ship comes in, I'm really going to give a lot to charity" or "I'm really going to give a big check to my church"? You've heard that, haven't you? We all have.

But somehow that ship just never comes in. Those checks just never get written. Why? Those people have life in the reverse order. You don't reap first and then sow. Sowing must come first.

Ask the farmer. He knows he must first plant tomato seeds before tomatoes can grow. Corn must be sown in the ground before a crop grows. Wheat must be planted before it can be harvested. So it is with money. Hey, I know we don't like to hear it, but that's the way it is.

Here's another fact farmers know well. You have to plant a big crop to get a big harvest. If you want abundance, you have to plant lots of seeds. If you want a financial harvest, it will take giving. Planting financial seeds is a must. But here's the best news of the century—you can't outgive God.

When you plant time, love, compassion or money into other people's lives—into the gospel—God is faithful to multiply your seeds. He promises it in His Word. If you don't have seed to sow, ask Him for it. He promises that He'll give you seed to sow. Sound too good to be true? Check out 2

Corinthians 9:10: "Now he that ministereth seed to the sower both minister bread for your food, and multiply your seed sown, and increase the fruits of your righteousness."

You take a risk on Wall Street. Some investments pay off. Others don't. But with God, every seed sown in good ground is multiplied back to you. How can you beat those odds?

OUT OF LACK

Moses led the children of Israel out of captivity in Egypt. As slaves in Egypt, they lived in the Land of Not Enough.

As he led them through the desert—even though they wandered around for forty years—God provided just enough for them every day. Clouds covered them by day, and fire warmed them by night. And God provided enough manna from heaven to feed them every day.

Moses spent forty years leading the children of Israel toward the Promised Land, the Land of More Than Enough. The Promised Land is what God has provided for us. We don't have to wear out three pairs of shoes to get there or wear out knee pads praying to get in. The Promised Land has been willed to us right here—not when we get to heaven, but right here and now. After all, in the Lord's Prayer He said, "Thy will be done in *earth*, as it is in heaven" (Matt. 6:10, emphasis added).

Are you living in the Land of Not Enough, but not the Land of More Than Enough? Do you want in? Do you know how to use the key to gain entry?

WHAT TO DO

Start planting seeds. Assess your current circumstances. Make a list of the things in your life that are in short supply. Then:

1. Begin sowing seeds. If you need money, sow financial seeds. If you need time, sow time. If you need discipline, sow some self-control.

2. As you sow your seed, lift it up as a sacrifice to God and pray over it. Sow it in faith by quoting God's multiplication scripture (2 Cor. 9:10).

3. Every day, water your plant with praise for the answer, thanking God that He has multiplied your seed back to you. (Yes, thank Him before

you see your harvest.) When you pray in faith, it's a done deal in the spiritual world. Your challenge is to receive your harvest when you pray, water it with your praise every day and wait in faith for the manifestation.

4. Rejoice when your seed is multiplied back to you. Then plant some more.

You can't save enough to bring about your harvest. Sowing is the only way to receive. It may seem backward to us, but I concluded a number of years ago that if God set it up that way, He did it for a reason. And as hard as it is for me to admit, He *is* smarter than I am. And certainly smarter than the High Priestess of Guilt and Condemnation, who tries to prevent me from lining up with the way God set it up.

A BACKWARD KINGDOM

Make all you can. Can all you get, then sit on the can. It's the world's way, and it makes sense to our natural minds.

But how many stories of disaster do we need to hear, stories of families whose houses were blown down by tornadoes, of people who've lost their life savings through bank failure, of business owners dragged into bankruptcy court? How many disasters do we have to read about before we start to wonder if there is a better way than what the world has to offer?

THE PA SYSTEM

Hey, who needs more enemies when you have one living in your head? Every time you ignore the wisdom presented in newspapers or on television, the enemy tells you you're committing an act of personal insanity. That's right, the High Priestess of Guilt and Condemnation from her microphone station in your head alternately beats you up when you spend too much money or when you don't spend enough; when you extend a hand to someone else or when you don't; when you operate apart from conventional wisdom or when you follow it. If you think you can't win, you're right. The wench with the microphone has a mission—to make you feel lousy about whatever act you perform, whatever deed you execute, whatever word you say, whatever thought you have. You can't win with her, so give it up.

But this just in: What works (God's way) is exactly the opposite of the way the world works. For instance, the world says to get revenge. God says to forgive. The world says to hoard your resources. God says to give them away: "Give, and it shall be given unto you" (Luke 6:38). The world says to accept what happens to you. God says to take authority over what happens to you. The world says other people make you complete. God says you're complete in Him. The world says you can make things happen through your own power. God says that if you turn loose and entrust your plans to Him, His power will bring your plans to fruition. See, it's all backwards, isn't it?

MEAT AND POTATOES

Are you ready for some real meat? We're not taking baby formula here, or even strained carrots. We're talking about the tough stuff. Ready? I'm going to give you God's twelve laws of sowing and reaping. I learned them from John Avanzini's ministry. John is a teacher of biblical economics. He's a bodacious teacher of the Word, and he also has a wonderful sense of humor.

Sharpen up a pencil, get some paper and let her rip. Here are the twelve laws:[1]

1. My seed must be planted (John 12:24).

Stop wishing and start acting. The biblical principles of sowing and reaping can be applied to anything—money, time, love, property and possessions. You name it.

Make a decision to act and then follow through on that decision by taking what you're in short supply of and giving away some of what you need. For instance, several years ago I was desperate for a breakthrough in my business. I needed clients and revenue. I took what little money I had and sowed it into my church. I needed money to come to me, so I also found a small company that badly needed my services for a two-day planning session. They couldn't afford my fee, so I made a decision to sow a seed by doing the planning session for free.

I believed God for the increase. Sowing my money into my church and my time into another business created the breakthrough I needed. Within a month, clients and revenue were coming at me from all directions.

2. I must render my seed useless (Mark 10:29–30; John 12:24).

Go ahead. Look up the scriptures. Jesus isn't telling you to take a powder from your family and possessions. He's talking about inconveniencing yourself for the sake of the gospel. And isn't that what sowing seed is all about—inconveniencing yourself? Notice that He says you'll receive a hundredfold return *in this lifetime.* He's not talking about heaven. He's talking about here on earth.

Letting go of your seed means that what you sow has no strings attached to it. If you sow money into a church, don't tell them how they should use it. Once you give it, it's not yours anymore. It belongs to the Lord. Even if you sow money into someone's life and they choose to use it for drugs or alcohol, that's not your issue. You sowed in obedience to God's Word. He's responsible for bringing in your harvest, not the person who received your gift.

3. I must plant what I expect to harvest (Gen. 1:12).

Every seed produces after its own kind. If you want to grow cucumbers in your backyard, don't plant squash. No matter how much you like watermelon, planting tomatoes won't grow melons. Therefore, what you need is what you must plant.

Let me give you an example. I desperately needed some new carpet in my living room, dining room and in the hall leading back to the bedrooms. Yet every time I priced carpet, I gagged. I needed to buy the carpet pad, too. To get really good stuff was going to cost several thousand dollars.

Someone at church had wanted carpet for a long time. I wrote a check to put toward her carpet. That was a seed sown. And I named the seed with God when I sowed it. I said, "Lord, I'm sowing seed into her life for her carpet, and it's a privilege for me to do so. Right now I name my seed, and my seed is new carpet for our house. I believe that You will multiply back to me my seed sown. I thank You right now for my harvest."

Within six months, the Lord had brought me some unexpected business, which gave me the money to buy new carpet. But on top of that, the Lord gave me the ability to purchase my new carpet through one of my clients. I got the best carpet on the market at the wholesale price.

I needed carpet, so I sowed carpet. Get the idea?

4. My harvest size is established when my seed is sown (2 Cor. 9:6).

That scripture says it all. Forrest Gump might say, "Stingy is as stingy does." The size of your seed determines the size of your harvest.

In addition to that, God also says in His Word that He measures the magnitude of your gift not by the size of what you sow but by the size of what you have left. Remember the story of the widow with two mites? She gave everything she had to Jesus. Although He had received many large gifts, He made an announcement to the crowd when the little woman threw in her two mites. Jesus took note of the size of her offering, and He blessed her richly.

When you don't have enough and you sow what you have, you're saying to God, "I don't have the power, but You do; I'm trusting Your power to bring forth Your blessings for me." So if you need a big harvest, sow a big seed.

5. My seed must be planted in good ground (Matt. 13:8).

Ask the farmer if he would spend time planting seed in rocky ground or in soil parched by the sun. He'll say, "No way. I'd be wasting my seed."

And so will you. If you sow seed into a church that doesn't produce results, a ministry that doesn't bear fruit or a charity that doesn't actually help people, you're wasting your seed. If you're sowing all your time into the television set or the latest movies from Hollywood, you're not sowing in very good ground, either.

The seed that you sow is precious. It's your life. It's your substance. Make sure when you plant your seed that you're planting into ground that has a demonstrated track record for producing results. As for churches, are people saved, healed and set free from bondage there? Do you hear testimonies of people who have been set free from drugs and alcohol, sickness and lack? If not, then perhaps it's not very good ground.

What about ministries? Do they regularly share their results with you? Are there testimonies of changed lives, people who are now productive members of society? Are the poor not only fed and clothed, but also ministered to? You see what I mean. Ask some questions before you start sowing your seed. There are thousands and thousands of worthy churches, ministries, organizations and charities that will be blessed by your substance. But contribute to those that produce results. That's the kind of ground you want to sow in, whether you're sowing your money, your time, your expertise or your goods.

6. I must always wait a period of time between planting and harvesting (Mark 4:26–27).

Crops don't grow overnight. Neither will your harvest come in overnight.

I remember planting tomatoes when I was a little kid. Two days after planting them I was out rooting around in the garden, and I dug down to where I had planted my seeds to see if anything was happening. I remember being really disappointed to see that nothing seemed to be going on with those roots. (Sometimes I'm still impatient.)

Farmers will tell you that when they plant seed, they have to turn loose the seed, let it go and forget about it, water the ground and expect their seed to grow roots. The seeds we sow work the same way. Whether it's time, property or money, there's always a waiting period between the time we plant and pray over our seed and the time it springs forth. Sometimes the time is short. Sometimes it can take weeks, months or even years, but the harvest always comes if we don't turn loose the faith we exercised when we planted the seed—or cease giving God thanks for the harvest before we actually see that harvest with our eyes.

7. I must properly maintain my crop and Christian life to experience a proper harvest (Matt. 6:33; 13:7; Mark 4:19).

Check out these scriptures. God tells us what can choke off our harvest and prevent it from coming to pass. He's pointing out how the cares of this world—worries, anxieties, the deceitfulness of riches, the lust for worldly things—can bring weeds that will choke off our seeds. He is also encouraging us to seek His kingdom *first,* and then all these things (all the goodies we want) will be added unto us.

In short, we're supposed to live worry-free, trusting God to perform on our behalf. But we can't trust unless we seek Him first and spend quality time with Him and His Word.

Without His Word, we don't have anything on which to hook our belief. (Seeking Him first will also prevent us from falling into other traps like unforgiveness, bitterness, judgmentalism and deception—all of which can delay, if not destroy, our harvest by preventing this power of God from working in our lives.)

By the way, God is not watching you like a hawk, making a list and checking it twice. One little slip won't choke off your harvest. God knows your heart. When you slip up, all you have to do is repent, ask for His forgiveness, receive it, forgive yourself and keep going. God wants to see progress, not perfection.

8. I must always sow to my harvest size, not from my harvest size (Gen. 26:12).

This law works in concert with number four. It means that you shouldn't look at your current crop to determine your future harvest. Walking in God's abundance in all things is a process. If you want a big harvest, continue to sow big seeds. If your current harvest is little, don't take a little seed from it and sow it. Sow a seed consistent with the harvest you need.

Let me give you an example. Several years ago I was in tremendous need of time. I had none. I raced from sunup to sundown and never seemed to get everything done. What I needed was another six hours a day.

God began to urge me to tithe my time to Him. Ten percent! Gulp! That's 2.4 hours a day! Gulp! That's almost seventeen hours a week! Gulp! *Impossible*, I thought. I needed a big harvest. So I began by keeping a log of how I was spending my time for two weeks. (What a humbling experience!) Yes, I had more time to spend than I thought I did.

Then I took a look at how much time I was giving to God. I was already attending church Sunday morning, Sunday night and Wednesday night. So I added the Tuesday night intercessory prayer group to my schedule. Then I made a commitment (a *real* seed, I mean we're talking *seed*) to get up at six o'clock in the morning and spend an extra hour of time in prayer and fellowship with God. It all added up to seventeen hours a week.

I sowed to the harvest size that I needed (lots of time), not *from* the harvest size I had (very little time). Almost immediately, I noticed that my schedule began to smooth out, and I had more time than I ever thought possible. When I put God first, He made my schedule work. It still does. And I have more energy than any twelve people I know!

9. My expense is always highest at harvest time (Matt. 20:1).

This scripture talks about a property owner who goes out early in the morning to hire laborers to work in the vineyard. It's an expense. This man apparently knew that he wasn't going to get any wine without paying someone to pick those grapes and stomp them into wine. All his expenses were up-front, before he took his first sip. It's the same with us.

Farmers know that before they get paid for their crops, they must bear the expense of seed irrigation and combining and packaging and shipping …money spent before money is earned. Manufacturers know they must incur expenses in technology, manufacturing equipment, labor, packaging, marketing, advertising and public relations before they can turn a dime. Corporations have to keep focused on the long term while they incur short-term expenses. It is the same with us.

When we plant seeds, we're doing it out of shortage. It's inconvenient for us. It's expensive. If nothing else, we incur the expense of patience, fortitude and determination, the effort of watering our seeds with praises to God and thanksgiving to Him for the answer. But the answer always comes if we faint not. It's part of our covenant!

10. A portion of my harvest is to be used for sowing again (2 Cor. 9:10).

You may have heard someone say, "Don't eat your seed." That simply means that after your harvest comes in, don't consume it all on yourself—you need to continue to plant seeds. You want a continuous harvest.

Back to our farmer again. He'd be an idiot to rejoice over his crop, harvest it all, sell it and then go to his house, put his feet up and expect corn to drop out of the sky for the next year. Nope—he has to plant more seed for a crop next year. It's a continuous process.

11. A portion of my harvest is for me to keep (2 Cor. 9:7).

We probably all groove on this one. It doesn't require much explanation. God does want to pour out His bounty on us. He *desires* for us to prosper and be healthy, even as our souls prosper (3 John 2).

12. My harvest is a miracle (1 Cor. 3:6).

Every seed sown has the power to bring about a harvest, if it is watered with praise and faithfulness.

Do you know that archaeologists have found seeds in ancient Egyptian tombs that never germinated? The seeds had been planted in the ground, and centuries later, they sprouted. God's power is a miracle, and it's waiting to spring forth. All we have to do is plant it.

Here's a tip. I keep a list of my seeds sown so that periodically I can look at my list and give God thanks and praise for the answers. In this way I can water my seeds with my praise and thanksgiving. As my harvest springs forth, I cross the items off my list and give special honor to God. I like to be able to keep up with my seeds so I can pray and rejoice over them.

BRISKET

I told you—strong meat, right? There are many, many other scriptures that verify these principles of sowing and reaping. I can tell you from my personal experience that they work. All of them work in a way that's opposite of conventional wisdom. But what do you care as long as they work? God knows what He's doing, and He knew what He was doing when He set these principles in motion. They work for me, and if you'll use them, they'll work for you. God is no respecter of persons (Acts 10:34).

If someone gave you a map to buried treasure, you'd fall over your boots getting there, wouldn't you? This is better than a treasure map. It's a treasure that never runs out—it just keeps on giving. So put these laws to work for you. Come on—you know your way isn't working. God's way will. Go for it!

Progress Check

1. What have you learned about the relationship between what you say and the circumstances that dominate your life?

_____

_____

_____

2. What actions have you taken that have contributed to the problems in your life?

_____

_____

_____

3. What has been unfamiliar and surprising to you about what you've read so far?

_____

_____

_____

4. Are you willing to take what's new to you and confirm it through prayer and study to arrive at your own conclusions?

_____

_____

_____

5. Are you willing to build your faith and begin to trust God in areas of your life that you've not had faith in before?

_____

_____

_____

6. Are you willing to endure the discomfort of breaking out of your religious tradition in order to have a more powerful and sustaining relationship with God?

_____

_____

_____

7. Where are you going to begin stretching your faith—finances, family, health, freedom from worry? How will you do it?

_____

_____

_____

_____

_____

_____

_____

8. What are your biggest questions for which you need answers from God?

_____

_____

_____

_____

_____

_____

_____

19

LESS IS MORE

Most members of my family know I'm kitchen-challenged. My ex-mother-in-law stood over me patiently until I could make a perfect pie crust from scratch. But years of not practicing, plus a lack of interest in cooking, have made me the queen of carry-out.

Here's a clue to my level of interest: My husband, Chuck, gives me an occasional pop quiz on kitchen appliances, just to make sure I can still recognize them. Getting a microwave was one of the most important events in my life. Now I can make bad food faster.

One Saturday, Chuck dashed into the house around noon and found me putting something into the microwave. "What's that?" he said. "It smells funny."

I said, "It's chicken noodle soup, but it didn't have enough chicken to suit me, so I added a can of tuna." Somehow, tuna noodle soup didn't cut it for him—plus it smelled like something the ocean left when the tide rolled out.

Perhaps my most famous kitchen mishap was deciding to make homemade yeast rolls. I had all the ingredients except the yeast, but I thought, *Oh well, how bad can they be without it?* When the rolls came out of the oven, they looked like small spaceships. One of the kids wondered whether we were going to have an after-dinner game of Frisbee or use them for coasters. If anybody wants to know what bread looked like back in Jesus' day, my yeast rolls are a modern-day prototype.

As much as I like to take shortcuts, I've learned that there are some rules you just can't break if you want results. For instance, cookbooks don't lie. Without yeast, rolls don't rise.

GOD'S YEAST

Just as there are rules for baking, there are rules for money. Now don't hyperventilate, but we're going to talk about tithing. Like it or not, tithing is to the rest of your money what yeast is to rolls. Tithing is what God uses to keep your needs continuously supplied. Contrary to conventional wisdom, God didn't design tithing to take your money from you. He designed tithing to get money *to* you.

God feels so strongly about tithing that in Malachi 3:10 He says, "Go ahead—challenge Me to see if I won't come through for you!" God says that if you're faithful in tithing 10 percent of your income to Him, you have a right to put pressure on your covenant with Him to continuously supply your needs. Tithing is mentioned prominently in both the Old and New Testaments. Your faithfulness in giving God 10 percent of your earnings is a symbol of obedience, and it is the leavening that God uses to multiply the rest of your finances.

Many Christians don't want to hear about tithing. They say things like, "Oh, that's just religious bondage." "That was only in Old Testament days." "The only thing preachers want is your money." "God knows I'm just getting by now; He can't possibly want me to live on 10 percent less."

If you've said or thought these things, hang on. This chapter will illustrate why and how tithing blesses your finances. You'll see how less can be more.

THE PROCESS OF EXCHANGE

Tithing is talked about thirty-nine times in God's Word—meaning He's very serious about it. Why do you think God is so focused on tithing? It's not that He needs the money. He already owns all the money in the world. It's just that much of it is in the hands of the unrighteous, not in yours. Getting money into your hands takes submitting to God's financial system and proving yourself to be trustworthy. God can't trust you with great riches until you've proven yourself to be a faithful steward of small riches. Think about it this way: Would you trust your house, furniture and every cent in your bank account to your sixteen-year-old child? Get real! Your offspring would have to demonstrate years of responsible behavior before you'd even consider it.

The Word says that the tithe is the Lord's (Lev. 27:30). Your obedience in giving back to Him what is His allows Him to guarantee to you what is yours. In Philippians 4:19 God promises that He'll meet all your needs in exchange for your responsible faithfulness to Him. But the first step is yours—you tithe; He delivers. I know what you're thinking: *Why does God need my measly 10 percent? Tell Him to go get it from Ross Perot, Ted Kennedy or Donald Trump.*

God wants your heart. That 10 percent is a symbol of your faith in Him as your financial source. You offer God's 10 percent back to Him in exchange for His promise to bless your finances. It says you trust Him to come through for you. When you operate in trust, you operate out of your heart.

TRUST

Trust is given willingly. It's not the product of coercion. For example, have you ever bludgeoned one of your kids into doing something they really didn't want to do? If they finally relented, did they do it willingly? Of course not! I remember arguing with my mother over a party dress that ended up making me look as if I were wearing a telephone booth. She kept saying, "If we just take some of the material out of the skirt, it will look lovely on you. You'll be the belle of the ball." I wasn't buying it. I wanted the skirt just the way it was. She nagged and cajoled. I fought and rebelled. She finally prevailed and took a hunk out of the skirt. I wore the thing all right, hating every minute of it and the party, too. Did I wear the dress willingly? About as willingly as if someone had dropped a grenade down my shorts—but I wore it. Both my mother and I wound up being miserable over the entire encounter. I didn't trust her decision, and she didn't trust mine. Since I didn't trust her advice, I didn't freely choose my response.

GOD IS NOT YOUR MOTHER

God doesn't argue and cajole. He doesn't wear you down. He just asks you to choose because He's given you the greatest gift of all—free will. That includes the ability to live your life the way you want to live it, with the choices that you want to make. Choices, of course, come with rewards or consequences. At all times you have two systems from which to choose: God's operating system (the kingdom of God), which is described in your Bible, and the world's operating system, which is described through intellect, experience and conventional wisdom.

God loves you regardless of what you choose, even when you make bad decisions. Every day of your life, you have the option to choose His way or the world's way. One decision leads to victory, the other to defeat.

Tithing is God's operating system of victorious finances. Tithing gives God permission to access your finances and fix your problems. Your obedience to His Word and your faith in His promise says, "I'm making You Lord over my finances, and I trust You as my source."

Where did tithing come from? It's been around since the Garden of Eden. Let me show you.

Have a Nice Life

In Genesis 2:8, God breathed the breath of life into Adam and created the Garden of Eden. In verse 9, God grew "every tree that was pleasant to the sight and good for food." He also put the tree of knowledge in the garden. In verse 15 He put Adam in the garden to dress it (take care of it) and to keep it. In verses 16 and 17, God gave Adam an instruction: "Of every tree of the garden thou mayest freely eat: but of the tree of the knowledge of good and evil, thou shalt not eat of it: for in the day that thou eatest thereof thou shalt surely die." Dying means spiritual death— separation from God. God gave Adam a choice and revealed the consequences for a bad choice.

In the same chapter, God formed every beast of the field, every fowl of the air and brought them to Adam to name. In verse 22, God created woman. Adam had it all. God created paradise for him and essentially said, "Have a nice life."

But take a look in verse 25. It says that "they were both naked, the man and his wife, and were not ashamed." They were completely at peace and comfortable before God Himself. Then guess what happened? In chapter 3, the serpent (the devil) conned Eve into eating from the tree that God had set apart as a symbol of their obedience to Him. That tree is a picture of the tithe. The serpent deceived Eve by saying, "Surely you won't die if you eat of the tree. After all, God knows when you eat of it your eyes will be opened and you will be as gods." (Get it? You'll be as smart as God is.)

Eve went for it. She was deceived by the temptation, but Adam wasn't. He knew better, but he disobeyed anyway. Bad choice. When God showed up in verse 8, suddenly Adam and Eve hid themselves from the presence of the Lord. In verse 10, Adam said, "I heard thy voice in the garden, and I was afraid, because I was naked; and I hid myself." Before their disobedience, Adam and Eve were not ashamed at being naked. Now they were. That act of disobedience separated Adam and Eve from God's best for them. Everything had been set up for their pleasure, enjoyment and dominion, but by their actions they said, "No thanks. We know better."

The Great Robbery

Before you say, "But that took place way back in the Garden of Eden," look at Malachi 3:6. God says, "For I am the LORD, I change not." In verse 7, He says, "Even from the days of your fathers ye are gone away from mine ordinances, and have not kept them. Return unto me and I will return unto you, saith the LORD of hosts." Check out verse 8, "Will a man rob God? Yet ye have robbed me. But ye say, Wherein have we robbed thee? In tithes and offerings." Notice . . . tithes and offerings.

Then in verse 10, God issues a challenge, the only one I know of in the Bible. "Bring ye all the tithes into the storehouse that there may be meat in mine house, and prove me now herewith, saith the Lord of hosts [the Lord is saying, 'Prove Me, challenge Me'], if I will not open you the windows of heaven, and pour you out a blessing, that there shall not be room enough to receive it." Verse 11 says, "And I will rebuke the devourer for your sakes, and he shall not destroy the fruits of your ground; neither shall your vine cast her fruit before the time in the field, saith the LORD of hosts."

Who is the devourer? The devil. The Hebrew word *akal* means "to eat, to consume, to burn up." It was used by Bible writers to define the actions of drought, famine, war, pestilence and plague. To "rebuke the devourer" is to check, curb or deter what consumes your time, energy or cash flow. And think of it—the only three things you have that you can give God are your time, energy and money.

THE RECIPE WORKS

When you bake bread and include yeast, it rises and multiplies the volume of your loaf. When you tithe, you demonstrate your obedience to God and your acknowledgment of His system of operation vs. the world's system of operation. God uses your tithe to take care of the people in His family (Christians...that's you, too) and to fund the teaching and preaching of the gospel around the world. In return, He pledges to bless your finances.

WHAT TO DO

So 10 percent supplies me abundantly, right? Wrong. Your tithe guarantees that you operate under an open heaven. But tithing isn't giving to God—it's returning back to Him what is His. You haven't given until you've given over and above your tithe (more about that in a later chapter). For now, concentrate on getting in line for abundance.

1. Study the scriptures in this chapter.

2. Tell God you're going to take Him up on His challenge.

3. Make a commitment to tithe 10 percent of your income. By the way, your tithe should go to your local church, if that's where you are being fed spiritually. If you're not being fed spiritually at your church, that's another discussion. Tithe to wherever you are being fed—a television ministry or a Bible teacher or a ministry that publishes God's Word in teaching booklets.

4. Offer your tithe up as a memorial to God. As you do, pray over it and confess Malachi 3:10. Thank God that He has opened the windows of heaven for you and that you are now operating under an open heaven.

5. When circumstances come about to make it look as if you can't tithe, tell the devil to get off your finances in Jesus' name. Then say aloud, "I have a covenant with almighty God. His covenant with me tells me in Philippians 4:19 that He meets all my needs according to His riches in glory through Christ Jesus." Then pray, "God, I am

trusting You to bring forth finances to supply my needs. You promised it to me, and I know You'll do it in Jesus' name."

6. If you just can't start with 10 percent, start with something less—3 percent or 5 percent. Then work your way up. It's faithfulness He's after.

Rejoice, because you've just given the Lord permission to grow the 90 percent you have left. And remember:

- "Trust in the Lord with all thine heart; and lean not unto thine own understanding" (Prov. 3:5).

- "Your glorying is not good. Know ye not that a little leaven leaveneth the whole lump?" (1 Cor. 5:6).

- "A little leaven leaveneth the whole lump" (Gal. 5:9).

Since I've begun tithing, I've never been without the funds I needed. Oh sure, the enemy has come a number of times to make it look as if I wouldn't make it, but I know I can trust in my covenant. When I confess the Word and thank Him for His provisions, He'll literally move heaven and earth to keep my pipeline going. He is faithful—less is more!

A little yeast makes the whole batch of rolls rise. A little obedience in giving back God's 10 percent makes the rest of your money grow and puts you in position for more than enough.

20

UNCLE

It was like something out of a sitcom, something that would happen to Lucy and Ethel. I went into a weight-loss center and noticed a work crew in the lobby laying floor tiles. What a mess! Inside, I began the ritual of taking off jewelry, belt, accessories and anything that might add weight to the number that would appear on the menacing scales. After all, those silk scarves can really add pounds.

As I left an hour later, I forgot about the floor-tile work and the thick black glue used as adhesive. Thinking only of the huge number on the scales and how fast I could lower that number, I stepped out onto the freshly spread adhesive. A step turned into a slide—and then, with my elbows and feet flailing, I fell right in the glue. I was covered in black goo from the top of my left shoulder all the way down my leg to the bottom of my feet. It wasn't pretty.

The workmen were awfully nice, dabbing at me with wads of paper towel, but the paper towels stuck. Big Bird would have been proud.

Driving home while sitting on my right hip was a challenge, but not as challenging as prying my left hand off the steering wheel when I got there. The nail file in my purse created enough leverage to pry my hand off the wheel. But that was the easy part. The tough part was yet to come. Inside, I peeled clothes off like a maniac, but there was one big problem: My pantyhose was permanently bonded to my leg.

You've heard of bonded building material, extra strength to withstand extra stress? My Hanes could have withstood a riptide. Trying to pull them off my body was excruciating. After several aborted attempts, I broke down and called my husband. He had to come home from work to get me out of pantyhose jail. We had to use towels soaked with lighter fluid to free me.

Like every other time in my life, I thought I could handle the problem with no one the wiser (except the workmen). I was wrong. I finally had to ask for help.

I'VE FALLEN DOWN AND CAN'T GET UP!

Asking for help has never been at the top on my skills inventory. It's something I've had to learn to do. Asking for help always made me feel too powerless, too vulnerable. I guess my greatest fears were that people would think less of me and that I wasn't worth inconveniencing someone else.

So I lived with my false pride, thinking I could deal with whatever came along. What a lie! I was worthy enough to ask for help, although I didn't think so. My pride deprived me of assistance from others and deprived them of the opportunity to sow into my life. (Remember sowing and reaping?)

Worst of all, my false pride formed the basis of my early relationship with the Lord. I thought that even with Him I had to do everything myself. So I'd pray, and then assume I had to think through all the possibilities to figure out the best solution. Then I had to make sure I manipulated all the pieces of the solution into place. It never occurred to me that my process meant I was operating in my own strength and not God's strength. Here's a news flash: God wants to help us. The only thing He asks in return is that we believe His Word and trust Him to follow through, no matter how bad the circumstances look—because it's not over until we win.

TRUST THE CREATOR, NOT THE CREATION

Why did I think I had to help God do His job? One by one all my heroes had let me down. No one in my life had ever been an example of unconditional commitment and follow-through—the kind of person who said what they'd do and then did it. I'd had a lifetime of men and women betraying my trust. Although some people are more trustworthy than others, human beings are imperfect. Even the best ones fail us. When they do, it's really brutal. So many had failed me that I didn't know how to trust. That's because I'd spent a lifetime trying to depend on other people (God's creation) to fill my needs.

Psychologists say that your first relationship with God is patterned after the one you had with your earthly father. If your dad abandoned you, you think God will abandon you. If your dad was judgmental or accusatory, you think God is critical and vengeful, too. If your dad was controlling and manipulative, you think God is the same.

Some of my friends had fathers who loved them but who didn't protect them from other family members. Some had fathers who were never around. The daughters of these fathers picture God as One who loves them but won't come through in the clutch. Whatever your circumstances, if your earthly father was less than expected, you shrink from commitment to God, fearing the same consequences.

Can you relate? Do you have trouble asking for help from your friends, family members or coworkers? Do you shrink from asking God for help because you think you're supposed to be able to do everything on your own? Do you ask God to take charge and then take the responsibility back from Him, fearing He won't honor your request? If so, you're like millions of other women. But I have great news for you.

God will never leave you nor forsake you. He promised that in Hebrews 13:5. Look it up and see for yourself. He says He's our refuge and our strength, a very present help in trouble (Ps. 46:1). Your friends or family may lie to you—they're imperfect. But God is perfect...He won't lie.

SATISFACTION GUARANTEED!

Have you ever bought a product with a manufacturer's guarantee? If anything goes wrong, the manufacturer replaces it free of charge...no hassles? Not likely. Most guarantees include tiny print describing the circumstances that void the guarantee. That's when you find the guarantee applicable only on alternate Tuesdays in leap years. And only if you're a Vietnam veteran.

God doesn't work that way. His guarantee is good. "God is not a man, that he should lie" (Num. 23:19).

But wait, there's more proof:

- "If ye abide in me, and my words abide in you, ye shall ask what ye will, and it shall be done unto you" (John 15:7).

- "Therefore I [Jesus] say unto you, What things soever ye desire, when ye pray, believe that ye receive them, and ye shall have them" (Mark 11:24). There are only two conditions to this promise: Verses 25 and 26 say that when you pray, forgive. If you're holding grudges against anyone, your prayers won't work. Also, "when ye pray, believe that ye receive"; you have to come to Him in faith, not in doubt.

- "For I the LORD thy God will hold thy right hand, saying unto thee, Fear not; I will help thee" (Isa. 41:13).

See—this is the real thing. A 100 percent unconditional guarantee from the Creator of the universe. Don't think the High Priestess of Guilt and Condemnation doesn't have a stroke when she hears you say these words. Her whole mission in life is to make you think God's promises won't work for you.

WHAT'S THE CATCH?

There isn't one. You only need to understand the following truth: Your faith is what brings your victory. You're the asker...God is the giver. Your faith is the messenger.

If you ordered a Domino's pizza and the kitchen staff prepared your order without a way to deliver it, you could sit home hungry all day. Without a messenger, the pizza won't move from the store to your table. Crying won't help. Only a messenger will. Your faith works the same way. Faith is your messenger to God's throne to bring back the goods. It's the currency you use to change your circumstances.

For instance, here's a *Jeopardy* Bible question: Did Jesus heal everyone who came to Him in New Testament days? No. But He did heal every single one who came to Him in faith. Every single one! Don't take my word for it—look it up for yourself.

Why is faith so important? Because it is your spoken commitment that your source for the answer is God alone. Not the world, not science, not wishful thinking, not positive affirmations. Your faith is the messenger that demonstrates to God that you believe what He said in His Word and that you trust Him to honor His Word.

Let's see how important Jesus thinks faith is:

- "But without faith it is impossible to please him: for he that cometh to God must believe that he is, and that he is a rewarder of them that diligently seek him" (Heb. 11:6).

- "But the just shall live by faith [My righteous servant shall live by his conviction respecting man's relationship to God and divine things, and holy fervor born of faith and conjoined with it]; and if he draws back and shrinks in fear, My soul has no delight or pleasure in him" (Heb. 10:38, AMP).

- "That your faith should not stand in the wisdom of men, but in the power of God" (1 Cor. 2:5).

- "According to your faith be it unto you" (Matt. 9:29).

- "But what does it say? The Word (God's message in Christ) is near you, on your lips and in your heart; that is, the Word (the message, the basis and object) of faith which we preach" (Rom. 10:8, AMP).

Faith is the runner that delivers your answer from God. Faith gives God permission to come into your life, fix the problems and loose His blessings on you. Faith is the substance that enables you to tell the High Priestess to take a hike while you wait in victory for your answer.

WHAT TO DO

Since faith is your messenger, take the necessary steps to build that dude up, to make him as strong, quick and tenacious as a bulldog. Here's how to put your faith on steroids:

1. Choose life. Where you go to church is a life-and-death decision.

Don't be led to where your relatives go, where you feel comfortable or where it's convenient or socially acceptable. What feels good will always be easy on your flesh, but that won't build your faith. There are clues to identify churches that will build your faith.

- Do people walk into church carrying their own Bibles?
- Does the pastor, minister or priest preach the power of the blood of Jesus?
- Does the church believe healing is for today? "Jesus Christ the same yesterday, and today, and for ever" (Heb. 13:8). He healed then, and He heals now.
- Do you regularly see people healed? Hear reports of financial blessings? Listen to testimonies of those set free? See evidence of miracles?
- Do people in the church love on you the minute you walk in the door? Do they make you feel welcome? If not, beat feet until you find a church that does.

Can you answer *yes* to all these questions? If not, change churches. If you don't, you're making a conscious decision to settle for less than God has provided for you. Do you have to change churches? No. Will God still love you if you don't? Of course. But staying in a church that doesn't demonstrate evidence of healing, restored lives and freedom from addiction and bondage will keep you in bondage. Hosea 4:6 says, "My people are destroyed for lack of knowledge." Staying in a church that doesn't teach the reality of the Word will rob you of your complete victory.

2. Listen to Christian teaching tapes. Make your car a rolling library. Why invest your time listening to secular music when there's no return on your investment that will change your circumstances?

3. Study God's Word every day. You eat every day, don't you? Your spirit man is just as hungry as your natural man. Both need to be fed daily.

4. Go to church at least twice a week. Don't let the High Priestess tell you that you don't have time. Jesus loved you enough to suffer agony on the cross. He's given you one hundred sixty-eight hours a week. Don't tell me you can't give up four of them to worship Him and learn how to receive the inheritance He's purchased for you.

5. Learn how to praise God—and how to consistently praise Him—for the answer even before you see it with your own eyes.

Go ahead—cry "Uncle!" You know your way isn't working anymore. God is right there waiting to pick up the slack. He loves you unconditionally and wants to bless you. He cared enough to put it in writing and seal it with the blood of His Son. It's our manufacturer's guarantee of performance.

21

BLACK BELTS AND HOCKEY PLAYERS

Someone once asked hockey great Wayne Gretsky the secret of his success. "It's simple," he said. "I skate to where the puck is going, not to where it is." Gretsky knows that if he is fixated on the current position of the puck, he'll be out of position to take control of it. Winning takes thinking ahead in order to score. Scoring is the difference between winning and just playing the game.

What about you? Are you focused on the goal, or are you all tangled up in your current circumstances? Does the High Priestess have you focused on the here and now, with your eyes riveted on lack, loneliness, failure or trouble? That's her job, you know—to scare you into submission to the bleakness of your reality.

Have you ever watched martial arts experts break through stacks of concrete and wonder why the medevac helicopter wasn't there to pick them up? I had always been mystified by that performance skill until one of the performers explained to me how the process works.

It's Not Brute Strength

When a martial arts expert stands in front of a stack of concrete blocks preparing to split it in two, he doesn't focus his attention on the blocks. If he did, breakthrough would be impossible. Instead, he focuses on the

97

floor beneath the concrete. Then the energy of the blow takes him right through the blocks to the point of focus. Prayer works the same way.

Do your prayers cut through obstacles? Listen to yourself when you pray. Do you sound something like this? "O God, please help me! I don't have enough money to last until the end of the month!" "Help, God! My daughter's an alcoholic, and I don't know what else to do! I'm at the end of my rope!" "My husband's been diagnosed with cancer. Please heal him, God. I don't know how I'll survive without him!" "O God, I've tried everything I know to do, but I can't get rid of these cigarettes. Please take the desire to smoke away from me!"

Sound familiar? If so, you have focused your attention on the concrete blocks, not the floor beneath them. You're hung up on the obstacles, speaking your inability to break through them, crying out to God to get them out of your way. You're speaking the problem, not the solution. I know...I've been there, done that! Much anguish, little relief.

MOVING GOD

Do you know God is not moved by your need? If He were moved by need, India and Somalia would be the richest nations in the world. If He were moved by need, sick babies would never die. Terrorists would never prevail. People would never be bound in chains of poverty, hate, disease or failure. Why does tragedy exist? Two reasons. Watch out—this is going to hurt.

1. God does not have permission to come in and fix your plight— not until you speak His Word, which frees Him to be on the scene.

I know, you think I'm nuts. You've heard God is in control of all circumstances. He is, but only if you speak His Word in faith.

Why? God is not a contract breaker. He's bound by His Word. By His Word He spoke the universe into existence. (See Genesis 1.) By His Word He put Adam and Eve in the Garden of Eden, gave them dominion and gave them free will to make their own decisions. Unfortunately, they chose to rebel against God's instructions and brought forth the consequences described in Genesis 3. In disobeying God, Adam and Eve gave up their dominion of the earth to the serpent (the devil), who became the god of this world (2 Cor. 4:4). Bummer.

But God had a backup plan. John 3:16 tells us that He loves us so much that He sent His Son to purchase our freedom and to reestablish our choice to give God dominion in our lives. When we choose to become born-again believers, we gain access to God's power through His Word. We have access to dominion over our circumstances through Him. How?

When we speak God's Word in prayer, we give Him access to fix our problems. We see it in Revelation 12:11: "And they [Christians] overcame him [Satan] by the blood of the Lamb, and by the word of their testimony."

2. God has already done all He's going to do about your finances, health, family, career, wisdom, power, relationships and possessions.

Your victory in every area of life has already been bought and paid for by the blood of Jesus. You have the instruction manual (His Word) that guarantees everything to you that Jesus purchased. If you're not walking in victory, it's not God's fault…it's yours. Ouch! "My people are destroyed for lack of knowledge" (Hos. 4:6). "He sent his word, and healed them, and delivered them from their destructions" (Ps. 107:20).

So what is it we need to know? Knowledge of His Word. How to speak it over every negative obstacle in our lives. Speaking His Word (not speaking the problems) builds our faith, sends it out as a messenger and gives God the green light to bring forth the answer. It's your inheritance. The centurion in Matthew shows us how it's done. He approached Jesus and asked Him to heal his servant. Although Jesus was willing to go to the centurion's home, the centurion replied, "Speak the word only, and my servant shall be healed" (Matt. 8:8). In verse 13, Jesus says, "Go thy way; and as thou hast believed, so be it done unto thee. And his servant was healed in the selfsame hour."

Can It Be This Easy?

It's not easy, but it is certain. Building your faith, speaking the Word and placing God in first place in your life takes time and discipline. But while you're doing it, you're building up a faith arsenal that works. Wouldn't you rather invest your time and energy in something that works than spend the same amount of time wringing your hands and worrying? Of course, the High Priestess would love you to spend every moment of every day tied up in knots, praying helpless, powerless prayers. But that's exactly the wrong thing to do.

So strap on your skates. Skate to take control of that puck. Cinch up your waist and your black belt of faith and focus past the obstacles. Fix your eyes on the solution—on Jesus, the author and finisher of your faith. After all, "[Faith] is the victory that overcometh the world" (1 John 5:4). The word *victory* in the Greek text means "the conquest." Jesus is your means of conquest.

WHAT TO DO

Pull out your paper and pen, and let's take a test.

1. Write down everything that is currently causing you pain, distress, anger, worry or defeat.

2. Say aloud, "I have a choice. I can focus on this list and watch the problems grow, or I can find out what God has to say about this list in His Word and focus on that instead. I choose to focus on His Word."

3. Spend some time in your concordance looking up scriptures that say the opposite of your laundry list of circumstances. Write the scriptures down.

4. Say aloud, "Lord, thank You for giving me the victory that overcomes the world. I choose victory over defeat; therefore, I choose to speak Your Word only and not speak my problems." Then speak your list of scriptures every day.

5. Thank Him and give Him praise that He has given you the way out. Thank Him for bringing His promises forth in your life. Don't quit speaking the truth and thanking Him for the answer until you see the complete manifestation of each and every answer.

It's a formula that works. Just as guilt is the "gift that keeps on giving," the Word is the power that keeps on delivering.

22

THROUGH A GLASS DARKLY

D o you ever wonder why you're here? Why you've been put on this planet? Growing up, I used to think my purpose was to please others. By doing so, I would honor my family. Then I went through a phase of thinking that I was on earth to please myself. That phase convinced me I couldn't please anyone else until I learned to first please me. Pleasing others or pleasing myself? Which was right? Both strategies were wrong. Neither was fulfilling.

Why? Because you can never please everyone. You can turn yourself inside out, work yourself down to a nubbin serving, entertaining, performing and earning points with others, but it's unfulfilling both for you and those whom you are trying to please. And you can never please yourself. Trying to please yourself is an endless task. Your body, your mind and your quest for comfort never stop. Your flesh never shuts up. The High Priestess makes sure of that. She makes sure your soul (mind, will and emotions) and body are constantly doing a two-on-one fast break on your spirit. As long as she can keep you intent on pleasing your flesh, she has you in a race with no finish line. The more you pamper yourself, the less fulfilled and the more empty you become.

Spick and Span

One day I found one of my stepchildren trying to sweep out the dogs' room with a mop. "It doesn't work very well," he said.

"No, it sure doesn't," I acknowledged as I watched him spread the dirt around the room in swirls. "You know, sweeping is not really the purpose of a mop. Its purpose is to wash the floor. What you really need for sweeping is a broom."

"Why?" He looked at me round-eyed.

"Because brooms are designed to sweep away dirt by using the stiff bristles. Since you're trying to remove the dirt, a mop won't work."

The misuse of the mop came to mind several years later. Responding to all the fashion magazines, I was attempting to add some luster to my dried-out hair. So I combed mayonnaise through it and let it sit before I shampooed. (Yes, I know how stupid that sounds, but that was the current *Vogue* wisdom.)

My husband walked through the door, took a whiff and said I smelled like a BLT. He was right. The mayonnaise never worked very well as a hair conditioner. Small wonder—it wasn't designed to be combed through split ends. It was designed to make tuna salad stick together. It wasn't long before I rejected conventional wisdom and saved my Miracle Whip for sandwich bread. (That is, after all, its purpose.)

Abnormal Use

If you don't know the purpose of something, you'll abuse it. Consider what happened to one of my closest friends from school. When she and her husband took off on their honeymoon, they faced a long flight to England. By the time they arrived, they were exhausted. No sleep and too much champagne made unpacking in their London hotel room too much of a chore. So clothes, mementos and flowers ended up strewn all over the room, along with the luggage.

While my friend's brand-new husband was taking a shower before bed, she couldn't resist pulling one of the luggage labels off her suitcase, sneaking behind the shower curtain and placing it firmly on his bare skin. It stuck all right—stuck so well that he had to spend the next two hours sitting in water, soaking the label off.

Once again, the purpose of a luggage tag is to mark luggage, not to stick on another person's bare skin.

You're Not a Luggage Tag, Either

Wife abuse. How can anyone think another human being loves them when that person beats the tar out of them on a regular basis? How can the abuser think he can maintain control over someone else by brutalizing them? It isn't rational. It's twisted thinking—an example of not knowing the purpose of your mate.

By the same token, the purpose of a wife is not to be used as a tackling dummy, any more than the purpose of a husband is to be the jailer. But if you don't know the purpose of a thing, you'll abuse it. Drug addiction? What's the purpose of that? What's rational about destroying your body, losing your family, lying to your friends, frying your brain and bankrupting yourself? Nothing—but if you don't know what your purpose is, you'll try it.

Do you know what the word *abuse* means? It means "abnormal use."

Are you abusing yourself with too much food, too much work, unhealthy relationships, too much alcohol, too many cigarettes, too much gambling, too much anger or guilt? Do you make too many decisions based on fear? Do you beat yourself up because you never seem to perform as well as you'd like? Are you depressed or lonely, feeling sorry for yourself? If the answer to any of these questions is *yes,* you are abusing yourself; you don't know your purpose.

The Meaning of Life

Do you know what your real purpose is? It's to fellowship with your Creator and to serve Him. Jesus laid down everything for you. He risked it all, suffering unimaginable torture to pay the price, just to fellowship with you.

Hebrews 12:2 says, "Looking unto Jesus, the author and finisher of our faith; who for the joy that was set before him endured the cross, despising the shame, and is set down at the right hand of the throne of God." Do you know what that joy was? The ability to fellowship with you! You are the joy that was set before Him. He loves you that much. He thinks you're special. You're the harvest of Jesus, the seed God sowed into the earth. You—becoming a born-again child of the living God. You—making Jesus your personal Lord and Savior. You—receiving the full power of the Holy Spirit. You—with the ability to hear from God Himself.

You are His joy. Isn't pleasing God better than pleasing the neighbors? Isn't that pursuit a more wonderful purpose than a career or hobby? Why does God fervently want communion with you? Because He gave each one of us certain talents, strengths and interests to use for His glory. You may be artistic, athletic or technically proficient. You may be a nurse, a waitress, a politician or a teacher. You may be great with your hands, with your muscles or with the clarity of your mind. Whatever talent you have, it's because God put it there Himself. He has a plan for you. He has a plan for each one of us. And none of His plans include failure.

YOUR PURPOSE IS...

"And we know that all things work together for good to them that love God, to them who are the called according to his purpose" (Rom. 8:28). Now read verses 29–39. Go ahead—it'll bless your socks off!

Now you know that nothing can separate you from the love of God. So let's deal with this purpose thing. The Greek word for *purpose* is defined as "a setting forth." His purpose is to set you forth. *Purpose* is defined the same way in Ephesians 3:11–12: "According to the eternal purpose which he purposed in Christ Jesus our Lord: In whom we have boldness and access with confidence by the faith of him." Now read verses 13–20. Almost overwhelming, isn't it?

Check out 2 Timothy 1:9: "Who hath saved us, and called us with an holy calling, not according to our works, but according to his own purpose and grace, which was given us in Christ Jesus before the world began." His purpose for you was planned before the world was created!

IT'S ABOUT INFLUENCE

The high calling, the purpose of our existence is to influence the world for Christ. How? By fellowshiping with the Lord and using our talents in His service. It's a joy to do so. He multiplies our time, money and energy back to us. And as you just read in one of the earlier scriptures, He won't let us fall. Besides, with purpose comes provision. If you're faithful to His vision, He'll be faithful to yours. First John 1:3–4 says, "Truly our fellowship is with the Father, and with his Son, Jesus Christ. And these things write we unto you, that your joy may be full." That means you'll have no room for guilt, anger, loneliness, self-hatred, unforgiveness or the rest of the world's pain.

Now, if you've got your mouth open to say that you don't have any gift or talent to give to God, put a lid on it. Each one of us has something to give to God, starting with time. (After all, God isn't interested in your skill. He's interested in your availability.)

Bill Wilson ministers in the ghettos of New York City. His purpose is to serve God, and his high calling is to demonstrate the love of God to abused, abandoned and lost children. One year a Hispanic woman from the neighborhood came to him and wanted to help. She indicated through a translator that she didn't have any special talent but wanted to contribute anyway. Bill Wilson told her she could start by riding the bus that picks up children and brings them to church on Saturdays and Sundays.

Wilson told her she didn't have to do a thing, just be there and love the children. She began riding the bus that weekend and loved being with all the children, but one little guy stole her heart.

In the only English words she could speak, she told each of the children, "Jesus loves you, and I love you." Some of the children would let her hug them, but the little boy who stole her heart was afraid. For weeks she smiled at him, always saying, "Jesus loves you, and I love you."

After a couple of months, the boy finally inched closer and sat down next to her. Two more weeks of telling him that "Jesus loves you, and I love you" enabled the boy to climb up on her lap. She stroked him and held him all the way to the ministry outreach building and all the way back. She cuddled him and crooned over and over, "Jesus loves you, and I love you." That day, as he got off the bus, the little boy gave her a huge hug and said, "I love you, too."

The next day, the boy was found dead in a garbage can, beaten to death by his parents. But that Hispanic lady had sown a gift into his life that no other human being had. Because of her, the little boy knew there was a God who loved him—and another human being who did, too. This woman may not have been able to sing and dance, teach or preach—but she demonstrated one of the greatest gifts of all, God's unconditional love. You have that same ability to give, to demonstrate God's purpose. It will fill you with greater joy than you have ever known, joy that the world can't copy.

SUPERCHARGED LIVING

WHAT TO DO

Your individual calling has to do with your purpose. Your purpose isn't to enjoy life—it's to influence the world for Christ!

1. Look up and say aloud the following: Ephesians 1:18; 2 Timothy 1:9; 2 Peter 1:10.

2. Confess these scriptures daily. God will reveal your purpose as you build your faith. As you line up your talent and your will with His, you'll live a life of joy.

3. Close your eyes and see yourself being cuddled and loved on by Jesus Himself—just like the little boy on the bus.

4. Spend time in prayer sitting quietly before the Lord.

5. Be obedient and become faithful to His ministry by being obedient to your pastor's ministry.

6. Go to your church and ask your pastor in what capacity he could use you. Be willing to start at the bottom. That's what faithfulness is all about.

7. Sow your time, your expertise and your money; offer it up as a memorial to God. Pray over your seed. Whatever you give to the gospel, He'll multiply back to you.

God says it's His decision to pour out His Spirit upon all flesh. Who will carry it to all flesh? Not the unbelievers. Who then? Those of us who believe. If not you—then who? That's what being a part of the body of Christ is all about, "that they may know you, the only true God, and Jesus Christ" (John 17:3, NIV).

Look in your mirror and see whom God sees. He sees you as His perfected work, equipped with His power and strength, ready to bring the Good News of the gospel to others.

23

HAIR SHIRT, SIZE MEDIUM

By now you've probably figured out that I've got it all together, that I've practiced all these steps, have perfect recall of God's Word and never let the High Priestess of Guilt and Condemnation get under my skin. Right? Wrong!

Yes, I've practiced every one of these steps. In fact, I live it on a daily basis. That's how I know it works. But I don't have perfect recall of the entire Bible, and when I pull away from my power source, the Word, the High Priestess gets under my skin. Then I end up in trouble just like everybody else. Trouble used to be a daily occurrence, but now it almost never comes my way. But when it does, I'm reminded of all the pain, remorse, self-doubt and twisted thinking I lived with for decades.

I had a vivid encounter several months ago in Dallas. I was there to facilitate a two-day management meeting. I was also swamped with three other projects, all due at the same time. And I was running on empty. During the three weeks prior to showing up in Dallas, I had all but pulled my power cord out of the wall socket (God).

My pattern had degenerated into getting up at the crack of dawn, giving the perfunctory nod to God (about fifteen minutes of quick prayer) and eliminating study of the Word and quiet time with Him. "He loves me," I'd say to myself. "He understands I'm working eighteen hours a day. He won't be mad at me."

Well, I had that part right—God is never mad at us. He loves us with *agape* (unconditional) love, and He grieves when we don't line up with His ways, because He knows we take ourselves out of position to receive His best. He wants His best for us always. But I had deceived myself. It never occurred to me that I was doing myself in by placing number one priority on my work, not on God.

The first day of my two-day meeting was a nightmare. I had overestimated the flexibility of the participants. They were hostile, and they never opened up to discuss anything all day. They were actors right out of the movie *Coma,* and I was sweating bullets. I never tap-danced so hard for so little response. That night after our dinner—three hours not exactly filled with clever gambits and sparkling conversation—I was so upset that I got lost driving back to the hotel. Totally, completely, desperately lost. Even three stops to ask for directions didn't get me back on course. Only by going all the way back to the airport and starting over did I get back to the hotel.

THE OLD TAPES

Not only did I lose my direction, but I also lost my identity that day. The old lies were spinning on new CDs in my head: "You're a fraud. They don't like you, and you made yourself look foolish today. You'll never work with this client again. You're nothing but an empty suit. They're laughing behind your back; what made you think you could guide this crowd anyway? If you had been better prepared, this wouldn't have happened." The CD was on continuous play.

I tried to pray, but my prayers were like boomerangs. They came right back and stuck to me. Attempting to take authority over the High Priestess increased the velocity of the accusations. And just for a moment, I fell in that pit again where I was consumed with work as my identity and the dread of being found out as a fraud.

Over and over again, I asked for forgiveness and repented for not spending enough time with God, as if He were going to send me to the principal's office or something. I had totally lost it.

YOUR LOVING, FORGIVING DADDY

I had forgotten the basics, like the words of Romans 5:7–10:

Now it is an extraordinary thing for one to give his life even for an upright man, though perhaps for a noble and lovable and generous benefactor someone might even dare to die. But God shows and clearly proves His [own] love for us by the fact that while we were still sinners, Christ (the Messiah, the Anointed One) died for us. Therefore since we are now justified (acquitted, made righteous, and brought into right relationship with God) by Christ's blood, how much more [certain is it that] we shall be saved by Him from the indignation and wrath of God. For if while we were enemies, we were reconciled to God through the death of His Son, it is much more [certain], now that we are reconciled, that we shall be saved (daily delivered from sin's dominion) through His [resurrection] life.

—AMP

Now look at Romans 5:17, which opens with a reference to Adam's sin: "For if because of one man's trespass (lapse, offense) death reigned through that one, much more surely will those who receive [God's] over-flowing grace (unmerited favor) and the free gift of righteousness [putting them into right standing with Himself] reign as kings in life through the one Man Jesus Christ (the Messiah, the Anointed One)" (AMP). See, you're in right standing with God. When you accepted Jesus Christ as your Savior, He forgave all your sins. You're forgiven. Now if you mess up, all you have to do is say, "Lord, I repent. I ask for Your forgiveness, I receive Your forgiveness and I forgive myself." Then go on.

Isaiah 38:17 says, "You have put all my sins behind your back" (NIV). When we confess our sins to God, not only is He faithful and just to for-give our sins—as 1 John 1:9 states—but He also removes them from us and puts them behind His back. Now man may think he has eyes in the back of his head, but God doesn't. Confessed sins are removed from us and from God's gaze by a process that puts them right out of His sight forever. Since God puts our sins out of His mind and view, we need to learn to do the same. Yet I constantly meet people whom God has forgiven but who have never forgiven themselves. These people continue to wear a hair shirt, beat themselves up and let the High Priestess condemn them on a daily basis.

I have a friend who is still haunted by the memory of an abortion she had when she was a teenager—thirty years ago. I have another friend who had a physically abusive first husband and has an emotionally abusive second one. Both of these women are convinced that they're guilty and deserve the abuse that comes their way. Another friend thinks her inability to have children is God's punishment for past offenses. All these women carry backpacks of self-imposed guilt. None of them have to.

Jeremiah 31:3 says, "Yea, I have loved thee with an everlasting love: therefore with lovingkindness have I drawn thee." Does this sound like someone who is issuing behavior citations? I don't think so.

THE ROAD HOME

Lost and driving around Dallas, I picked up my old backpack. After two and a half hours of driving on unfamiliar highways and side roads—punctuated with intermittent sobbing—I finally reached the hotel, backpack and all.

As soon as I got to my room, I called my friend Joanie. Receiving a phone call from a sobbing, sniveling friend was a clear indication something was wrong—big time. After she asked what happened and I sobbed out the whole mess, she, as usual, had the wisdom to put Humpty Dumpty back together again. Joanie said, "Apparently, you have forgotten who you are and who your Daddy is. Let's do a back-to-the-basics course."

1. Joanie said, "You are the righteousness of God." She then quoted Romans 14:17: "For the kingdom of God is not meat and drink; but righteousness, and peace, and joy in the Holy Ghost." And 1 Corinthians 1:30: "But of him are ye in Christ Jesus, who of God is made unto us wisdom, and righteousness, and sanctification, and redemption."

2. Joanie then reminded me that condemnation doesn't come from God. She quoted Romans 8:1: "There is therefore now no condemnation to them which are in Christ Jesus, who walk not after the flesh, but after the Spirit"; John 3:17: "For God sent not his Son into the world to condemn the world; but that the world through Him might be saved"; and 1 John 3:20: "For if our heart condemn us, God is greater than our heart, and knoweth all things." Condemnation is not allowed. It only comes from the witch on guard duty in our heads.

110

3. Joanie reminded me of how much God loves me—not love by man's standards, but *agape* love, the kind that only God can give. The unconditional, overwhelming love of the Father looks past your defects and wrongdoings and sees only His perfect work in you. (Look up *love* in your concordance. It's alive with scriptures that talk about how much God loves you.)

4. Joanie then asked me if I had repented to the Lord for removing Him from first place in my life. I said yes. As I said that, I immediately realized how I had made work my god for the previous three weeks, so I repented for that, too.

After that, Joanie said, "So you've asked for His forgiveness, and you know He's given it, right?"

I said, "Right."

She said, "Have you forgiven yourself?"

"Um, er, well, ah, not really," I stammered.

To her everlasting credit, Joanie said, "So let me get this straight. Jesus' sacrifice on the cross was good enough for every other person in the world, but not quite good enough for you, right?"

"Well..."

"So the blood of Jesus is available to cover every sin for every person on the face of the planet, but you're such a bad Mamma Jamma that it's not quite good enough to cover you. Do I understand this right?"

"Well, gee, that sounds pretty...uh..."

Joanie said, "So you might as well go ahead and repent for pride and arrogance while you're at it."

She was right. What a doofus I had become. You see how perverted my thinking had become? I knew my next step was to receive my forgiveness from Him and to forgive myself.

NIGHTTIME ADVICE

But I still didn't know how to carry off day two of the meeting, how to pull the pieces together. The last wonderful thing my friend said before she prayed for me was, "Don't worry about it. Cast the care of day two onto God and let Him figure it out." She read me Job 33:15–16: "In a dream, in a vision of the night, when deep sleep falleth upon men, in slumberings upon the bed; then he openeth the ears of men and sealeth their instruction." I claimed that scripture as my own before I went to sleep.

The next day I went into the meeting without a clue about what I was going to do. But as I opened my mouth, God's wisdom rolled out. Day two was an overwhelming success, pulling together day one (as difficult as it was) and day two into a triumphant outcome.

THE MORAL

That very day I plugged my power cord back into the Source. It's OK to be swamped as long as God is my first priority. Then He makes everything else work. I've learned that whatever it takes, no matter how improbable it seems, if I put aside the proper amount of time for study, prayer and fellowship, I have unlimited energy and wisdom to get the job done.

It'll work for you, too.

WHAT TO DO

1. Read over this chapter again and look up the scriptures. Write them down on a piece of paper and read them over.

2. Practice sitting perfectly quiet for fifteen minutes and visualize yourself sitting in Father God's lap with His arms wrapped around you. As you slowly confess the scriptures in this chapter, think of His unconditional love for you. It's your personal inner picture of your Daddy and His grace.

24

PROMISE MADE, PROMISE KEPT

Weddings are about promises. Two people stand and look into each others' eyes, and then they promise to be together "until death do us part." Few couples actually make it. For many, marriage is a trial run. If mate satisfaction isn't guaranteed, you trade in the one you've got for a new one. When couples break up, the last thing on their minds is the promise they made at the altar.

Take my first wedding, for example. The fact that I bawled all the way down the aisle was a good indicator that the relationship wasn't exactly built to last. But for that one day, I was the star of a pageant. I looked good but felt bad. I may have looked like Cinderella on the outside, but my stomach felt as if I'd swallowed the glass slipper.

The reception was beautiful—wonderful food, beautiful flowers. Why is it that I remember most vividly the two gigantic platters of paté? They were round and shaped like grapefruit halves—each adorned with a huge black olive on top. Sort of like an X-rated buffet table. My brand-new groom got drunk and threw one out the ninth-story window. Can you imagine being summoned to court by the survivors of a family member crushed by paté?

Five years later my groom and I divorced. The thought of the promise I'd made never occurred to me. How easily I broke my promise!

SERIOUS STUFF

What is a promise anyway? It's a covenant between two people or groups. You promise to do for me, and I promise to do for you. The word *covenant* came from God Himself. In Genesis 17:2–4 God makes a covenant. Strong's Concordance describes a *covenant* as "a compact made by passing between pieces of flesh." This is industrial-strength stuff. Covenants were considered serious in Old Testament times. They were used as a way for two tribes to build on their strengths and diminish their weaknesses.

For instance, a tribe made up of expert warriors who were weak as merchants could seek out and make a covenant with another tribe of strong merchants who were weak as warriors. Together the two tribes were strong at war and commerce. The covenant they made was serious, binding and legalized by the shedding of blood.

When two tribes made a covenant with each other, they followed this procedure:

- A covenant site was chosen where all parties could observe the ceremony.
- The two tribal leaders came together at the center of the covenant site.
- An animal was selected, sacrificed and parted down the middle.
- Each leader took off his coat and gave it to the other. (The coats stood for authority—"who I am" and "all that I am.")
- Leaders exchanged their belts of weapons.
- They pledged, "Your enemies are mine; even if it results in my death, I will stand with you."
- The leaders walked twice through a path between the divided animal. Standing together in the center, each made promises that could never be broken.
- Each leader swore by God to keep his promises.
- Each cut his wrist. Then with arms lifted, they placed the two cuts together to seal the covenant.
- The two tribes then joined together to eat a covenant meal.

The commitment of a covenant was so serious that each member of each tribe pledged to fight to the death to protect any member of the other tribe. We're talking serious covenants. In those days, you didn't make one unless you were prepared to keep it.

FRIVOLOUS STUFF

Today we live in a world of broken promises. People walk away from written agreements in a nanosecond. Legal contracts are broken in the blink of an eye. Employee commitments go up in smoke. Rental and purchase agreements are voided. Treaties and accords between countries are regularly broken. Family members, friends and coworkers regularly promise to do something for you; when they don't follow through, their response is, "Oh well, I tried."

Like it or lump it, if you feel hemmed in today by an agreement, you get rid of it. No big deal. Hire a lawyer. Put together a protest group. Appeal to the government. Whine on television. Promises are made every day. It's easy. Promises are broken every day, too. That's why we don't trust anyone when their lips are moving.

THE ORIGINAL PROMISE KEEPER

God Himself was, and is, the original promise keeper. Listen to His promise to us in Genesis 12:2–3: "I will make you into a great nation and I will bless you; I will make your name great, and you will be a blessing. I will bless those who bless you, and whoever curses you I will curse; and all peoples on earth will be blessed through you" (NIV). That's a pretty strong promise. God is promising Abram that his name will be made great and that he'll be a blessing. And He's promising that all the rest of us would be blessed through Abram.

Abram was blown away. He couldn't imagine how God could make him into a great nation. He and his wife, Sarah, were already way up there in years. They didn't even have children. But in Genesis 17:4–5, God reinforced the promise to Abram that he would be a "father of many nations." "No longer will you be called Abram; your name will be Abraham" (NIV). Why do you think God changed Abram's name? Because the word *Abraham* means "father of many nations." Every time Abraham opened his mouth and introduced himself, he would be speaking God's promise into reality.

Don't forget that not only were Abraham and his wife childless, but Sarah's plumbing didn't even work anymore. Nonetheless, they grabbed hold of the promise. For years they stood in faith. When it seemed the promise wasn't working, Abraham and Sarah decided to give God a little help. So Abraham bedded Sarah's servant, Hagar. That union produced Ishmael. But Ishmael wasn't the son of promise; God told Abraham that. So once again they believed God and stood in faith for another eleven years!

GOD DELIVERED!

Sarah and Abraham believed God would come through, and He did. Their son was named Isaac. Not only did God make it happen, but Sarah became so beautiful that a king desired her as one of his wives. Abraham hung in there and got a son and a trophy wife to boot.

But what about the rest of the promise, "All the people of the earth will be blessed through you?" Let's look at a reinforcement of God's promise in Isaiah 61:1: "The Spirit of the Sovereign Lord is on me, because the Lord has anointed me to preach good news to the poor. He has sent me to bind up the brokenhearted, to proclaim freedom for the captives and release from darkness for the prisoners" (NIV). Now what does that word *anointed* mean? Strong's Concordance defines *anointed* as "to rub or paint on" What was rubbed on him? It was the Spirit of the Lord God. That means the power of the Spirit of the Lord God was rubbed all over him.

Isaiah was one of the major prophets declaring what God had told him to declare—the Good News to the poor, to the brokenhearted and to those bound up in darkness (ignorance). Isaiah was anointed—smeared on with the power of God to declare the Good News.

Isaiah was anointed by God to comfort all those in affliction. Look at verse 3: "To bestow on them a crown of beauty instead of ashes, the oil of gladness instead of mourning, and a garment of praise instead of a spirit of despair. They will be called oaks of righteousness, a planting of the Lord for the display of his splendor" (NIV). Wow! God is reminding us again through Isaiah that He made a promise that we could be free, prosperous, healthy and delivered from all kinds of affliction.

Here's some more proof, in Jeremiah 29:10–11: "This is what the LORD says... 'I will come to you and fulfill my gracious promise... For I know the plans I have for you,' declares the LORD, 'plans to prosper you and not to harm you, plans to give you hope and a future'" (NIV). God is reminding us of His covenant with Abraham and with us through Abraham. We are the seed of Abraham. How? Romans 9:7 reads: "Because they [believers] are the seed of Abraham, are they all children: but, in Isaac shall thy seed be called." Look back in Genesis 21:12: "...for in Isaac shall thy seed be called."

What's going on? God promised a son to Abraham and Sarah. They stood and believed for a long time, then began to doubt. (Ever done the same?) Ishmael wasn't the promised son—he was the product of Abraham and Sarah's thinking that they were smarter than God, that they had a better way to bring God's promise to fruition. But Isaac was the promised son.

God clearly said, "In Isaac shall thy seed by called." That was the promise. In Romans 9:8, God says that you can't be a child of God through reason in your mind; you become a child of God through faith in His promise. If you have declared the Lord Jesus as your Lord and Savior, you are part of the seed of Abraham through Isaac. God sowed Jesus as a seed into the earth. As you accept Him through faith, and His blood sacrifice for your sins, you become part of the lineage of Abraham through Isaac. God made a covenant with Abraham that all people on the earth would be blessed through him. Did He keep it? Acts 3:25 proves He did. Go ahead—look it up.

PROMISE KEPT

God promised blessings for us in Genesis. He delivered, as illustrated in Luke 4:18. How? God's promise was kept when He sent His Son Jesus to shed His blood to be the sacrifice for our sins, so that those of us who believe in Him could inherit the promise. "We do not want you to become lazy, but to imitate those who through faith and patience inherit what has been promised" (Heb. 6:12, NIV).

Take a look at what was delivered. In Luke 4:18–19, Jesus Himself says, "The Spirit of the Lord is on me, because he has anointed [there's that word again] me to preach good news to the poor. He has sent me to proclaim freedom for the prisoners and recovery of sight [spiritual sight] for the blind, to release the oppressed, to proclaim the year of the Lord's favor" (NIV). Did you notice that you saw these same words in Isaiah? God promised it in Genesis, the prophet reinforced the promise in the Book of

Isaiah and Jesus Himself proclaimed it in the Book of Luke. Promise made, promise kept.

THE ANOINTING

If we're blessed through Jesus, why do babies die? Why are people paralyzed and ravaged by disease? Why do thousands starve from lack of food? Why do some parts of the world tremble in terror? Because they don't know that they don't have to.

"My people are destroyed for lack of knowledge" (Hos. 4:6). The knowledge you need to overcome sickness, disease, perversity, poverty, pain, turmoil—everything that comes against you—is in the living Word of God.

God Himself said it in John 1:1: "In the beginning was the Word, and the Word was with God, and the Word was God." The Bible is God. The Bible is God's will. Jesus was the Word made flesh (John 1:14). If you have a problem, God has the answer. He sent Jesus. The answer is in His Word, and He sent Jesus to seal the deal.

CHRIST IS NOT JESUS' LAST NAME

Jesus means "savior." *Christ,* translated directly from Greek scripture, means "the Anointed One." Every time you see the words *Jesus Christ,* what you're seeing is "Jesus the Anointed One." And we know that His anointing means "smeared on with *supernatural* ability." Does that sound like someone who can take care of your problem? You bet it does.

The High Priestess of Guilt and Condemnation hates this truth. She loves to see you break promises and loves to make you think God breaks His promises, too. She constantly reminds you when others break their promises to you, but she can't change the fact that Father God Himself made a promise to you and kept it. All the fullness of His promise is waiting for you—to study, claim as your own and receive for yourself. The best she can do is to make you think that the promise is not real or that you're not worthy enough to receive it. But she's wrong—you are worthy, and you can receive it. It's been bought and paid for.

WHAT TO DO

1. Study the full meaning of the words *anointing* and *covenant*.

2. Study the following scriptures: Isaiah 10:27; Luke 1:72; John 9:6–11; Acts 3:25; 4:27; 10:38: Romans 8:6–12; 11:27; Hebrews 1:9; James 5:14; 1 John 2:27.

The truth is better than a money-back guarantee. Your covenant with God through Jesus means you can trade your strength for His. It doesn't get any better than that.

25

WHAT, ME WORRY?

Earl Nightingale once said, "Whenever we're afraid, it's because we don't know enough. If we understood enough, we would never be afraid."

Listen to the conversations around you: "I'm scared to death of..." "What terrifies me is..." "She was just scared stiff..." "Yes, but what I'm afraid of is..." "Things seem to be under control, but I'm scared that..." Some of these comments are just figures of speech. Often, though, they are indicators of what lies within. Real fear—fear of people, things, events, circumstances, reactions or changes.

Regardless of the conditions under which these phrases are spoken, words have power. As innocent as a simple phrase seems, saying "I'm scared to death" cements fear in your mind. And worse, it brings to pass what you're scared of. God spoke the whole universe into existence. Look at the first chapter of Genesis. It says "God said" over and over again. Now look at what it says in the last verse of that chapter: "God saw." God saw what He said. Like it or not, what you speak brings about your circumstances. The words that come out of your mouth control your world.

If we understood the power of speaking God's Word over our circumstances, we'd never be afraid of anything. Instead, we speak fear, which is the devil's talk. You choose to speak fear or faith. Fear-filled words come between you and the success God wants for you. Faith-filled words bring about God's success because you're plugged into His power.

FIVE LYING PERSONALITIES

When you're afraid, you don't perform up to your potential. The High Priestess of Guilt and Condemnation knows that and uses fear as a weapon to make sure you don't succeed. The weapon of fear takes on five different strategies. John Avanzini of His Image Ministries calls them "personalities," and he wrote of them recently in one of his magazines. Let's see what they are:[1]

The fear of lack

All over the world people fear not getting enough of what they need, or they fear losing what they have. Fear of shortage to meet demand can be paralyzing.

Sometimes fear of lack manifests itself in overwork (you never know when you'll need it) or in hoarding. I admit to some hoarding myself. I don't buy just the three-roll toilet-paper pack; two nine-roll packs is my kind of starter kit. And this is for a house with two people in it. Right now I could supply an entire army unit—even if they all had food poisoning.

Then there's lipstick. When I finally find that shade of Revlon that works for me, one is good, two is better, so I buy three. You never know when they might discontinue it.

In 1 Kings 17:8–16, the widow at Zarephath had the fear of lack. Scripture reveals that she was ready to fix her last meal when Elijah showed up and asked for food. "And Elijah said unto her, Fear not..." (1 Kings 17:13).

The widow made a decision and gave her last food to God's prophet. When she believed and obeyed the prophet, "...the barrel of meal wasted not, neither did the cruse of oil fail..." (v. 16). Her supply of ingredients was multiplied continuously. The widow turned her fear of lack to abundance by obeying and offering God her faith.

The fear of criticism

All too often we're afraid someone will judge us for making a mistake or not doing something perfectly. But people learn by making mistakes.

Abraham Lincoln failed twelve times before he became president. Thomas Edison plotted his path toward success by recording the thousands of methods by which his experiments didn't work.

Don't forget, Romans 8:31 says, "What shall we then say to these things? If God be for us, who can be against us?"

The fear of poor health

Some worry about the day when they won't be able to work anymore. Others fear that small ailments will turn into terminal disease. Many are so focused on health concerns that they sabotage their own path to success. I have a friend who loses about 20 percent of her work week every week. If it's not hormone problems, sinus headaches, colitis or depression, it's cramps, blurry vision, irregular periods or lack of energy—or a combination of several problems. I'm serious. Her mind is filled with thoughts of bad health, coupled with fear of declining health. Her mind and mouth create a constantly self-fulfilling prophecy.

The Bible is full of examples of healing and God's reminder that He is "no respecter of persons" (Acts 10:34). That means if He healed one, He'll heal all. When we receive salvation, He makes provision for our total healing as well. First Peter 2:24 says, "...by whose stripes ye were healed." The stripes (wounds) on Jesus' back and the terrible beating He endured was for you. He took your sickness, disease and infirmity on Himself so you don't have to put up with it.

The fear of abandonment

Most people operate out of need. They need other people to make them feel complete. Needy people operate in great fear that their spouse or boyfriend will leave or the children will stop loving them or friends will desert them. Needy people don't share relationships; they take hostages—or they are taken hostage by others. If taken hostage by others, the needy one will do anything to avoid being dumped. The emotionally needy person who takes hostages will manipulate and "guilt-trip" them until they get the desired response, a response that allows the needy one to feel blameless and worthy.

Fear of abandonment often stems from childhood experiences. Dad left, or mom died. Or dad or mom was a drunk or emotionally unavailable. The children feel rejected and often live their lives trying to win approval from family and others. In so doing, they manipulate others—and drive others away.

Fear of abandonment always brings just that—abandonment. The ones who flee the needy are sucked dry by the needy one's insatiable requirement for acceptance.

Neediness is a trap. Neediness expects others to supply self-worth. Yet fellowshiping with God, learning who we are in Him and learning His Word are the only tools that supply our self-worth. You are whole when you know He loves you unconditionally. Being whole in Him means you can enter into a relationship with another person from a position of giving, not in a position of desperation to receive.

Jesus promised He would never leave us: "Who shall separate us from the love of Christ? Shall tribulation, or distress, or persecution, or famine, or nakedness, or peril, or sword?" (Rom. 8:35). Verse 37 says, "Nay, in all these things, we are more than conquerors through him that loved us." If we firmly believe what the Bible says, we can live in peace while depending upon Jesus to be with us, always providing for our needs (Phil. 4:19).

The fear of death

The fear of death is an effective tool against anyone who is not certain of their salvation, not sure their name is written in the Book of Life. Yet the flame of this fear is fanned by many churches that teach that the way to salvation is through works. They tell you to work hard and earn your way to heaven.

It's a perfect setup for the High Priestess of Guilt and Condemnation, who can then remind you every hour on the hour that you haven't worked hard enough to be worthy to go to heaven. But that's a lie! Check out Ephesians 2:8–9: "For by grace are ye saved through faith; and that not of yourselves: it is the gift of God: Not of works, lest any man should boast." See, His grace doesn't have anything to do with you—it has everything to do with Him.

Believers who rest easy in their salvation—convinced that their destination is heaven—don't walk in fear of death. They know that "to be absent from the body...[is] to be present with the Lord" (2 Cor. 5:8).

SUPERCHARGED LIVING

GET THE FEAR OUT

Second Timothy 1:7 says, "For God hath not given us the spirit of fear; but of power, and of love, and of a sound mind." If you're experiencing any of the five types of fear, identify the author. Timothy tells us God doesn't give us the spirit of fear. Therefore, if we have fear, it's not from God.

That leaves the author of fear as . . . guess who? You've just fingered the High Priestess—the author of fear. But you don't have to put up with her influence. Revelation 12:9 elaborates: "And the great dragon was cast out, that old serpent, called the Devil, and Satan, which deceiveth the whole world: he was cast out into the earth, and his angels were cast out with him." Satan is the real messenger of fear; the High Priestess is his hand puppet. Now read verses 10–11. See how the accuser is cast down by Christ. "And they overcame him [the accuser] by the blood of the Lamb [Jesus], and by the word of their testimony."

See? Words have power. Speaking God's Word instead of the devil's words brings all the power of God on the scene. But it won't work unless you know God's Word and speak it with authority.

WHAT TO DO

1. Start by dedicating twenty minutes a day to study God's Word. Get yourself a daily devotional and start using it.

2. Follow your daily devotional and look up all the scriptures in it. Open your mind to hear what the Spirit of God is saying.

3. If what you read and study bumps up against what you've been taught, don't reject what you're reading in the Word. Let's face it—God is smarter than man. Man makes mistakes; God doesn't.

4. As you study a little day by day, you'll begin to see a complete picture of God's love for you. And you'll begin to separate God's will from your tradition.

And don't forget that the High Priestess of Guilt and Condemnation will try all kinds of tricks to crowd your schedule and clutter your life. She'll try to make you think you don't have time for God. Just reject the clutter. Put first priority on your twenty minutes a day in the Word, and your schedule will take care of itself.

26

THE ENFORCER

Sometimes I think I've seen too many gangster movies. You know, the kind where the mobster boss is surrounded by dozens of heavy-set, lantern-jawed tough guys ready to do his bidding at the slightest raise of an eyebrow. The kind where missing a commitment or falling short of what the boss has commanded results in being fitted for cement overshoes by one of the boss's enforcers. In these movies the enforcers rule by violence.

MOVIES: FACT OR FANTASY?

Were you ever taught that God is an enforcer, too? OK, maybe not a cruel one like the boys from *The Godfather* movies, but a stern judge who watches to see if you step out of line and then metes out punishment. If you were, then you're probably living your life with the notion that all your troubles are caused by your inability to be good enough. If you believe that God is an enforcer, the films cranked out of Hollywood have reinforced your view of Him as a vengeful, fearful God of retribution.

I used to view God not so much as a figure to be feared, but more as a hands-off critic who wished I'd do better and was constantly disappointed in my failure to do so. Well, guess what? God as an enforcer and God as a critic are both incorrect interpretations. They are pure fantasy.

The God of the Bible is a loving Father who wishes "above all things that thou mayest prosper and be in health, even as thy soul prospereth" (3 John 2).

According to Matthew 10:30, God cares about every hair on our heads. He sees us not as flawed human beings but as His sons and daughters (2 Cor. 6:18). He's always ready to defend our cause and live up to the commitment expressed in Romans 8:31: "If God be for us, who can be against us?" He's a loving enforcer who will not tolerate the devil working through people or circumstances to rob us of what belongs to us. And that's a fact.

Now You See It, Now You Don't

I recently sold my house and bought a condominium, a big change after having lived in the same house for twenty years; it was a decision I didn't make lightly. One of the reasons I liked the condo was its security alarm system, already installed and listed as part of the property disclosure document provided by the sellers and their real estate agent. The instructions from the sellers were simple: "Wait until you move in, call the security alarm company and get a new code. Then the system will be set up and ready to go."

That sounded good to me, so I complied. Just a few problems...the system was not operable, the parts were so old they couldn't be repaired, the smoke alarm wasn't hooked up and the company that had supposedly been monitoring the system had been out of business for nine years. To put in a system that worked would cost at least a thousand dollars. To put it bluntly, I'd been stiffed.

On advice from my lawyer, I wrote the previous owners a nice letter outlining the circumstances and giving them the name of the man from the security alarm company who declared the alarm system inoperable. I also told them I felt the alarm was their responsibility, and I was sure they didn't realize the unworkable condition it was in. What I got in return was a message through their real estate agent, saying the system worked just fine when they left and the security alarm was no longer their problem. To add insult to injury, they had even removed the battery when they left. (I've heard of people removing light bulbs but never a dead security alarm battery.)

Well, pursuing legal action would have been more costly than the installation of a new system. That left me with a choice: Get angry and gripe about the previous owners, or forgive them and let the Lord replace what had been stolen from me. I chose the second option. Did my flesh feel good about that? Are you kidding? I would have liked to toss cherry bombs into their new mailbox. But I've learned there's nothing that can be stolen from me that my God won't replace. I've also heard that strife will only stand in the way of my prayers being answered.

THE CHOICE

I said, "Lord, You are my righteous judge, and the Word says that You rebuke the devourer for my sake because I'm a tither (Mal. 3:11). I bought my condominium with the full understanding that a working security alarm system was part of the purchase price. Now the devil has used deception to rob me of that part of the bargain. I forgive the previous owners for trying to cheat me, and I ask You to forgive them, too. I pray Your blessings into their lives and ask that this incident be used to show them Your manifested love. Now I ask You to replace what has been stolen from me. I cast the care of it onto You in Jesus' name."

Then I thanked Him for the answer. Five days later my phone rang with one of those annoying "You have been selected to win a free..." calls. I was ready to hang up when I realized that the person on the other end was telling me I'd been chosen at random to receive a free security alarm system. After obtaining verification of the call and doing a background check on the company, I discovered the offer was legitimate.

Four days later my new home was completely protected with an all-new state-of-the-art system installed by a reputable security alarm company. Total cost to me: $175.

A LOVER, NOT A FIGHTER

God is so faithful. He's not about to let His children be taken advantage of. The only requirement is that you don't allow your feelings to take over. God's promise is this: "Vengeance is mine; I will repay" (Rom. 12:19). The lesson you must learn is to trust Him to rectify wrongs in His way, not in yours. Then fully expect Him to come through with blessings on your behalf.

And He will come through, because He loves you more than you can imagine. In fact, Father God loves you as much as He loves Jesus. I know you don't believe me, so prove it to yourself. Look it up in John 17:23. See? Furthermore, God isn't an enforcer looking for excuses to hold out on you. He approves of you! He says in Jeremiah 1:5, "Before I formed you in the womb I knew and approved of you [as My chosen instrument], and before you were born I separated and set you apart, consecrating you..." (AMP).

He knew you and approved of you before He ever formed you in your mother's womb. He approved of you before anyone else got a chance to disapprove. Tell *that* to the High Priestess of Guilt and Condemnation the next time she says you're not good enough to expect God to answer your prayers!

WHAT TO DO

1. Learn to stay away from strife by learning to forgive. Study Matthew 6:12, 14–15. The first verse should be very familiar to you. The rest will reinforce the concept. Now I know these verses may make the Lord sound grumpy, but He's giving you the straight scoop so He can bless you. Besides, if Jesus, having been tortured and hung on the cross to be ridiculed, can say, "Father, forgive them; for they know not what they do" (Luke 23:24), you can forgive that sister-in-law who drives you nuts.

2. Create a mental picture of the way God is on your side. Say aloud, "God is on my side. God is in me now. Who can be against me? He has given me all things that pertain to life and godliness. Therefore I am a partaker of His divine nature." Now look up John 10:10; Romans 8:31; 2 Corinthians 6:16 and 2 Peter 1:3–4 to see that you've spoken the truth according to your heavenly Father.

3. When you ask God to replace something the devil has stolen from you, don't try to help Him. He can handle it all by Himself, better than any scheme you can dream up. Expect Him to do it then refuse to worry. Say aloud several times a day, until it gets down in your heart, "I let the peace of God rule in my heart, and I refuse to worry about anything." (See Colossians 3:15.)

4. Thank Him every day that He has restored everything that has been stolen from you. And watch Him work miracles in your life.

27

WHICH WATER
ARE YOU IN?

Remember the *I Love Lucy* episode of Lucy and Ethel working in the candy factory? They'd been hired to wrap bonbons and were desperately trying to keep up as candy came down the conveyer belt. But the belt was moving too fast, and they couldn't match the pace. Lucy resorted to stuffing bonbons down her uniform—and that was after she'd already filled her hat with them. Ethel's mouth, hat and pockets were stuffed with bonbons. They were both so stuffed with chocolate they looked like runaway balloons from Macy's Thanksgiving Day parade. But they still couldn't keep up.

Does your life sometimes feel like that—full of problems that never cease and a frantic pace that never ends? You have so many obligations and "gotta do's" that you can't keep up either. If so, you're in the wrong body of water.

STAGNANT WATER

I have a friend who's so negative she could make suicide look good. A mutual acquaintance of ours calls her "Black Cloud." Never one to mince words, Black Cloud can tell you what's wrong with her surroundings, her dinner, her family members, her boss, her last trip to Wal-Mart and the last thing you said to her. Although she's attractive, financially sound and has a great husband, she can only see the bad side of everything. Consequently, she has more than her share of bad luck.

Any attempt to redirect this woman's attention to the bright side makes her defensive and promises an onslaught of world-class, award-winning whining. (I don't know about you, but whining from either a child or an adult makes me automatically want to call a cab.) By now you're probably wondering about my mental acuity; why would I have a friend like this? I'm not as dumb as I sound; in fact, I rarely see this woman anymore. Having given it my best shot, I decided I had a choice between remaining a close friend or climbing to the top of the tallest building in town with a high-powered rifle. Talk about getting on your last nerve!

Here's the problem: Black Cloud is caught in a trap. It's a trap of her own making, but it was inspired by the High Priestess of Guilt and Condemnation. As long as the wench with the guilt trip can get us in the habit of looking at the dark side of our circumstances, she can prevent us from knowing there's another way to live. It's like being in stagnant water.

You know what stagnant water is like...dark, yucky, smelly, filled with pond scum and dead fish. Why? Because there's no movement in the water, no fresh spring water that feeds the pond and causes the circulation that allows life. It's a picture of my former friend's existence. She has wrapped herself in a blanket of negativism and cut herself off from any source that could bring fresh thinking into her head or her heart. She is planted in a dead church that doesn't teach the power of the gospel. She won't consider counseling, and she hangs out with people who reinforce her bad opinion of herself.

I had become an offense to her. She didn't want to hear from me or anyone else who tried to open up positive possibilities to her. Unless she takes some action, her stagnant state will never change.

WHIRLPOOL

Another friend of mine—I'll call her Sally—is married to an emotionally abusive husband. He cheats on her, screams at her, tells her she's no good, pouts for days and informs her that every bad thing in the solar system is her fault. She's been married to Prince Charming for almost twenty years, so unfortunately she believes a lot of what he says. Although she's thrown him out twice that I know of, he always comes back with the promise he'll do better. Right. And you're already a winner in the Publishers Clearing House sweepstakes.

Sally is caught up in a vicious marital cycle: "He's turned over a new leaf this time...God is showing me what I'm doing wrong and need to learn...I've seen some encouraging signs...You won't believe it—he blew up last night over nothing...Why does he have to make me feel like a worthless fool?...He makes me so mad I could use his toothbrush to scrub the toilet, then gleefully watch him polish those pearly whites... Cutting the sleeves off his suits would be too good for the bum...If he yells at me one more time he'll be wearing that Gateway 2000...I'm going to kill that miserable, lying so-and-so...He's turned over a new leaf this time...God is showing me..."

If Sally's not functioning in a whirlpool, I don't know what you would call it. Think about it. The dictionary defines *whirlpool* as "water moving rapidly in a circle so as to produce a depression in the center into which floating objects may be drawn." Well, that about sums it up. Sally's the floating object in that whirlpool. Unless she's willing to make some changes in herself, she'll be sucked into that vortex and stay there.

A Rushing River

Then there's my friend Grace. She has overcome physical and emotional abuse as a child, a painful divorce and alcoholism. She's been completely healed of cancer, a bad heart and back problems, plus she has come out of mountains of debt and is totally debt free. How did she do it? She didn't, but she knows the One who did. And she put herself in the right place—right in the middle of a rushing river.

Grace walked away from tradition and the dead church she was attending and went to a church where the Holy Spirit is given freedom to operate. Now I know I'm going to step on some toes here, but ask yourself this: Are people miraculously healed in your church? Has anyone been set free of alcohol or drugs? Are there regular testimonies of God's faithfulness and the impossible circumstances He's changed? Does the teaching there put a demand on you to change and come into the revelation knowledge of God's Word? If not, you're not in a rushing river where the Holy Spirit can change your life.

Now, I know everyone as far back as your great-grandmother went to your church, but if you want results like the ones that Grace gets, you're going to have to place a higher value on finding out more about the Holy Spirit and His power than you place on keeping up the tradition in your family.

A MENTAL PICTURE

Last year I met a military chaplain and his wife at a conference in Virginia. We clicked at once and had a wonderful time sharing stories about all that the Lord had done in our lives. The chaplain related a story about walking in the woods and coming upon a tributary that led into a river. What caught his attention was a beautiful maple leaf that fell into a stagnant pool cut off from the tributary. He watched the maple leaf settle into the stagnant water and watched in amazement as a gust of wind caught the edge of it, elevating and then dropping it into a whirlpool at the mouth of the tributary.

At first, the leaf began to move slowly around the outer ring of the whirlpool and then picked up speed as it moved more rapidly around the rings and finally into the center of the vortex. Down it went, several seconds later popping up further out in the whirlpool—only to be drawn toward the center, down the vortex, then out to one of the outer rings again. Fascinated, he watched the maple leaf make this same trip a dozen or more times. After a while the leaf became wedged against a log blocking the entrance to the river.

The chaplain walked over to the log just in time to see the leaf move slightly, then slowly, slowly the current moved it under the edge of the log and finally into the river. There the leaf broke free. As he viewed the leaf floating down the river, the Spirit of the Lord spoke to him, saying, "My people are living in three distinct pools. The ones in stagnant water continue to live with their problems because they won't change. The ones in the whirlpool create lots of activity but no results—they just go around in circles not making any progress. But My children who desire Me enough to risk change and go where the power of My Spirit is live in peace, health, prosperity and power."

What about you? Most people don't change until the pain of their experience is worse than the fear of the unknown. If you've got the same problems you've had since TV was only in black and white, or if you're living amid painful circumstances you can't think, spend or whine your way through, consider making a change.

WHAT TO DO

1. Study the Holy Spirit and His gifts. Ask God to reveal Himself to you through these scriptures. Look up the following:

   - Jesus will give it: Matthew 3:13–17; Mark 1:9–11; Luke 3:16
   - Jesus receives it: Matthew 3:11; Mark 1:8; Luke 3:21–22; John 1:29–34
   - Jesus describes it: Luke 4:18; John 7:37–39; 14:26; 15:26; 16:5–16
   - It's a gift from the Father: Luke 11:11–13
   - Jesus instructs the disciples: Acts 1:4–5, 8
   - The disciples receive it: Acts 2:1–21
   - Other people receive it: Acts 2:38; 8:14–17; 11:15–16; 19:2–6
   - Purpose of the baptism of the Holy Spirit: Romans 8:26–27; 1 Corinthians 2:10–14
   - Praying in tongues explained: Isaiah 28:11–12; 1 Corinthians 14:1–25; Ephesians 5:18–19; Jude 20–21

2. Pray and ask Father God, in the name of Jesus, to fill you to overflowing with the Holy Spirit.

28

MOUNTAINS
OUT OF MOLEHILLS

Have you ever noticed that the more you worry about a problem, the bigger it gets? You may be very good at "projecting"—something psychologists call the habit of imagining the worst, then looking ahead and projecting the future based on the worst possible scenario. Know what I mean? When you project, your picture of the future is all gloom and doom, based not on facts but on fear.

It's one of the High Priestess's main strengths. She likes to get you into a state of anxiety where you lose sight of God's Word, fixate on troubling circumstances and then take on the responsibility of working out the details yourself. When you do that and follow her road map, you remove the ability to solve your problem from God's job description and put it in yours. Now whom would you rather have working on your case—you or the God that created the universe?

My friend Sandy had an encounter with a snake (the reptile kind, not some bad guy) several years ago that provides a useful illustration of projection. Sandy and her husband had just moved into a new house in a new city. One afternoon, as she was sweeping out the garage, a snake slithered across her path. Terrified of snakes, she screamed and did her best roadrunner impersonation into the house. She called her mother, who asked what kind of snake it was. Sandy didn't know.

Her mother said, "Stick a broom handle in front of its mouth; if it snaps at the handle, it's venomous." Sandy crept out to the garage, broom in hand, sneaked up to the snake and poked the broom handle down toward the snake's mouth. The snake snapped. Horrified, Sandy grabbed the first thing in sight—a large flowerpot—and dropped it over the snake.

Back in the house and shaking, Sandy called the police and reported a large venomous snake in her garage. The wait was interminable. Her greatest reason for fear was the size of the thing. That hideous creature could easily get tired of wearing the flowerpot for a helmet and push it over. And her children were due home from school any minute. What would happen if the snake got one of her children? She'd never have the strength to fight him off. She'd read that within ten minutes after a venomous snakebite, breathing becomes impaired and the lungs begin to shut down. She would never even be able to get her child to the hospital in time. And she'd never forgive herself for not being able to help her poor defenseless children stave off such a brutal attack. Why had they moved to this state anyhow, a state where snakes could just slither up out of nowhere and take over your house? It was all her fault; she was the one who wanted to move here, and now her selfish decision was going to end the life of one of her children.

About ten minutes later, two police cars pulled into the driveway, lights flashing. They screeched on their brakes and got out with pistols drawn. Sandy, crying, gratefully led them into the garage. After surveying the situation, the officers surrounded the snake's position and told her that on the count of three, she'd have to snatch the flowerpot and run into the house as fast as she could. The officers waited in a crouched position, guns pointed and ready to kill the snake the minute the flowerpot was lifted. Sandy didn't like getting that close to the monstrous snake, but she knew it was the only way to make certain the police had a sure shot.

They started counting: "One...," Sandy's heart was pounding; "two...," her hands were sweating, and she was afraid she would drop the flowerpot; "three!" She grabbed the pot and flew into the house. The door slammed behind her. What followed was silence, total silence. Then... laughter.

"Uh, ma'am, would you mind coming out into the garage?" asked one of the officers. Sandy obliged, just in time to see the other officer pick up the snake with his bare hands. "Uh, ma'am, was this the snake you were referring to?" the officer asked as he opened his shirt pocket and dropped the snake into it. "This is only a little garden snake that wouldn't hurt a flea." Then the officers all began to laugh again.

"Well, you might think it's funny, but that thing was much bigger before he went under that flowerpot. Or maybe it just looks small in comparison to you, because you're so tall," Sandy stammered defensively.

"I think you're safe from harm now, ma'am. He's caged up and unable to eat you or your children. Will that be all?" he asked.

Mortified, Sandy said that was all she needed, but she was still shaking an hour later. When fear takes over, emotions run wild. What began as a small garden snake had grown into a dry-land version of the Loch Ness monster, because Sandy projected the worst from an incorrect initial assumption.

MONSTER CHECK

How many monsters are lurking in your mind? How much dread are you projecting into the future? Not only does this practice take its toll on your physical body, but it literally puts the wheels in motion to bring about your worst nightmare. I have a friend who has always had a mortal fear of ending up broke and alone. He has always made an extremely good living, but he's now on his fourth wife. She seems determined to squeeze all the cash from him that hasn't already been squandered by his irresponsible children, who play him like a slot machine.

The new wife, who has enough money of her own to bankroll an emerging Third World country, doesn't like to use her cash for anything—only his. See a pattern here? My friend is well on the way to becoming broke...and alone.

WHO OPENS THE CAGE?

You do. The monsters in your life are manifestations of your own lack of self-esteem. If you feel no confidence in who you are and how you're loved and accepted by God, you automatically gravitate toward others to affirm you. In the process, you sell your soul. Looking to others for validation places all the power to establish your security in the hands of another person. If the other person doesn't act in your best interest, you're toast.

You don't need another human being to affirm you. The simple truth is that you're accepted by God. Jeremiah 1:5 says, "Before I formed you in the womb I knew and approved of you [as My chosen instrument], and before you were born I separated and set you apart, consecrating you..." (AMP). Before you were even born, Father God chose and accepted you. God approved of you before anybody else ever got a chance to disapprove.

Here's more good news: Ephesians 1:5–6 says, "For He foreordained us (destined us, planned in love for us) to be adopted (revealed) as His own children through Jesus Christ, in accordance with the purpose of His will [because it pleased Him and was His kind intent]–[So that we might be] to the praise and commendation of His glorious grace (favor and mercy), which He so freely bestowed on us in the Beloved" (AMP). Think of it: God planned for you in love, before you had parents, siblings, friends or relatives. He guarantees that even if you can't get what you need from your loved ones, He'll be your loving mother or father, sister or brother. He'll build in you what others are unable to give you.

By Grace, Not Works

His love for you is a free gift. You don't have to earn it. You don't even have to accept it, although God's love for you is unchanging and overwhelming whether you choose to accept it or not. You can't make God love you any more or cause Him to love you any less by what you do. His love (unlike man's) is unconditional. When you begin to get a picture of God's love and approval of you, fear is impossible, because it can't co-exist with love.

WHAT TO DO

1. Look up and meditate on 1 John 4:18. God's perfect love casts out fear.

2. Make a list of all those from whom you've tried to receive validation. If they've disappointed you, forgive every one of them, with the Lord's forgiveness.

3. Read the Book of Ephesians. Count how many times the phrase "in Him" appears there and meditate on what that says about you.

4. Write down Ephesians 1:5–6 and carry those verses in your purse. When you're feeling "less than" or "different from," pull out what you've written to remind yourself of how precious you are in God's sight.

5. Based on your reading in Ephesians, begin to form a mental picture of who you are in Christ. Practice seeing that picture several times each day.

6. Now, go tell the devil to take a hike the next time he comes to torment you with thoughts of insecurity.

29

AND THE HORSE YOU
RODE IN ON...

W hat would you do if you went to work one day and found a
Federal Express package on the desk containing a bunch of love
letters and cards from your husband—addressed to another woman—
along with one of her nightgowns? Would manslaughter be a viable
option? Arson? How about a quick phone call to Jack Kevorkian to
arrange the assisted suicide of your spouse, without his permission? Or
would you just sit there and bawl until your eyes became slits and your
face swelled up like a jack-o'-lantern?

Actually, I didn't do any of the above—I just sat there with my heart
pounding, silently screaming. It's funny what you think about in times of
severe shock and hurt. I had a friend at the time who had a real hang-up
about men, and the first thought that shot across my mind was how this
incident would only reinforce her belief that all men are pigs. How
strange—as if I were responsible for her feelings about men. How odd to
be thinking about that instead of how I was going to deal with the situation. I began to shake. I shook so hard that I couldn't pick up my coffee
cup or the phone.

I began to read one of the letters, and it sounded just like a soap opera
script. It read something like this: "So you see, it's really a bad time for
me. I've had a lot of pressure on me, and it's just not the time to tell her.
You'll have to give me some time..." I almost gagged; the dialogue was so

trite, I could have finished the sentence myself without having to read it. It made me even madder that he couldn't come up with anything more clever than excuses from Adultery 101. What kind of blockhead had I been married to all these years?

CALL 911

My first call was to my pastor. Thank God for men of God who can keep us from destroying ourselves by our stupidity. The first question he asked me was this: "How do you want to handle this: God's way or the world's way?" Long pause. Choke. Longer pause. "G-G-God's way," I stammered, taking a deep breath.

"OK," he said. "I'll support you either way, but God's way will minimize the hurt and put you in a position to walk in the fullness of what He's provided you. The world's way is more emotionally satisfying at first, but it will tangle you up in revenge, remorse and self-doubt. You'll be calling your girlfriends, telling them what a no-good dirtbag he is, verbalizing your own 'Somebody Done Somebody Wrong' song and plotting how to get back at him. And you'll be holding yourself hostage with your own bitterness."

"No thanks," I said. "I hurt enough already; I don't need to add to it. Besides, doing it my way all the years before I had a relationship with the Lord got me nothing but emptiness. I want to do it God's way." So my pastor prayed for me and told me the following:

First, I had to forgive my husband and the other woman. This doesn't mean I had to accept the betrayal or the behavior, or settle for anything less than a change of behavior on his part. But it did mean that with God's forgiveness I had to forgive both of them by saying aloud, "Lord, with Your forgiveness I forgive them, and with Your love I love them, and I ask You to bring about Your answers in our lives." Sometimes I had to say it a hundred times a day, because what I really wanted to do was pour gasoline on both of them and light a match. But remember, forgiveness is a gift you give yourself.

Second, I had to come to terms with the fact that what was going on with my husband had nothing to do with me. Not that I'm any trip to Dixie as a wife, you understand, but his betrayal was caused by the pain inside of him and his unwillingness to deal with it. He was simply trying to run away from the pain by changing the scenery. I could understand that. God knows that I tried for decades to control my external environment, vainly hoping to get all the people and circumstances lined up so I could control my internal environment. No dice.

I'd like to tell you I responded to this advice perfectly. I didn't. There was the day I threw a cereal bowl at him so hard that it shattered and put a big dent in the side of the refrigerator. I was only sorry I missed and hadn't put a big dent in the side of his head. Then there was the day his car was blocking my path and I told him to move his (expletive deleted) car or I would run over it—sounding every bit like a longshoreman. But God was so good to me during this time. I leaned completely on Him, and He filled me with "the peace of God, which passeth all understanding" (Phil. 4:7). My church family rallied around me, covered me in prayer and reminded me of my covenant with God and His promise to take care of me.

ALL'S WELL THAT ENDS WELL

I'd like to tell you this story had a happy ending. It did, but not the kind you may be expecting. After we had been separated for five months, he filed for divorce. Divorce was not my idea, and I stood in faith for a restored relationship. But God does give us free will. My husband was afraid of facing the pain in his own life because it required some change, so he ran. He can run from me, but unfortunately he can't run from himself.

Through it all, the Lord kept me calm, and although it was painful at first, I can truly say I have no bitterness. Besides, I've learned from this experience, which reinforced some of the things I already knew and provided new information that I've needed to unravel some of my own problems.

If you're in a similar position—or if you are staying in an abusive marriage because you're afraid you can't take care of yourself—listen up. You can't take care of yourself. But your loving heavenly Father can and will. He has blessed my business, provided me with a debt-free condominium, surrounded me with friends and taken care of my every need. He'll do the same for you because He has a covenant with you, too.

WHAT TO DO

If you have been abandoned by your husband, know beyond the shadow of a doubt that the God who made heaven and earth loves you more than you can possibly imagine. He's there to wipe every tear, calm every fear and provide for you.

1. Look up the word *covenant* in your concordance. The word appears in thirty-one books of the Bible.

2. Study the scriptures in which the word *covenant* appears. Write them down.

3. Meditate on these scriptures. You'll never be the same.

30

I DID IT MY WAY

My name is Jane, and I'm a food addict. Do you have any idea how hard it is to admit that? Particularly since Jesus has already delivered me from it through His sacrifice on the cross. But knowing I'm delivered and walking in the physical manifestation of it are two different things. Why the conflict? Because quite simply, I've had myself on the throne trying to cure this addiction myself instead of admitting I'm powerless over it and letting God deal with it.

STINKIN' THINKIN'

For years I've used food as a way of insulating myself from pain. As a little girl I used food to rebel against my mother's attempts to control me. Food became the only area of my life where no one could control me. When I was angry or sad, I could always find a way to mainline sugar into my system to temporarily numb myself to circumstances I didn't like.

Cream horns were my special favorite. As I recall, they were long cone pastries shaped like Saturn 5 rockets, just filled with globs of sickening-sweet whipped cream guaranteed to turn thighs into ham hocks. I could eat several of them at one time. Naturally, by the third grade I looked like the kid on the front of the Dutch Boy paint can—straight bangs, moon-shaped face and all.

By the seventh grade, my height had mercifully saved me from being eternally shaped like a Buick, but food was still my nemesis. Until several years ago, food dominated my life. I've spent more man-hours consumed in conversation with the committee in my head about what not to eat than it took to compile the entire World Book Encyclopedia. And I've spent more man-hours being shamed by the same committee for having eaten what I wasn't supposed to than it would take to read the entire World Book series. The thing is, I always lost the debate, gave in, porked up and then devised ridiculous schemes to try to avoid the consequences.

I have vivid memories of eating hot fudge sundaes with my friend Susie as we rocked back and forth from side to side—as if that rocking motion would eliminate a thousand calories and at least that many carbohydrate grams. (Funny—I've never seen that move in any Jane Fonda exercise video.) I can also remember sneaking downstairs at the sorority house at college to clean out the brownie tin. Everyone always wondered what happened to all those sinkers. (I acted appropriately mystified as well. It's a good thing no one ever caught me with brownie crumbs on my mouth.)

THE SIZE DU JOUR

I've never been what anyone would call fat, although at times I could easily have been labeled with a sign reading "Wide Load." At five feet eight inches, my frame has gained and lost the same forty pounds so many times that I'm like "accordion woman." And I've deceived myself into some of the dumbest diets known to man.

One all-meat-and-fat diet made me so dizzy that I fainted in downtown Cincinnati. Another delightful plan of cheese, onions and eggs made my breath strong enough to take the paint off a passing bus. One of my favorite miracle fat-burning schemes turned my purse into a toxic waste dump—I had to carry with me kelp pills, cider vinegar and two other ingredients I don't recall that were probably also used in the manufacture of bombs. At least, that's what it felt like when I had to down this junk with a nice big glass of carrot juice four times a day.

I ordered fat pills from TV infomercials that were supposed to take the weight off while I got a good night's sleep. Right. All they did was cause me to make forty trips to the bathroom every night, preventing any sleep whatsoever. Then there was a microbiotic diet plan, consisting of little envelopes of dehydrated food to be mixed with water and eaten several times a day. The food was supposed to bulk up in your stomach and keep hunger pains away. It bulked up all right—and caused excruciating pain.

Meanwhile my closet turned into a department store with sizes ranging from six to fourteen. I allowed the number on the scale and the size of my attire to dictate my emotional state. No one has ever developed as many techniques for sneaking onto the scale as I have. You can experience a five-pound variance based on how you lean, where you step, how you slide on and off, where you place the scale and what you wear when you step on. We professionals know never to weigh at any time other than first thing in the morning, after using the restroom and before taking vitamin pills.

If you think this behavior is sick, you're right. What started out as childhood rebellion turned into a full-blown addiction. Food became a coping mechanism to deal with anger, fear and rejection. Instead of learning how to express my emotions, I used food to stuff them down. By the time I hit forty my stomach was a mass of knots, and I had refined worry into an Olympic event. My ex-husband could tell what kind of day I'd had based on the size of the Popeye's biscuit bag I carried in the door at night. I tried to eat like a normal person, but I couldn't. I was just like an alcoholic.

IT'S NOT WHAT YOU EAT; IT'S WHAT'S EATING YOU

Ten years ago I got desperate enough to get help. I walked into a twelve-step program for people with eating disorders. When I heard others referring to their Higher Power, I almost ran out the door. I was an atheist at the time. But I discovered that I was broken physically, emotionally and spiritually.

After that first meeting, I came home to an empty house. I sat in the den, looked heavenward, cleared my throat and said, "Uh, God, if You're up there and You're real—please help me, because I can't live like this another day." Astoundingly, help came one day at a time. It was my first step to a personal relationship with the Lord—and to freedom from the bondage of food.

I've learned that food was never the problem; it was only the manifestation of the problem. The real problem was what was eating me—and an inability to surrender control to a power greater than myself to solve it. I thought I could minimize any risk by controlling every detail of my life. I did it my way for forty years and had nothing to show for it but a five-alarm addiction and a stomach full of knots.

TRY IT; YOU'LL LIKE IT

If you can relate to any of this, I've got some advice: Give it up and get a clue. If your life isn't working under your control by now, it isn't going to. Give your loving heavenly Father a turn at bat to soothe your hurts and plan your path. He's utterly faithful, you know. God is not a man, that He should lie (Num. 23:19). He's incapable of lying. And He has promised to take care of you. Psalm 34:10 says, "The young lions do lack, and suffer hunger: but they that seek the LORD shall not want any good thing."

WHAT TO DO

1. Surrender. If food, alcohol, drugs, gambling, smoking or any other substance or activity has taken you hostage, give up. You can't control it with either will power or self-knowledge. You're whipped. Letting the High Priestess of Guilt and Condemnation continue to deceive you into thinking you can control your obsession will only guarantee you more shame.

2. Admit to God and yourself that you have no control over _____ and that your life has become unmanageable. Ask Him to take over your life and show you how to break free one day at a time.

3. Participate in a church-sponsored addiction-breaking program or a twelve-step program (built on Christian principles).

4. Meditate on the following scriptures: Psalm 55:18; 103:5; 145:18; Proverbs 18:20; Isaiah 26:3; Philippians 4:7; Hebrews 10:35.

31

FEET, DON'T FAIL ME NOW!

I n every area of my life, I'm surrounded by people who are *running away* from something out of fear. Here are three examples; see if you can relate to any of them.

The Friend: "I'm not going to get into an argument with her," my friend said. "Every time I take issue with her or try to offer another opinion, she just gets mad—so I'll just go along and not make a big deal out of it. Like the other day—she bamboozled me into volunteering for a community project, and I ended up in a room full of women that sounded like a bunch of magpies talking, talking, talking. No one could seem to make a decision about anything, but everyone wanted to be in charge. It was like a real-life telecast of *Crossfire*—everyone bellowing at the top of their lungs at the same time, no one listening. I'm surprised there was any oxygen left in the room. So I suggested an executive committee to narrow down the focus, and she hit the ceiling.

"I wanted to be involved in this thing like I wanted to run naked through O'Hare Airport. But I can't seem to say no—especially to her—so I just go along and try not to make too big a deal of anything. Anyway, why back her into a corner? Life is too short; who needs more aggravation?"

The Client: "He's so slick that he can out-manipulate me even before I know I've been had. He's a master at making me feel guilty over things he's done. I catch him red-handed with another woman, and before I can snap my fingers he has convinced me that my behavior drove him to it. I guess if he robbed a 7-Eleven it'd be my fault, too. Why is everything my fault?"

"How do you deal with it?" I asked my client.

"Oh, I just don't," she answered. "It's a no-win situation. Every time I try to interject some reason, he works it around so I'm to blame. My only defense is to try to stay on his good side."

The Couple: "We're so tired of being one paycheck away from the poorhouse," one of them wailed. "Every time we get a little in the bank for a rainy day, some crisis comes up and wipes us out. I just wish we'd taken that job out of town last year, but it was such a big change and so much responsibility."

All these people are Christians, yet they're either shrinking from risk or doing everything possible to avoid conflict...*running away*. What's wrong with this picture? If anyone should be able to live a peaceful life and boldly pursue opportunities, it's the blood-bought children of the living God. So what's the deal?

You may see yourself in one or more of these examples. If so, it may be because you're running from things in fear instead of facing them in faith. My friend in the first example is fearful of saying no to projects in which she really doesn't want to participate and afraid of establishing boundaries with a dominating and defensive associate.

My client is afraid of confronting her husband with his inappropriate behavior and establishing consequences for that continued behavior. And the couple in the final example stays at the poverty level because they're afraid of change. How does this happen?

SELLING OUT

Let's look at Genesis 25:30–33. Esau was starving, and he said to his brother, "Feed me, I pray thee, for I feel faint." Jacob said that he would, but only if Esau would sell him his birthright in exchange. Esau agreed, and he sold his birthright for a bowl of lentil stew.

Now, back then a birthright was a big deal. The birthright consisted of the rights of the firstborn son. The firstborn was awarded a double portion of the inheritance and operated as head of the family. It was a position not to be taken lightly. Yet Esau gave it all away for a bowl of stew. Exactly how hungry could the boy have been? Could he not have waited one more day for some grub? But you know what? I sold out my birthright too, until recently.

As a child of God in covenant with Jesus Christ, I have firstborn rights. So do you, if you have asked Jesus to come into your life and be your Lord and Savior. What are those rights? Romans 14:17 says, "For the kingdom of God is not meat and drink; but righteousness, and peace, and joy in the Holy Ghost." That means I can live a peaceful and serene life, joyfully enjoying all the provisions of health, prosperity, healthy relationships, protection from harm and everything else that my heavenly Father has promised me. But until recently I wasn't, because my head was filled with worry, fear and self-criticism.

My particular torment involved food. Because I couldn't control my eating, the High Priestess of Guilt and Condemnation had a loudspeaker set up in my head, constantly broadcasting shame to me. Food was a continual source of pain and defeat for me. That's not living in righteousness, peace and joy in the Holy Ghost. That's living with a running conversation with the committee in my head over what I didn't want to do but did, and then felt shame over. You see, I had given up my birthright for dozens of brownies, pizzas, chocolate chip cookies and other binge foods. And do you know why? Because I was running from dealing with whatever was causing the pain I was trying to numb with food. I was just like Esau.

THE QUEEN OF DENIAL

Sure, learning to confront issues and people is scary, but it's a lot less punishing than the pain of staying in denial and feeling like a victim. The discomfort of getting to the root of unhealthy behavior is temporary; the discomfort of staying in denial is permanent.

Why is it so hard for you to confront your past? Remember the Serenity Prayer:

> God, grant me the serenity
> to accept the things I cannot change,
> the courage to change the things I can,
> and the wisdom to know the difference.

Many people suffer from growing up in a world of conditional love, which breeds compulsivity, self-centeredness, attachments, addictions, fear, shame, resentment and broken relationships. We will never find healing until we first acknowledge the existence of unconditional love. Conditional love is not freely given. It's a demand note that requires certain actions, decisions or behavior from the receiver before love is granted. Conditional love puts the giver in control and turns the receiver into a puppet. It explains much about my former (and sometimes current) behavior—and perhaps yours.

My friend who ends up involved with people and projects that suck her dry is running away from the need to say no, because she's afraid of the anger and rejection of others. My client is running away from confronting and taking action against her husband because she's afraid of abandonment. The couple I mentioned is running away from added responsibility because of fear of failure and fear of the unknown.

And I was running away from the fear of not measuring up, constantly in search of external acceptance, which never came in quantities large enough to dispel the feelings of inadequacy. I used food to stuff all that down. Not a pretty picture, is it?

Now, the Good News

None of us have to live this way any longer. It takes rigorous honesty. It takes a willingness to admit we can't fix it, humility to surrender our pain and futile fix-it attempts to God and faith to ask Him to take over. And, you won't see a quickie result. But if you're hungry for answers, the Lord has them.

WHAT TO DO

OK, it's time to stop being Cleopatra. Take out your paper and pencil and start writing.

1. Make a list of the situations and people from which you shy away—situations that make you uncomfortable, people who seem to always get your goat.

2. Next to each situation, write down your feelings about those experiences. Next to each name write down what you feel like when

you're with them. Write words like *anger, helplessness, fear, hostility, anxiousness* and so forth.

3. Now pray and ask the Lord to reveal to you why you feel that way about each circumstance and each person.

4. Read the next chapter and see what comes to mind while you're reading.

32

FEET, DON'T FAIL ME NOW! (THE SEQUEL)

Have you ever screwed up your courage to do something, and even though you thought you had all the elements of success in place, it flopped? Don't feel bad—it's happened to many of us. Often failure is a result of either ignorance or arrogance.

Consider these bloopers committed by those who didn't understand the subtleties of foreign languages:

- The milk industry's huge success with its "Got Milk?" ad campaign prompted the industry to expand its advertising in Mexico. But it was soon brought to their attention that the Spanish translation for "Got Milk?" can be interpreted, "Are you lactating?"
- The Coors slogan "Turn it loose" was translated into Spanish as "Suffer from diarrhea."
- An American T-shirt maker in Miami printed T-shirts in Spanish promoting the Pope's visit. Unfortunately, instead of "I saw the Pope" (*el Papa*), the shirts read "I saw the potato" (*la papa*).

If you read the last chapter—and followed the steps at the end—you should have a list of people and situations that make you feel uneasy and fearful. If you prayed and spent some quiet time with God, asking Him to show you why—you should have the beginning of some possible answers.

And you have a choice: You can ignore the need to do anything different from what you're doing now, hoping against hope that you can live with the discomfort these people and situations cause. Or you can confront your fears and find out God's way of overcoming them. Prepare for change.

EMOTIONAL COP-OUT

Many Christians run away from things under the banner of faith. In so doing they're just like Esau, selling out their birthright for short-term relief. On one hand, they say, "O God, I'm believing You to take care of this-or-that and to protect me from so-and-so." On the other hand, they're running away from confronting the truth and setting boundaries with so-and-so. That's not operating in faith; it's operating in fear.

I can relate. For years I avoided confronting difficult people, thinking if I could limit my exposure to those people who frightened me or made me angry—and could grit my teeth to survive when I had to be with them—that I was doing the right thing. What I was really doing was copping out for what I thought was short-term relief.

PRESSURE POINTS

I recently listened to a tape by the founder of a ministry that has blessed my life. The founder, who had been sexually abused by her father for years, came under enormous pressure by her parents to send her daughters to stay with them on weekends. Her mother in particular pressured her, saying, "I don't understand why you never let my grandchildren come spend time with me." As if that wasn't bad enough, she was also under pressure from her daughters, who asked continually, "Why can't we go see Gramma and Grandpa?"

She felt manipulated from both sides, but she was terrified of telling her mother the truth. And she was still afraid of her father and what his reaction would be if she confronted him. One day she decided to let them go and trust God to protect them! The girls went several times, and it seemed that nothing negative happened.

Years later she found out *both* her daughters had been sexually abused by her father. The rage that washed over her was almost more than she could bear. She cried out to God, "How could You let this happen? I trusted You to protect them. I was operating in *faith!*"

The Spirit of the Lord rose up in her and said, "No, child, you weren't operating in faith. You were operating in fear. You were afraid of confronting your parents and telling them the real reason you didn't want your girls to spend time with them." She discovered that believing and faith are two different things.

Faith comes from the spirit. It comes from having heard the Word (Rom. 10:17). You meditate on the Word until it drops down from your head into your heart (spirit). Then you know beyond a shadow of a doubt that what God promises is true.

Believing comes from the will. It comes from making up your mind to do something. But you can believe something without having the faith to bring it about. As an example, lots of folks believe God can heal, but they don't have the faith to get their *own* healing from God.

The decision to send her girls to see their grandparents was not based on Spirit-led faith, the kind of faith developed over time and grounded in the study of God's Word and promises of protection. It was driven by a decision of the mind grounded in fear over the consequences of dealing with truth.

COUNTERFEIT FAITH

Fear is the High Priestess's stock-in-trade. She'll deceive you into seeking an easier way out by using mind games to avoid pain, if you let her. For instance, I've been praying for years, asking God to deliver me from cravings for food, confessing the Word over this area of my life and believing God for deliverance. But it's only been recently that I've gotten the picture. God has shown me that I've wanted Him to drop deliverance on me like a blanket, but I haven't been willing to change my behavior and turn loose of food as a coping mechanism for avoiding fear. Now that I've got the truth, true deliverance is coming.

What about you? Are you willing to experience the short-term discomfort to be free?

WHAT TO DO

1. Begin to build your faith to walk free of the fear surrounding the people and situations on that list you just developed.

155

2. If you're not in a good church that teaches the uncompromised Word of God, break your traditions and find one.

3. Concentrate on finding out how much God loves you. Until you understand that, your faith won't be strong enough to kill a gnat. Begin by looking in your concordance for scriptures on the love and care of the Father and for scriptures on righteousness. That's what you are in Him.

4. Meditate on these Scriptures day and night until you begin to see a vision of how special and powerful you are through your covenant with God.

5. Keep a journal of your feelings each day; be honest with yourself about whether you're handling them or they're handling you, causing you to run from confrontation.

6. Thank God every day for making you what He sees you to be—His perfect vessel.

33

LIGHTS, CAMERA, ACTION

O K, admit it. All your attempts to arrange and run your life have come up empty, right? Every time you think you've got your husband, your "significant other," your children or your boss in just the right place to accomplish what you need accomplished, something happens and everything goes haywire, doesn't it?

Before I knew the Lord, I used to hear people say "let go and let God," and I'd want to hurl a shoe at them. How could anyone be so dense to think that turning loose of everything and trusting some universal power to solve all the problems would produce anything more than chaos? I remember saying, "Those people who just turn over their lives to some deity must be weak-minded and need a crutch. I guess it's okay if it makes them feel better, but *I'm* sure not going to live that way." (Translation: I'm terrified of not getting mine, so I'll devote every waking moment to making sure I get what's coming to me, if that's what it takes.) Well, that's what it took all right, but I was never satisfied.

STEVEN SPIELBERG LIVES

One of the first requirements for recovery from any life-controlling problem is to be convinced that a life propelled by self-will is doomed to failure. If you're living on self-will, trying to motor your way through life, you're always on a collision course with somebody or something. It doesn't matter whether your motives are as pure as the driven snow—you're still setting yourself up for the big crash.

Most of us try to live through self-directed strength and fortitude. We are like actors who want to run the whole show—producing the play, directing the other actors, placing the lights and scenery, choosing the costuming, writing the dialogue, delivering the lines. And if people would only stay put and deliver their lines the way we've written them, our arrangements would go off like clockwork. Life would be terrific. Everyone would benefit from the arrangements we've set up.

What usually happens? The play doesn't come off the way we've planned it. The other actors miss their cues, the scenery changes don't happen fast enough, the costumes don't look right, the lighting throws shadows on the faces of the cast, the plot is confusing—and worst of all, the critics pan the production as one of the worst of the season. That's when we begin to think life doesn't treat us right. So we redouble our efforts and become more demanding.

But the play still doesn't come out right. We blame ourselves some but reserve the majority of the blame for others. After all, they're more culpable than we. Couldn't they see what a wonderful opportunity this was? Couldn't they follow directions well enough to accomplish what was laid out before them? Why were they careless about details, and why did they try to change the pattern that had been established?

What comes next is anger and self-pity. What's the *real* problem here? We're deceived into thinking we can create happiness in this world if we only manage the details of our lives. It's a deception borne of selfishness and self-absorption. The author of the deception, of course, is the High Priestess of Guilt and Condemnation, who uses the lie as an artful snare into fear. Motivated by fear, we try to manage our lives by controlling the lives of others around us—and they retaliate. Hurt, we're unable to see how our actions were self-centered in the first place.

HE'S GOD, AND YOU'RE NOT

What's the way out of this vicious trap? You can't just decide to stop being selfish, to stop being afraid. Your own power isn't enough, no matter how strong you think you are. So the first step is to stop playing God. That's decision number one. Decision number two is to fire yourself as director and hire God as the Director of your life and loved ones. Decision number three is to believe He has your best interests at heart and will daily provide everything you need. He has promised you that in Philippians 4:19.

This is a daily decision. You'll find the Lord faithful beyond your wildest dreams in providing for you, and best of all, you'll be liberated from having to orchestrate all the people and situations in your life to get what you need. It's the quickest shortcut to relieving stress that I know. And don't tell me you don't have stress—I know better.

MIRROR, MIRROR ON THE WALL, WHO'S THE MOST SELFISH OF THEM ALL?

As you begin to live this way, one day at a time, you'll begin to see how self-centered your actions have been. I remember, for example, how stunned I was to realize what my real motive had been for all those hospital visits, all those casseroles I'd delivered, all those favors I'd given. It hadn't really been to demonstrate love and care for others; it had been to receive praise and thanks in order to make me feel better about myself. Ouch! It's hard to admit that each act of kindness had a string tied to it that was anchored to my emotional neediness.

But here's the miracle: God has filled that emotional hole with His love and acceptance of me. Now I can perform acts of kindness purely for the joy of extending them, whether or not I receive thanks. In fact, I've learned the most satisfying kind of giving is giving that is done anonymously. That way it's God's and my little secret. Now that I think of it, that's scriptural. Matthew 6:6–7 illustrates the same principle as it applies to public and private prayer. Look it up and see how it works.

WHAT TO DO

If you'd like to turn in your Screen Actors Guild card and put someone else in charge, someone who can change your disappointment to joy, then follow these steps:

1. Study these verses about dependence on God: Deuteronomy 33:27; 2 Chronicles 20:6–12; Psalm 127:1; 139:1–5; Jeremiah 10:23–24; Matthew 28:18; John 3:22–27; 15:5; 2 Corinthians 3:4–5.

2. Get out your trusty pen and paper and write down what all these scriptures are saying to you. Then be honest with yourself and write down how big the gap is between what God is saying to you and what your current actions are.

3. Commit to trust God to follow through for you one day at a time. See how much better your life works.

34

BULL'S-EYE!

It was a direct hit. My friend Dan and a couple of his buddies from high school were working part time as waiters at one of the snooty hotel restaurants downtown. They were all dressed up in tuxedo-like outfits with starched collars and bow ties—the whole nine yards. They were serving guests at an important civic event, trying not to appear as flustered and inexperienced as they really were.

Dan was serving the head table, where a former Secretary of Defense and his wife were seated among the local big cheeses. Everyone was dressed to the nines, including the former cabinet officer's wife, who was wearing a beautiful dress with a plunging neckline. Dan was carrying a big tray as he walked behind her. He lost his balance and lost control of the tray. One of the sauce boats containing Thousand Island dressing tumbled forward off the edge of the tray, spun around in slow motion and emptied its contents directly down the front of the cabinet officer's wife's dress.

Silence followed. Stunned, the lady looked down, then up, then around at her tablemates who were about to explode. Then she burst out laughing. The whole table fell out. Dan was looking for a pistol to use on himself, but he soon realized her gracious reaction might actually save his life.

One can only imagine what it feels like to think you look pretty snappy and then suddenly have an entire gravy boat of Thousand Island dressing poured down your dress. What's your next move? Stand up and let it slither through to the floor? Or do you try to catch it in a container and mop up later?

IT'S HOW YOU RESPOND THAT COUNTS

Because of the unexpected that happens in our lives, you need to be aware of two realities:

1. *The unexpected always comes around, engineered by the High Priestess of Guilt and Condemnation, to try to steal the Word from you* (Mark 4:14–15). The drill works like this: An unpleasant surprise occurs, you get your stomach tied in a knot and you begin to worry and fret, snap at your family, project the worst and speak gloom and doom. You open the door for the Priestess to bring the words of your mouth into existence. We've already shown how you reap what you sow with the words of your mouth. Never forget—words have power.

2. *Your attitude determines what happens to you.* Just as freshly baked bread produces an aroma, your attitude is the savor of your character. It provides a clue about who you really are. People who give off negative vibes draw negative people to them. People with chips on their shoulders, waiting to be offended, attract offenses like flypaper. If you're touchy and thin-skinned, prepare to have more than your share of unexpected calamity.

A GREAT CATCH

The cabinet officer's wife could easily have made a big stink. Instead she was gracious enough to laugh. That decision to laugh in the face of adversity put her tablemates at ease and saved the waiter from complete mortification. It was an elegant gesture. It also said a lot about her character.

How about you? What is your response when you find yourself in an embarrassing or stressful situation? Do you take it out on others by playing the blame game, or do you take an inventory of your own attitudes that may have brought the circumstances about? It's a useful exercise to write down the unpleasant surprises you've had over the last several years and analyze them in terms of your response.

I drew three columns on a sheet of paper and titled them "Incident," "Response" and "Outcome." To my amazement, my angry or blaming response always produced a more negative outcome than the original incident had produced. I either lost a friend, began a turf war or tied myself up in knots. On the other hand, I found responding in love (even when the other person was wrong—how difficult!) nullified the negative impact of the original incident.

WHAT TO DO

If you'd like to secure an insurance policy against more than your share of unpredictable calamities, follow these steps:

1. Turn to 1 Corinthians 13 in your Bible. It's the chapter about love, the one that's often read at weddings.

2. Read it aloud. As you do, insert the word *I* throughout. For example, "I am patient; I am kind." Don't think I've got this mastered—I don't. At a recent Bible study my teacher read the chapter with *I* inserted. When she finished I said, "Just shoot me!" But she reminded me that I'm not the one who can pull this off; only Jesus living in me is capable of it.

3. Write the verses (with *I* inserted) on cards to carry with you and confess them several times a day. Prepare for positive changes in your attitude.

35

ROOM TEMPERATURE IQ

I t was like working in a haunted house. I never knew what mood my boss was going to be in when he hit the door. Sometimes gregarious, sometimes withdrawn—he always kept everyone guessing what his demeanor would be. Living on that roller coaster was one thing, but what made me particularly crazy was the fact that he'd just as soon tell a lie as the truth. In fact, even when the truth was *easy* to tell, he'd replace it with a falsehood. Maybe he actually *believed* all those lies he told, but it sure was hard to report to him when you never knew if he was giving you the straight scoop.

What causes behavior like this? Or the kind of behavior that promises the moon and never follows through? Or the kind that never accepts responsibility because it's never their fault? The answer is IQ.

NEW GAME, NEW RULES

No, not the kind of IQ we were all tested for in grade school or the kind reflected in college SAT scores or GMAT tests. I'm talking about emotional IQ. It's one of the hottest subjects among leadership scholars today. An impressive emotional IQ is the most desirable quality sought by corporations hiring MBA graduates.

In his groundbreaking book *Emotional Intelligence,* Daniel P.

Goleman used research to show that IQ (the kind we're familiar with) is far less important as a predictor of success than what he calls emotional intelligence. He defines emotional intelligence as attributes of self-awareness, impulse control, persistence, confidence, self-motivation, empathy and social deftness. The research strongly indicates these attributes separate people who do well in life from people who fail or who simply never seem to get off the dime, despite smarts and skills.

The rules for work are changing, and although there's a high premium placed on technology and technical skills, we're all being judged by a new yardstick. Today it's not how smart you are but how well you handle yourself with others that makes the difference in who gets promoted, who gets passed over and even who *doesn't* get laid off.

Goleman gathered information from hundreds of human resources training and development specialists targeting one hundred eighty-one jobs and one hundred twenty-one companies worldwide, representing a cross-section of millions of employees. The results were compelling: Two out of three abilities considered vital for success were emotional competencies like trustworthiness and adaptability—and a talent for collaboration. That conclusion has been supported by other studies revealing that emotional competencies are twice as important to people's success today as raw intelligence or technical know-how. Plus, emotional intelligence is of paramount importance to any management or leadership position.[1]

"AND THIS AFFECTS ME HOW?"

Your financial and social picture is largely impacted by your own emotional competency. Your skill in persuading others, articulating a goal or mission and creating buy-in to get everyone on board are critical success factors. And that doesn't mean twisting their arms off or using kickboxing techniques, either. Even your ability to take the pulse of a group and to understand the unspoken agendas is critical to communicate effectively at home or at work. But here's the catch: Most of us aren't very aware of or honest about our need for improvement.

What is your emotional IQ? Ask yourself a few of these questions:

- Do I usually stay positive in difficult circumstances?
- Do I admit mistakes?

- Do I hold myself accountable for meeting my goals?
- Do I expect to succeed or fail?

GAP ANALYSIS

Most shortcomings in emotional intelligence are a result of habits of the mind. They're deeply rooted because we learned them early in life. They become survival tactics and coping mechanisms. As an example, you may be reluctant to admit your own mistakes because you learned as a child that mistakes were punishable by painful consequences. Or, you may find it hard to hold yourself accountable for meeting your goals because you've had a history of failure; you have learned it's more painful to try and miss than not to try in the first place.

If you're interested in elevating your emotional IQ, it's going to take some guts. The Serenity Prayer that we talked about a couple of chapters ago applies here:

> God, grant me the serenity
> to accept the things I cannot change,
> the courage to change the things I can,
> and the wisdom to know the difference.

Choosing to raise your emotional IQ is one of the things you *can* change. It involves identifying and modifying those mental habits. It also requires overcoming the fear behind the development of those habits. The good news is that your loving Father has provided a way for you to do it and an instruction manual to guide your way.

MAKING CHANGE

I once saw a slogan that read, "Courage is fear that has said its prayers." Courage is a direct result of making a decision to venture beyond your comfort zone, acknowledging your inability to do it on your own strength and asking God to do what you can't. Courage comes from knowing that there's someone more powerful than you who is involved in your effort. Remember, 1 John 4:18 says, "Perfect love casts out fear" (NAS). Simply put, if you know how much God loves you and how faithful

He is to perform on your behalf, you need have no fear.

Fear is a dark, murky poison in the minds of all those who haven't come into the fullness of union with Jesus Christ. It's developed by being loved conditionally by others and results in the creation of two selves—a mask we show to the public and a different reality inside. We develop defenses to keep this fear out of our awareness. And we begin to pursue the things of this world to attain peace and eliminate our discomfort. But those pursuits bring only short-term relief. And here's the kicker: We never conquer our fears by avoiding them or trying to distract ourselves from them.

The journey to peace and serenity is a journey through fear, which is the fundamental roadblock to emotional intelligence. Sometimes you just need to face your fear and do the thing you fear anyway! Your heavenly Father is with you every step of the way, holding your right hand (Ps. 139:10; Isa. 41:13). And when you face your fear and do it anyway again and again, you overcome your fears.

WHAT TO DO

If you want to improve your marketability by increasing your emotional IQ, here are some steps you can take:

1. Make a list of your fears. Some common ones are failure, financial lack, sickness, the disapproval of others, abandonment and death.

2. Ask yourself, When do I experience this fear? How does this particular fear limit my lifestyle and the choices I make? What consequences do I experience because of this fear?

3. Meditate on these scriptures: Deuteronomy 31:8; Psalm 23:4; 27:1; 34:4; 91:5; Proverbs 18:10; Isaiah 41:10; Matthew 28:20; Luke 12:7; Romans 8:15; 2 Thessalonians 3:3; 2 Timothy 1:7; 1 John 4:18; Revelation 21:7–8.

4. Now make a list of ways you can act more courageously and commit it to action. Remember, you're after progress, not perfection.

Progress Check

1. What have you identified as your biggest fears?

   _____

   _____

   _____

2. How have you let the High Priestess of Guilt and Condemnation use your head as a battering ram for torment?

   _____

   _____

   _____

3. What have you learned about who you really are, not who the High Priestess says you are?

   _____

   _____

   _____

4. How big was the gap between a loving God who only wants what is best for you and your perception of Him when you began this book?

   _____

   _____

   _____

5. What steps are you willing to take on a consistent basis to develop spiritual maturity?

   _____

   _____

   _____

   _____

   _____

6. Make a list of all the problems in your life that need resolution.

_____

_____

_____

_____

_____

_____

_____

7. Commit to paper how you're planning to build your faith in these areas.

_____

_____

_____

_____

_____

_____

_____

8. Make a gratitude list of all your blessings and the things for which you're thankful.

_____

_____

_____

_____

_____

_____

_____

36

AIN'T NO BIG THING

I missed my flight. But it sure wasn't for lack of effort. My plane from Phoenix sat on the ground an hour and fifteen minutes waiting for rain to pass through so we could take off. By the time we got to Dallas it was the exact departure time of my connecting flight.

It's funny how you look for little shreds of hope, signs indicating that all is not lost. The gate and flight numbers for my connecting flight were announced, which seemed a sure sign that other flights were delayed, including mine. Then there was the announcement requesting those without tight connections to stay seated so the rest of us could deplane first. Even the gate agent who met us was encouraging, telling me to hurry because my plane was still at the gate.

I'll bet you could write this script. Of course I arrived at gate number two. And naturally my connecting flight was departing from gate number thirty-five. By then beads of sweat were breaking out under my hairsprayed bangs. And I was dragging a tote bag full of books that made me feel as if I were carrying the Chrysler Building under my arm. Add to that a purse weighing the same as a sumo wrestler and a cowboy hat (that's a long story), and you can imagine how aerodynamically sound I was for the sprint. After doing a mental calculation of the number of gates I'd have to run, I decided to go for it.

I did my best Wilma Rudolph imitation, weaving among people as I ran, no doubt leaving a trail of carnage behind as I took people out with that deadly tote bag. By gate twenty, I looked down and noticed my skirt was turned around backwards, caused by friction from the tote. By gate twenty-six the former beads of sweat had become rivers, and I looked like a grape with my hair plastered to my head. Two gates later my big toe popped through my pantyhose, causing a giant run directly up the front of my leg. (This is the time for a silent prayer you don't run into anyone you know.)

By the time gate thirty-five appeared in view I was a candidate for an ugly man contest at any major university. Undaunted, I rumbled up to the gate, just in time to see the plane pull away from the jetway. Manslaughter came to mind. But that was actually too moderate a punishment; something like death by leeches seemed more in line with my sense of fairness. Almost as quickly, I regained my sense of proportion, repented for taking offense and asked the Lord to get me home. A gate agent with a clipboard appeared almost instantly. What I wasn't prepared for was the reaction of the other travelers who arrived at the gate shortly after I did.

THEATER OF THE ABSURD

A young mother with a small child was bawling at the top of her lungs. No, not the child—the mother. "I'll never get home now!" she wailed. "How could you do this to me?!" She carried on and on; I checked to see if she was wearing ruby red slippers and was trying to get home to Aunt Em. A middle-aged woman with an extremely loud voice and a thick New York accent was bellowing at the top of her lungs, "This is a disgrace! A disgrace, I tell you! This airline is going to hear from us, big time! (Like they weren't already hearing from her!) You knew this flight wouldn't wait, and yet you deliberately let us run all the way down here for nothing! We'll never fly this airline again, will we, Arnold?" She looked toward her beleaguered husband, who had just stumbled up carrying enough bags to open a lost and found.

Arnold looked sort of embarrassed but evidently decided his wife was more terrifying than his own discomfort. "No, dear, we won't," he said. As the gate agent began to speak, Mrs. Arnold shouted him down, "Do you hear me? We'll never fly this airline again! This is an outrage, an absolute disgrace, and I'll not be taken advantage of like this!"

By now the young mother's child tuned up and began to scream, matching her mother decibel for decibel. I asked the gate agent what he suggested we do to reroute ourselves, but before he could respond, Mrs. Arnold was at it again. The poor gate agent looked as if he were ready to commit suicide. It was then that both mother and child sank to the floor crying at the top of their lungs, and I was beginning to think suicide wasn't a bad option either.

Do you ever hear yourself say something and wonder whose mouth it came from? Well, that's what happened as I heard a voice (mine) say, "Let's all calm down here, what's done is done—and it's not this young man's fault." The other travelers turned on me like Rottweilers. Finally I took the gate agent's arm, ushered him about twelve feet away from the crowd and asked about other flight connections. He told me he'd already put me on another carrier and showed me where to go.

FOLLOW THROUGH

As usual, my heavenly Father took care of me, and I got home only an hour and a half later than originally scheduled. For all I know the rest of my travel group is still standing in the airport bellowing and howling like losers in a cockfight. I say this not because I'm such a swell person—if you haven't identified my warts in this book, then you can't read—but I'm learning that getting all upset over something that isn't, in reality, such a big deal is counterproductive.

I know the difference. Getting upset was the way I used to live my life. When things went out of control and I was inconvenienced, I used to act just like the woman from New York. (In fact, I can remember reducing a Braniff gate agent to tears over an aborted trip to Washington.) All that my histrionics ever produced was acid indigestion and a list of people who would have loved to see me under the rails of a fast-moving train.

An acquaintance of mine apparently needs to learn the same lesson. She recently had to have surgery. Her doctor doesn't operate on Mondays, but she pitched such a fit that he made special arrangements for operating room time and scheduled her for a Monday surgery. Since then she has done nothing but complain about the job he did on her. Apparently, he left some extra skin around her incision that's causing irritation because it rubs against her clothing. She gripes about it constantly. I'm not saying the surgeon did it deliberately, but she was determined on inconveniencing him;

172

she may have reaped what she sowed. In any case, no one here was a winner.

BOTTOM LINE

All of this is about whether you are living your life based on trust or on your ability to muscle people and events into place. If you choose to trust God for your needs, you can remain calm in the midst of turmoil. One of my favorite scriptures is Proverbs 3:5–6: "Trust in the LORD with all thine heart; and lean not unto thine own understanding. In all thy ways acknowledge him, and he shall direct thy paths."

Face it. God is smarter than you are, and He has a better way to take care of you than you ever could imagine. But you have to be willing to stop consulting your head and turn things over to Him to work out. In other words, trust infinite God instead of finite you.

The Lord demonstrated this lesson powerfully to me about six years ago. I had spent the better part of two years raising money through a limited partnership to develop a product for the meetings and conventions market. I was close to the goal when the unforeseen happened. As a result, I ended up $100,000 in debt, with my business grinding to a halt. I was too ashamed to even tell my husband about it and was at wit's end. To complicate matters, my office landlord informed me I had to be out of my office in twenty-eight days because he had sold the building. That meant I would need money to move, and I didn't have any.

I kept confessing the Word, because I know I have a covenant with God. I'm a tither, and He has promised to provide for me, but the circumstances were beginning to get the best of me. Try as I might, I couldn't figure out where I was going to get the money. The inside of my head was beginning to feel like a wheel with small animals spinning on it. One day I walked into the office, and my secretary said, "Your pastor called, and he's got the answer to your problem."

I replied, "That's funny—he doesn't even know what the question is, much less the answer."

The next thing I knew my pastor was at the door with a book, which he said the Lord had impressed upon him to get to me immediately. The book was titled *Petitioning for the Impossible,* written by Buddy Harrison. I went home, read the book, followed the instructions exactly, put together a petition and held it prayerfully up to God. I even had my pastor and some of the church elders agree in prayer with me over it.

Then I gave the hamsters on the treadmill in my head a rest. I admitted to the Lord that my own ability had failed and told Him that without a move from Him, I knew I was toast.

Five days later I had a check in my hand for $57,000. It came from a client I had talked to not a month before about a project she had no interest in. Yet she asked a question that led me right back into the discussion we'd just had. It was as if she had never heard it before. When I finished explaining, she said, "We need to begin this process right away." The rest is history.

The balance of the $100,000 came in from places I could never have identified, and by the end of the month I was out of debt. It was an absolute, certifiable miracle! But do you know what? Our God is a miracle-working God.

WHAT TO DO

If you'd like to retire from being the air traffic controller for the world and all its people and turn the job over to God—take heart.

1. Get out your trusty pen and paper and list all the incidents you can remember over the last year that left you vexed from trying to force square pegs into round holes.

2. Then ask yourself if these incidents were truly win-wins for all concerned or if they caused you and others heartburn.

3. Check out the following scriptures to develop your trust level: Psalm 37:3–5; 91:4; 119:41–42; Proverbs 3:5–6; Isaiah 26:4. Write these scriptures on cards to carry with you. Read them several times a day.

4. Check out these scriptures to develop peace: Ephesians 2:14; Philippians 4:7; 2 Thessalonians 3:16. Write them down and meditate on them.

5. Practice taking baby steps by turning over pieces of your life to the Lord. Go ahead—He won't let you down.

37

TOO CUTE BY HALF

Bob had a drinking problem. Everyone knew it but Bob. His wife had left him and had taken the children, his coworkers knew he was in trouble and even his boss was beginning to suspect Bob liked alcohol far too much. Bob had an important job with a large corporation and was regarded highly for his business acumen, but every description of him was followed by, "He sure can drink!" Because he was a happy drunk, people cut him a lot of slack.

Bob promised himself that he would cut back on his consumption—after all, he could quit any time he wanted to. Besides, who could begrudge him a couple of drinks to soothe the stress he was under? If it wasn't the job and the incessant demands of his boss, it was his wife sounding off or one of the kids who needed something from him. What did they think he was made of—money?

The annual convention was coming up, and Bob had a major role in it. One of his responsibilities was a keynote speech in front of several thousand people. He was a bit nervous, but Bob was glib and good on his feet, so he knew he'd be able to wow the audience. At the welcoming party the night before his speech, he drank moderately—under the watchful eye of his boss. After dinner one of his friends took it upon himself to make sure Bob got to bed at a decent hour. They stopped at the hotel bar first, and Bob's opening move was to order two doubles at the same time. After plenty of admonitions (and two more drinks), the friend walked Bob to his hotel room at ten o'clock.

What Bob's friend didn't know was that after he left, Bob waited five minutes, took the elevator down to the lobby, hailed a cab and stayed out all night. The next morning, fifteen minutes before his presentation, Bob was nowhere to be found. Several of his managers began combing the hotel, frantically searching for him. The president of the company kept asking for Bob, wanting to tell him something before he went on stage. Bob's managers were running out of excuses.

Voilá! Four minutes before show time, Bob burst through the front door of the hotel—suit rumpled, tie hanging out of his pocket, sunglasses parked on top of his head and wearing a headband with chaser lights that went all the way around his head. He looked like a walking signboard—or like a human version of one of those yard signs announcing a garage sale.

Bob's self-appointed chaperon from the night before was horrified. He tried to get some coffee into him as he dragged him toward the auditorium. All Bob had to say was, "Don't worry—I'll be great. I've got everything under control." (Yeah, just the way Hurricane Andrew was under control.) His chaperon reluctantly went inside and sat in the second row. He started sweating bullets.

WATCHING A TRAIN WRECK

Have you ever noticed there are five stages to becoming totally drunk? Even if you've never been there yourself, you have surely noticed the process in others. My friend David said to me this is how it works:

1. *Smarter.* After a couple of cocktails, you feel yourself becoming wittier and more articulate than others around you. You can be found commenting on foreign policy and the Federal Reserve's last decision to lower interest rates. There's virtually no subject on which you cannot comment.

2. *Better looking.* You begin to think you're exceptionally fine looking. After all, those around you may appear to be giving you looks of approval. You stand up straighter since you feel you're establishing a more powerful presence in the room.

3. *Funnier.* You become convinced of your ability to tell a story. Everything seems amusing, and your talent for describing people and events feels more clever than ever. Everyone around you seems to be laughing at what you have to say.

4. *Bulletproof.* Nothing can stop you now. You can't possibly get in trouble, because you're too cute by half. The title *King* (or *Queen*) *for a Day* suits you perfectly. Who can resist you? You're invincible. Nothing can get in your way—not speed limits, traffic lights or dress codes. The word *exception* was made just for you.

5. *Invisible.* Not only do you feel unstoppable, you can do anything your heart desires. You commit outrageous acts of bad judgment and get away it because no one can actually see you. You can drive ninety miles an hour or walk into that hotel room with someone you're not married to because you're invisible. It's a perfect world.

Bob was at stage 4—convinced that his ability to dazzle the audience would quiet any potential criticism from those scout troop leaders, the CEO and the president.

The first paragraph of his speech went pretty well. Just one problem: Bob was still wearing the headband with the blinking chaser lights, and he looked as if he'd selected his clothes on the way out of a burning building. Warming to his subject, Bob began to deviate from the script in the TelePrompTer. He mispronounced a word and got a laugh. That emboldened him. He began to tell jokes and poke fun at some of the audience members. Bob's friend in the second row was now in total despair as he watched his friend's self-destructive meltdown.

Bob settled on the CEO and told another joke directed at him. The story was filled with profanities. Nervous laughter followed. Bob retorted, "Oh, come on! Loosen up—you look like you just sucked on a lemon. Let me tell you another one." From the second row came a voice: "The speech, Bob, the speech." "Oh—the speech," said Bob, apparently remembering he was supposed to be doing a corporate speech instead of a Henny Youngman routine. He tried to pick up where he left off, but by now the TelePrompTer operator was lost.

"This speech is boring anyway," Bob announced. "Let me just tell you what's really important. But first let me tell you the one about..." This was the final straw for senior management, who dispatched someone to escort Bob off the stage. The audience sat in total silence.

PICKING UP THE PIECES

The following Monday Bob was presented with a choice. Go into treatment and get help or leave the company. Fortunately, he chose the former; as part of the process he gave his life to the Lord. Since then he's left the company and has a successful business going. He's been in AA ever since and continues to work on his character defects. God has given him the peace and serenity he craved all those years—and best of all, the serenity doesn't come with a hangover.

You may think Bob's story is extreme, but there are many ways to get drunk without using liquor. You can get drunk on relationships. Think about it—if you're the type to get drunk on relationships, the process is the same:

1. The attention of a special person begins to make you feel smarter. Because that person wants to spend time with you, you make a special effort to explore his needs and stretch yourself to find ways to impress him. Positive feedback makes you feel insightful and on top of things.

2. If that special person happens to be male and he's fixated on you, it's tough not to break into a chorus of "I Feel Pretty" from *West Side Story*. The loving attention of Prince Charming always reinforces stage two—prettier.

3. Lighthearted doesn't even begin to describe it. As you become more inebriated with him, everything you say is funnier than ever before, and everything he says is hilarious. You tell everyone about his amusing anecdotes and your even more amusing responses. You can't stop talking about him.

4. Because you're loved and adored by a significant other, you feel bulletproof from harm. Nothing can get to you because you've placed all you trust in another human being to solve all your problems. So far he's been able to insulate you from criticism and self-doubt.

5. You're so besotted with Mr. Right that you've thrown everyone else in your life over the side. You don't have time for them anymore because they can't make you feel the way he does. You're convinced no one else has noticed that you're not there for them because after all, you're invisible. But standing in the reflected glory of Mr. Right, you're somebody. He gives you identity, purpose and meaning. You need him in order to be complete because without him you're nothing.

Prepare for a fall. Been there? If so, you know it's not long before you begin making boneheaded decisions just as Bob did. And it's not long before you sell your soul for the privilege of that high. Not only will that high eventually cause you to self-destruct, but it's a cheap counterfeit of the real thing. The real thing is a personal relationship with Jesus. There's nothing like getting high on the Holy Spirit. You may think that sounds crazy, but don't criticize it until you know what I'm talking about.

THE MIRROR TEST

Do you have a problem with relationships that you're not facing? Or another problem that's patently obvious to everyone around you, but something you don't want to admit to because you don't want to give it up? Food was like that for me. I wanted to give up compulsive eating—but not really, because I used it as a mechanism to deal with hurt, anger and fear.

A good way to get to the truth is to keep track of your time for a week and discover what you spend most of your time on. As you add up your hours, you'll find out what your true god is. And remember, desire follows attention. What you give most of your attention to will create its own force of desire. Look in the mirror and admit you've got the hots for whatever dominates your thinking. If it's not fellowship with the Father, the High Priestess of Guilt and Condemnation has got you snared right where she wants you. She only needs to watch while your significant other (or whatever your obsession might be) fails you—then she brings in the heavy artillery of blame and shame. It's a slam dunk for her; she knows everything fails at some point.

Are you tired of being played for a chump, wounded by a long line of people from whom you expected a lot but received little? Are you finding it difficult to be vulnerable because you're afraid of being hurt? When you get sick and tired of being sick and tired, look up, for your redemption is nigh (Luke 21:28).

WHAT TO DO

1. Get out your concordance and look up the words *drunkard, drunkards, drunken* and *drunkenness* and the scriptures associated with each. Remember that drunkenness applies to more than liquor. You can get just as drunk on food, men, work or TV.

2. See if what is described there sounds like you.

3. If so, notice the incapacitation associated with drunkenness.

4. Repent and ask God to show you a new way to live.

5. Look up the words *sober, soberness* and *sobriety,* along with the accompanying scriptures.

6. Notice that soberness allows alertness, flexibility and clarity of decision-making. No, it doesn't mean being an old prune, without humor. It means clearheaded.

7. Begin confessing that you are what the scriptures on soberness say you are. Keep confessing them no matter what you feel like. Over time you'll begin to see some positive change.

Set aside some time each morning to be quiet before the Lord and let Him love on you. He's better than a Broadway hunk any day.

38

GOT YA LAST!

Every elevator has a sign inside clearly stating its maximum capacity. Ignore it at your own peril. Most elevators won't operate with too many people stuffed inside, but some have actually plunged passengers to their deaths because the maximum capacity was exceeded.

Every building is constructed based on engineering knowledge of weight-bearing support beams and joints. The amount of force the structure of the building can withstand without collapsing is determined before the "skin" goes onto the structure. The construction industry is where the word *stress* originally came from, although today the word *stress* is used to describe everything from a bad medical report to a bad hair day.

God created our bodies to withstand a certain amount of stress. After all, He surely knew we'd be living among plenty of geeks and Murphy's Law events. But just like an I-beam, we're designed to handle only so much pressure. When we ignore the limit, we face meltdown and total collapse. When you think about it, you're no different from that pair of black silk pants you wore last Thanksgiving. After you ate like a truck driver who hadn't stopped for food in eighteen hours, the button on your waistband was under so much stress that one more bite of apple pie would have sent it airborne like exploding shrapnel. Your emotional stability may be in the same condition.

GETTING YOUR GOAT

One of the things that brings more stress into your life than anything else is other people, especially difficult people. If the High Priestess of Guilt and Condemnation knows you don't know how to handle them very well, she'll keep a steady stream coming your way to weigh you down, suck you dry, get you into strife and make you borderline homicidal. The High Priestess knows how to read your meter. When you're a quart low on patience, here comes a custom-designed dork with a special-delivery ribbon bearing your name.

I recently heard three secrets from a motivational speaker who guarantees you'll never have trouble with difficult people:

1. Never say no to them.
2. Never give them any feedback.
3. Never ask them to do anything.

Just let them rule your life without setting any boundaries around yourself. Let them run roughshod over you—you'll never have trouble with them. Of course, you can plan to spend the rest of your days at the rehab clinic of your choice. The speaker was only kidding about using the secrets, and if you're using them now without knowing it, your body is being pushed beyond its maximum stress capacity.

MACHIAVELLI WAS A SWELL GUY

Italian statesman Niccolo Machiavelli was the poster boy for difficult people. In the sixteenth century he wrote *The Prince,* a book that is considered to be his masterpiece. It emphasized power at any cost. Machiavelli's principles of conduct included cunning, duplicity and bad faith. He believed that any means to achieve power was justifiable, however unscrupulous. He also believed the only two human motivations were fear and greed—and he used them brilliantly to get what he wanted.

Sound like anyone in your life? If so, listen up; your elevator is going into the shop for repairs.

Difficult people know they can get their needs met by being difficult. They also know that the two most manipulative emotions in the world are guilt and anger, and they've refined their use into an art form. Don't even to try to beat them at this game—you're standing in the presence of Roger Maris, of Michael Jordan, of Picasso, of Bill Gates...towering champions of skill. Difficult people are pros at the game of guilt and anger. You're a rookie by comparison, so give it up.

Difficult people began honing this art form early in life. Put yourself in the role of the mother and let's see how guilt works.

"Mom, may I go to the movies?"

"No."

"Why not, Mom? All the other kids are going."

"Because you've been very busy this week, and I think you should stay home."

"But, Mom, I've only been busy because you're always at work and never seem to have any time to spend with me. Sally's mom doesn't work—I wish you didn't have to. Sally's mom stays home and cooks and helps us with school projects and stuff. She always seems to have time to talk to us and answer questions about boys and talk to us about what's going on at school and everything. But I guess it's really important to you to work so you can have pretty clothes for your boyfriend. I sure do miss Dad since he left, but I guess he was tired of never seeing you either. Maybe someday you'll have just a little free time and we can...oh, I don't know, maybe do some things together like a real mother and daughter" (small tear runs down cheek).

How do you feel right about now? Lower than dirt? That's the object of the game, so you'll say, "Oh, OK, I guess it's all right if you go to the movies tonight." Bull's-eye! She just pinned the tail on the donkey (that would be you). A performance like this turns your *no* into *yes*—and at the same time teaches the child that if you ask for something like an adult and don't get it, the way to score is to make the other person feel like pond scum in order to get your way.

If guilt doesn't work, difficult people know they can always rely on anger to get their needs met. Words like *always* and *never* are used like automatic weapons: "You've *always* liked Billy better than me. That's why you *always* listen to everything he has to say and agree with it. You've *never* had any time for me, and you *never* let me do anything I want. You're just a mean, horrible mother, and I hate you!"

Anger used like this is verbal abuse that has no basis in truth. It's simply based on the reality that someone wants something and can get it by attacking someone else. Who needs Machiavelli when you've got someone in your life like this? Attacking and abusing or whining and crying are major tactics difficult people have been using for years. The problem is that they have been rewarded for it

THROUGH THE LOOKING GLASS

I'll bet you've got some of these scenes going on in your house. What about this one for an example?

Your husband says, "I'm going hunting this weekend."

You say, "Oh, well if you have to, I guess it's OK. Of course, I was hoping to finally get to have dinner with you, but I can understand you think hunting is more important than having dinner with me." Then you put him in the deep freeze all day.

Four hours later he says, "Is something wrong?"

"No," you say and then sigh.

"Well, you're awfully quiet," he says. "Did I do something to make you angry?"

"No," you reply, "everything's fine." You won't level with him for anything. It might make him feel better, and you want to make sure he suffers to make up for leaving you in favor of the duck blind. After several futile attempts to soften you up, he gets mad because he's tired of living in the same house with yeti. (For those of you who may have botched this question during your last game of Trivial Pursuit, *yeti* is the Tibetan word for the abominable snowman.)

By bedtime, you've thawed out, and he's good and torqued—not exactly the perfect formula for a roll in the hay. Been there? Most of us have. All that angst for nothing. And all because neither of you can express to the other person what you need. Instead, in order to get what you want, you use guilt as a surrogate for the real thing—which is telling the other person how you feel and asking for what you want. Crazy, isn't it?

I used to be particularly skilled at sulking, pouting and other guerrilla tactics. Often my life resembled a scene right out of *Alice in Wonderland*, all because I didn't have the guts to express what I really meant and receive feedback without getting defensive. Instead, I was the local franchise for Manipulations R Us.

Psychologists say there are four distinct personality types:

1. *Assertive.* These people get their needs met without taking advantage of others. They know how to tell people what they need. For instance, they say, "It hurts my feelings when you leave me for the whole weekend. Can we work out a deal for part of the weekend? Or, if you go this weekend, can we spend some time together next weekend doing something we both enjoy?"

2. *Passive.* The term *doormat* was coined just for them. These people have "peace-at-any-price" personalities. They don't know how to express what they need and are afraid to do so for fear of the reaction. They spend their lives saying *yes* when they really mean *no,* then they silently resent the other person for it.

3. *Aggressive.* These folks are the terrorists all too many of us tolerate. Aggressive people use guilt and anger to get what they want, but unlike assertive people, they take advantage of others.

4. *Passive-aggressive.* These people operate like the stealth bomber. They have a need, but they won't tell you what it is. Because you're not Karnack the Magnificent, they wait to punish you by teaching you a lesson when you're with others. They take pleasure in embarrassing you by talking down to you or criticizing you in a crowd. It's the ultimate "got-ya-last" behavior. It's gutless, but effective—and of course, it makes you livid.

Do you know which of these personalities fits you? Do you have some aggressive and passive-aggressive folks in your life? Would you like to be able to set some boundaries so you won't get swallowed by these vultures?

WHAT TO DO

1. Come to terms with the fact that failure to set reasonable boundaries is driven by fear. It's a by-product of not knowing who you are in Christ and therefore feeling "less than" and "different from." Deep down inside, you don't feel worthy to establish ground rules because you're afraid of attack or abandonment.

2. Read Revelation 12:10. In this scripture you see that day and night Satan is accusing the brethren (Christians) while deceiving the whole world. Any condemnation you feel is from Satan.

3. Learn about the delegated authority you've been given by Jesus Christ. Meditate on:

- Colossians 1:13
- Ephesians 1:3
- Ephesians 6:12 (There are many heavens—terrestrial, celestial, heavens of the heavens and the throne of God. Although Satan is the prince of the power of the air [Eph. 2:2] and the god of this world [2 Cor. 4:4], Jesus placed believers far above the powers of Satan and his powers of darkness.)
- Ephesians 1:21–22 (It was all accomplished at the cross. You, as part of the body of believers, are the feet separated from the head [Jesus].)
- Ephesians 2:6 (Jesus doesn't sit in the middle of the kingdom of darkness. He sits above it all, and so do we as His body.)
- Ephesians 1:19–20
- Mark 16:17 (Believers have authority, which has been delegated to them in the name of Jesus, over all the powers of darkness.)
- Luke 10:19
- Matthew 28:18 (Power is given to all, not just to ministers or a certain few.)
- James 4:7

39

NO PLACE TO HIDE

hat do you know about Jonah, besides the fact that he spent three days and three nights in the belly of a whale? Did you know he was divinely commissioned as God's messenger in the early eighth century B.C. to warn the population of Nineveh of coming judgment? God told him to go to Nineveh and what to do when he got there. Instead Jonah went in the opposite direction to Tarshish. The Bible says in Jonah 1:3 that he *fled* from the presence of the Lord and boarded a ship for Tarshish.

Why did Jonah flee? Because he didn't want to do what God told him to do; he thought he could get away with rebellion by getting away from God. It didn't work, of course—any more than it works when you and I don't obey God. But before you laugh at the futility of Jonah thinking he could become invisible to the God who made heaven and earth, think how many times you've acted in defiance of God's Word and expected to get away with it. I know, you thought that His directions didn't apply today. After all, times have changed since the days of the apostles. Or you think that God will cut you some slack because you're a reasonably good person in other areas of your life. He will, but the devil won't.

OUT FROM UNDER THE UMBRELLA

God loves you all the time, no matter what you do. He is infinitely patient with you while He waits for you to make the right decisions consistent with His directions so He can bless you. As long as you're obedient to His Word, you're standing under the protective covering of His mercy and grace. But when you knowingly or unknowingly walk contrary to His written directions, you step out from under His umbrella of protection. That's when you place yourself in position to be a punching bag for the enemy.

Jonah learned that lesson soon after he jumped on the ship headed for Tarshish. A huge tempest with mighty winds came upon the sea. The captain came to Jonah and said, "Arise, call upon your god! Perhaps the god will give a thought to us, that we do not perish" (Jon. 1:6, RSV). Then the captain and the other mariners said to one another, "Come, let us cast lots, that we may know on whose account this evil has come upon us" (v. 7, RSV). They knew someone on board had sinned and was causing them all to be at risk.

They cast lots, and the lot fell on Jonah. The men knew he was fleeing the Lord, because he had told them so. They asked Jonah what they should do to him so they could be safe from the great storm. Jonah told them to cast him overboard since he had caused the tempest, but they didn't. In vain his fellow sailors rowed hard trying to bring the ship to land. The sea was too much for them, however, and they cried out to the Lord.

Finally, the crew tossed Jonah into the sea—and the moment they did, the storm ceased. Two points bear mentioning:

1. Neither Jonah nor the mariners could hide from God. They had no place to run.

2. Even though it was clear to everyone that Jonah's rebellion was the cause of extreme danger, they were reluctant to take the necessary action to free themselves from him. (How many times have you stayed in close relationship with someone who was involved with serious sin—and you knew it—and you were not willing to practice tough love?)

After Jonah was thrown overboard, the crew was safe, but Jonah was immediately swallowed by a huge fish. The Bible says, "The waters compassed me about even to the soul: the depth closed me round about, the weeds were wrapped about my head" (Jon. 2:5, NKJV). Yuck! How would you like to spend the weekend in Moby Dick's stomach among digestive juices, seaweed and whatever else he had to eat?

REDEMPTION

Jonah realized he was in deep trouble. He cried out to the Lord and repented, and God caused the fish to vomit out Jonah upon the dry land. That's when God called to Jonah the second time and told him to go directly to Nineveh. This time Jonah obeyed. As a result of his warning to the people, the entire city repented, and God extended His mercy in postponing the day of judgment.

Jonah was obviously back under the protective umbrella, so now God could work in his behalf while Jonah could operate in the anointing of his calling as prophet. Did God cause the storm and the three-day pass into the Whale Hotel? No, but the devil had license to bring destruction because of Jonah's rebellion. However, God is always ready to turn things around for our good when we admit our mistakes and seek His help.

TRICK OR TREAT

Do you ever wake up early in the morning when you're out of town and can't figure out where you are? It happens. I recently had this experience. I lay in bed for a few minutes trying to retrace my steps. I took a deep breath and smelled chlorine, so I figured I was in a hotel with an inside pool. I finally decided I was in a Holiday Inn somewhere. A look at the telephone reinforced my hunch. I was in West Virginia.

A friend of mine who's a hotel general manager tells of being the manager on duty at 2 A.M. in a deserted lobby and looking up to see a man standing in front of the desk in his birthday suit. The guest had gotten up in the middle of the night, and instead of walking into the bathroom, he had walked into the corridor. The door to his room locked behind him. He frantically looked everywhere for a linen closet or a discarded room service tray. Nothing. He got on the elevator, praying no one else would want a ride, and arrived in the lobby looking for a potted plant to duck behind. There was nowhere to hide. He was locked out of his room, and now the whole world knew he slept without pajamas!

You can thank your lucky stars if you have never had to experience this. Yet if you're running from something God told you to do or are living in rebellion, you're just as naked in His sight. You can con yourself, but you can't con God. He has seen it all, and He has seen all your antics. But unlike the High Priestess of Guilt and Condemnation, He loves you anyway, and He wants you to get your act together. Until that time comes, you may be naked for one of the following reasons:

Cowardice

You think you've figured out a better way than what God told you to do. The Lord impressed upon me recently to call someone and tell her something. I didn't want to do it because I knew she didn't want to hear it. I dragged my feet and dragged my feet, all the while praying for this person—hoping God would get the message to her. Is this dumb or what? If God had been able to get the message to this person, He wouldn't have needed me, would He?

Finally I screwed up my courage and told the woman what I was supposed to tell her. She cried. I figured I could kiss the relationship good-bye. Instead she said, "Oh, thank you. You just don't know how I've been crying out to God for the answer to this problem! I've been crying for days looking for the next step to take and asking for wisdom. I know this is it." I had made a mistake and consulted my head, thinking I had a better way to accomplish what God told me to do. *Wrong.* And my poor friend had spent several more days in torment because of my cowardice.

Selfishness

You're not willing to turn loose of the sinful behavior because it makes your flesh feel good. Earlier I told of my unwillingness to give up sugar because I wanted to hang on to it as a coping mechanism. What I was really afraid of was dealing with my emotions directly without using food to dull the pain. But failure to turn loose of something destructive is like an old oil filter ad I remember that said, "You can pay me now, or you can pay me later." Hanging on to bad habits opens the door for tempests and storms.

Ignorance

You are walking around in ignorance if you don't know what God's Word says. You're stepping into one pothole after another without realizing it. But ignorance is not bliss. Ignorance keeps you attired in your birthday suit before God and before the devil, who knows he can bring destruction on you that you may not be able to reverse.

Self-delusion

If you think you're fooling anyone, you're nuts. Repeated rebellion is usually obvious to anyone who knows you very well. You might as well pin a "Kick Me" sign on your back.

OUT OF THE BELLY

There's significance to the fact that Jonah spent three days and three nights in the belly of the fish. Matthew 12:40 says, "For even as Jonas was three days and three nights in the whale's belly; so shall the Son of man be three days and three nights in the heart of the earth." The Son of man is Jesus, and the heart of the earth is hell, where Jesus went to win the keys to death, hell and the grave (Rev. 1:18). There He was separated from God and endured all the fury of sickness, disease, lack, poverty, fear, torment and all the evil in the world so you don't have to. Jesus acted as your substitute, paying the price for all the sin in the world. When He rose from the grave and ascended into heaven, He had defeated all the power of Satan and placed His authority in your hands, the hands of all believers.

You serve a God who loves you enough to have endured the cross and hell for the joy that was set before Him (Heb. 12:2). *You* are that joy! Can anyone who endured that much for you deny you His very best? So why run from His directions? Why try to figure out a better way? He wants you to walk in the fullness of His promises. The answer is to look up—not stay focused on your own ability.

WHAT TO DO

If you want to get in line for His blessings:

1. Read the Book of Jonah.

2. Ask the Lord to reveal to you any areas of rebellion.

3. Spend some quiet time before the Lord so that He can show you areas needing improvement.

4. Write down what He tells you, and commit to make a small change every day.

5. Remember, practice makes perfect.

40

KISS ME, I'M IRISH

It was one of my best practical jokes. My former husband had a wonderful sense of humor, and we had several business and personal friends with whom we traded jokes—always at the others' expense. For instance, one couple looked out their window one Saturday morning to see a team of people measuring their house for aluminum siding. It's only funny if you know their house is in the most expensive part of the city. There isn't a piece of aluminum within twenty miles—we're talking strictly a brick, wood and marble neighborhood. They got us back. A week later, when my then-husband turned on the radio in his car, he could hear nothing but Chinese. No matter what button he pushed, the only sound was Chinese talk or song. (There's nothing like a creative mechanic when you need one.)

Among the group, no one was safe from surprise pizza deliveries or inexplicable Frederick's of Hollywood gifts. A pair of bright pink plastic flamingos regularly made guest appearances in our front yards. Thinking we had come up with the ultimate prank, my then-husband and I sent out an invitation to one of the couples for a St. Patrick's Day party. The party was allegedly being held at the home of an executive with whom I worked at the time. He and his wife were from New York City, very sophisticated and barely friends of the couple to whom we sent the invitation. Because of the St. Patrick's Day theme, the invitation clearly stated, "Wear green."

We waited. Thinking about our handiwork, we rolled on the floor laughing over the thought of our friends showing up attired in green leprechaun outfits at the home of two startled people who aren't having a party. Unfortunately, the invited couple couldn't attend but called to thank the "hosts" for the invitation, expressing regret over not being able to be there. They thought the host sounded a bit perplexed when they called, but they assumed his wife was doing all the planning and he didn't know much about the party. Two weeks later the husband ran into the "host."

"How was your St. Patrick's Day party?"

The response was one of those stares that indicates the people with the butterfly nets are on the way. "There never was a party. It was never planned, never implemented. Besides, we're Italian, as if that isn't patently obvious. Where did you get the idea we were having a party complete with green beer and 'Kiss-me-I'm-Irish' outfits?"

Our friend said he did a slow burn, realizing he'd been had and who did it. Only one thought crossed his mind—*revenge*.

WHO AM I?

One of the things we fear most is looking stupid in front of others. Since childhood the High Priestess of Guilt and Condemnation fills us with shame over any time that we've stood out from the crowd looking different. Rather than face the consequences of shame, teens learn to ask their friends for advice about what to do, whom to see, how to look and so forth. Wanting to be unique, they all end up flying in formation like geese because they want to be part of the "in crowd." Being considered out of the mainstream for a teenager is torture. By the time a person reaches young adulthood, the process of asking others what they think about people, events and priorities is ingrained. Independent thinking is risky. Consequences for mistakes are heavy. It's a pattern that ruins your life.

We end up not knowing who we are. We let others define our identities. We put on the mask we think others want to see; we try to stay in character, thinking our value is established by what others think of us. Asking for help is never an option. We don't want to appear weak or risk being considered too much trouble by those we're trying to impress. Confrontation is not an option either; it's frequently followed by rejection. Thus the pattern is set for seeking acknowledgment from others.

Rather than find out who we are from a source that really knows us, we try to find identity through others who are as fallible as we are. What we're really doing is asking the creature who we are instead of asking the Creator who made us.

Consider the lunacy of this pattern. Because we don't know who we are, we ask other people (who don't know who they are either) to define who we are. When we don't get the answers we like, we're filled with remorse over not being the people they want us to be. It makes my head hurt just thinking about it. All that the "creature" can tell us is based only on a little bitty snapshot of accumulated knowledge that is nothing compared to what God knows.

GOD KNOWS WHO YOU ARE

Look at Jeremiah 1:4–5. God says He knew you before He formed you in the womb. He knew you, approved of you and sanctified you before you were ever conceived. Study Psalm 139:14. You're fearfully and wonderfully made. You're special to God. He has given you special gifts and a unique assignment to bring forth in the earth. He has provided you with an instruction manual (the Bible) and the Comforter (the Holy Spirit, as stated in John 14:26). His Word tells you who you are, from Genesis to Revelation. You don't need another living soul to tell you who you are or how important you are.

I used to beat myself up because I wasn't any good at math. I had to be tutored in math all the way through college. As a businessperson, I've taken "Finance for Non-Financial Managers" twice, and I still don't get it. A friend of mine is fond of saying, "Jane knows how to make money; she just doesn't know how to count it." That always gets a big laugh, but in the final analysis it doesn't make any difference. Math just isn't part of my skill set. And I can hire people to count money for me, but I can't hire them to make money for me.

I've been blessed with extraordinary creative, verbal big-picture thinking and problem-solving skills. They're gifts from God to be used for the work of the gospel and to prosper me financially. No one gets all the skills, so I stopped berating myself over what I'm not and started appreciating what I am. (I'm still working on the body image part; I'm still too aware of the gap between Rachel Hunter and me.) I'm also learning through the Word who God says that I am and how He views me. God's appreciation for me is not conditional nor based on my ability to perform. It's a hard concept to understand initially, but once you see a glimmer of light, your whole value system begins to change.

BLUSH-FREE ZONE

When you know you're loved by God, that you're the apple of His eye, it makes you virtually immune to embarrassment. You have the ability to pass things off easily. Confidence rises up on the inside of you, and what people think isn't nearly so important anymore. It's liberating. You feel free to do what's right rather than what's expected. I even had the courage to dismiss one of my clients three years ago. This was a huge step for someone who used to think her whole identity was tied up in what she did for a living.

Every time I walked into this client's office building, I felt as if I were walking into a black cloud. I didn't recognize it at first. I only knew that my time there was always accompanied by a sinking feeling in my stomach, a feeling of impending doom. Something always seemed amiss, and it seemed as if it were my fault. No wonder—the head of the organization had a personality like a junkyard dog. He was a fountain of criticism that poured on everyone. Nothing was ever good enough. He controlled through fault-finding. I thought, *Hmm ... I've lived here before in one of my former lives.*

One day I walked into his office and said, "You know, I've worked with you for two years, and your organization has made progress. I think it's time for me to turn it all over to you." He looked surprised (this may be the first recorded act of a consultant canceling an annual retainer), but he said, "Well, if you really think we can take it from here, then let's try it." God had given me the words to say so I could do it with kindness and not burn a bridge.

When I got on that elevator I felt like Dr. Martin Luther King, Jr.—"Free at last, free at last, thank God Almighty, I'm free at last!" I walked away from several thousand dollars a month and a man who insulted people for entertainment. Within three weeks, the Lord had brought me a new client more profitable than this one, a client who treated me with respect and valued the work I did.

Without a growing understanding of who I am in Christ, I'd still be back with the original client taking ample scoops of abuse along with the rest of his employees. But God demonstrated His love and concern for me by giving me the courage to get out of a harmful situation. And He'll do the same for you. You see, you're the apple of His eye. He wants you to ask *Him* who you are—not your boyfriend or your boss or your mother-in-law. And when you know who you are, you'll begin to think the way He thinks, react the way He reacts and follow His directions, not someone else's.

CAN YOU TOP THIS?

There was, of course, payback for the St. Patrick's Day party. We returned from vacation to find our yard filled with those wooden ducks on sticks that have wings that flap around in a circle when the wind blows. Charming. The neighbors wanted to know if the yard art would be permanent. We told them yes, but only if we could add a few of those birdbaths with the shiny blue gazing balls in them. They looked horrified. Oh well, if they can't take a joke…

WHAT TO DO

If you're interested in finding out who you really are according to the One who made you and who ever lives to make intercession for you to the Father—as Hebrews 7:25 says—and if you want to develop immunity to feeling foolish, do the following:

1. Read the Book of Ephesians. Read it slowly—it's a short book—and picture yourself in the descriptions. In this book the apostle Paul speaks of the church (that's you) as being established by God in His eternal purpose through redemption in Christ. The conduct of the believer stands in contrast to his former way of life—referring to his spiritual life as "in the heavenly sphere," through the power of the Holy Spirit (Heb. 1:3, 20; 2:6; 3:10; 6:12).

2. Write down on a sheet of paper in your own words what you've learned as a result of your study.

3. When you begin to feel intimidated, read Ephesians again. You are blood-bought, special and in covenant with the Father.

41

LABELED

L abels. We put them on our clothes, our automobiles and our acquaintances. Consumers recognize brand names because they deliver a consistent image. Names like Coca-Cola, Nike, Harley Davidson, Kleenex, Comet, Xerox, Sony and Levi have credibility. Each of these brand names stands for something in the minds of consumers. Each targets the expectations of customers and meets or exceeds those expectations. Yet "branding" can go beyond products and services. Some people have even done a pretty good job "branding" themselves. Think about Madonna, Donald Trump, Bill Gates, Michael Jordan and Oprah Winfrey. There's no doubt what each of these individuals is famous for.

As human beings we love to put people in categories, even those who aren't famous. You remember—in school you labeled certain kids "cool" and others "geeks." There were the "brains" and the "teacher's pets." Some girls were considered "easy," some guys "trouble." Today, kids are also designated as either "druggies" or "straights." From childhood on, we're used to identifying others as belonging to certain groups. We learn to make quick judgments without much information and to put labels on individuals. Unfortunately, those labels often last a lifetime.

- "You're a loser."
- "Your father was rotten to the core, and so are you."

198

- "Your family was dirt poor, and you'll be poor as long as you live."
- "Your mother was a drunk, and you will be one, too."
- "You'll get heart disease because it runs in your family—none of the men have lived past forty-five."

The comments above are all labels spoken and affixed to people. The High Priestess reinforces them. Those who receive the labels as truth bring them to fruition. What's fixed in your mind as truth drives the choices you make, the actions you take and the results you achieve. If you're living with negative thoughts about yourself that have been planted in your mind, you are your own worst enemy. Changing your circumstances requires changing your mind, because your mind is the battleground that determines your victory or defeat.

WHAT'S YOUR LABEL?

If you think about and see yourself as a loser, that's exactly what you'll be. If you think of yourself as barely getting by, you'll never live much beyond the poverty line. But that's not God's plan for you. He didn't pay the price on the cross for you to live a defeated life. Second Corinthians 10:5 tells us to cast down "imaginations, and every high thing that exalteth itself against the knowledge of God, and [bring] into captivity every thought to the obedience of Christ." That simply means if your thoughts don't agree with what God says about you, you are to replace those thoughts with the truth according to God's Word. For instance, if the High Priestess of Guilt and Condemnation says, "You're broke, and you'll always be broke," you say, "Oh no, I refuse to stay broke because Philippians 4:19 tells me that my God provides for my every need according to His riches in glory by Christ Jesus."

What you think about and dwell on becomes your destiny. Philippians 4:8 says, "Whatsoever things are true, whatsoever things are honest, whatsoever things are just, whatsoever things are pure, whatsoever things are lovely, whatsoever things are of good report; if there be any virtue, and if there be any praise, think on these things." The apostle Paul is telling you to reject any thought that's negative and worrisome. Instead, fill your head with positive, empowering thoughts that come directly from the throne room of God.

Above all, you need a prosperous soul. What's that? 3 John 2 says,

"Beloved, I pray that you may prosper in every way and [that your body] may keep well, even as [I know] your soul keeps well and prospers" (AMP). Prospering in every way is dependent upon the prospering of your soul. Remember in an earlier chapter we talked about the soul being made up of the mind, the will and the emotions? The mind is your intellect, the will is your decision-making mechanism and the emotions are your feelings. Remember that the mind is your battleground. Romans 12:2 says, "Be not conformed to the world: but be ye transformed by the renewing of your mind."

A mind transformed from one that thinks "loser" into one that thinks "winner" through the renewing power of the Word of God grabs hold of the decision-making mechanism to make wise decisions. Wise decisions produce positive results. In time, emotions line up with the renewed mind. It's the process of building character. Jerry Savelle defines a prosperous soul as one in which the mind is renewed to God's Word, the will is conformed to God's will and the emotions are brought under the control of a reborn spirit. He adds that we are limited by what we create in our minds when we fail to cast down thoughts, ideas and concepts that are contrary to God's will. What we experience outwardly, Savelle believes, is in direct proportion to what we see and think about ourselves.

If you've labeled yourself as a failure inside, you'll never grow beyond that category at work, at home or with friends. Proverbs 23:7 says, "As [a man] thinketh in his heart, so is he." My personal opinion is that the translators put the comma in the wrong place in this scripture. Try putting it after the word "thinketh," and see how it reads. Whatever you think is what's produced in your heart. But no matter where the comma is placed (I'm perfectly willing to admit the translators knew a whole lot more than I do), the scripture says the same thing—your thoughts drop down into your heart, and what is in your heart is who you really are.

ZOO PARADE

I used to be group vice president of a large hospitality company. For some reason, corporate management frequently sent over potential job candidates for another vice president and me to interview. I guess they wanted another source of input before making decisions on people who would have responsibility for interacting with other parts of the organization.

Since the other vice president was one of the people involved in the practical jokes ring, this parade of job candidates presented a terrific chance for a sting.

I had a secretary at the time who wasn't much of a secretary, but she was a gifted writer, specializing in fiction. It was just too easy.

One day I ducked into my friend's office to announce that corporate management wanted us to interview someone who was being considered for the legal department. I handed him a resume, creatively prepared by my secretary. We named the fictional job candidate Bradford Simian Van Landingham. We knew with a name like that, he'd instantly be labeled as affluent, so we fudged the rest of his accomplishments to line up with the sound of his name. (The word *simian* was the only clue to the truth, but more about that later.)

Bradford was a graduate of Cornell with a law degree from Harvard. He was into Class A yachting, polo and tennis. His wife was named Buffie, and the children carried the monikers Heather and Skip. Get the picture? Isn't this someone you'd love to hate? See how easily we assign labels to people? As my friend read over the résumé, he said, "Is this guy for real?" I was concerned that I had overplayed my hand, but I responded, "Yep. He looks like an Ivy League dream, doesn't he? Corporate wants us to make sure he can fit into the culture here, since we're not as formal as the New York law firm where he's been practicing."

My friend said, "Oh, OK; how about next Wednesday at ten o'clock?"

"Fine. I'll bring Bradford by after we're finished talking," I said. Pay dirt.

Wednesday arrived, and so did Bradford Simian Van Landingham—except Bradford wasn't human. He's a trained chimpanzee named Zippy who performs at the local theme park. For a fee, his trainer lets him make special appearances, although I'll bet Zippy never tried out for a job as a corporate lawyer.

Zippy was all dressed up for his big interview, complete with necktie and roller skates. I held his hand as he skated down the halls with me to my friend's office. As we breezed by other offices, phones dropped, conversations stopped, people ran out of meeting rooms to stare.... It was hilarious! My fellow vice president was ready for the interview, seated on a couch in his office. I went in first, saying, "I'd like to introduce you to Bradford Simian Van Landingham"—and in skated Zippy. He promptly glided over, hugged his interviewer, sat down on the couch next to him, put his arm around him and with his other hand reached down to the coffee table and opened up the *Harvard Business Review*. It was the funniest scene I'd ever witnessed.

Zippy didn't get hired, but his résumé is on file in case legal needs anyone with his special skills. Not every corporate lawyer can balance torts with tax and hang out at the roller rink, too.

I probably deserve to have a hippopotamus show up in my living room some evening in retribution for all the clever stunts I've pulled. But here's my point: See how easy it was to spin a personal image based purely on a shallow description? That's how quick we are to form an opinion based on perceptions.

As a Man Thinketh

What dominates your thinking? Whatever it is will be what you become. If you remember the cripple from the Book of John who was lame for thirty-eight years (John 5:2–9), notice how Jesus ministered to him. Jesus ministered to his spirit, soul and body. He said to the man, "Rise, take up thy bed, and walk." Three commands: "Rise," "take up thy bed" and "walk."

Oral Roberts says Jesus was giving a command to each part of the man's makeup. The command to rise was directed to his spirit, because the man's spirit was down after thirty-eight years of being paralyzed. If you can't get a man's spirit to rise, his body will never respond. You've got to get up on the inside before you can get up on the outside.

The second command was directed at the man's soul (the mind, will and emotions): "Take up thy bed." Jesus was encouraging the man to change the image in his mind from the bed carrying him to him carrying the bed. Jesus was in essence saying, "Get a new picture of yourself! Get up, spirit; get up, soul—get a new image." Roberts says—and the Word verifies—that if you can get your spirit and your soul into agreement, your body has to follow suit.

The last command was to the body, "Walk!" When the lame man's spirit rose, his soul got a new image, and his body got up and walked. Jesus changed the ideas, concepts and thoughts the man had held for thirty-eight years! Almost four decades of stinking thinking done away with in an instant, all because of a new image.

What limitations have you established for yourself that are robbing you of the fullness of God? Limitations can be removed if you're willing to change your mind. Remember that you have control of your thoughts. Are you willing to trade in a soul that's in debt for one that's prosperous?

WHAT TO DO

1. Study the fifth chapter of John.

2. Make a list of all the directions offered by Jesus.

3. Describe how His directions impacted others.

4. Write out how His directions can change you.

5. Pray for willingness to follow His directions.

6. Paint a new picture of yourself on the inside by what you've learned in this chapter.

42

SHARKPROOF

A passenger boat pushes slowly through some tropical sea under a relentless sun. On deck, a well-travelled and evidently knowledgeable man in holding forth, surrounded by a circle of listeners.

"At this moment," he pontificates, "we are sailing through waters where, if by some mischance you should happen to fall overboard, it would be quite impossible for you to drown."

The audience is intrigued. "Really?" "That's surely impossible," and "How do you make that out?" they chorus.

The knowledgeable man's face hardens momentarily. He narrows his eyes and says grimly, "Sharks."[1]

Politics—a world filled with individuals driven by a lust for power, a world inhabited by sharklike motives and sharklike personalities. Politics is often described as the method for obtaining favor from people with the power to make decisions. Webster's definition of politics relates almost entirely to government. Webster, however, never worked in a corporate environment.

Politics is a survival technique in a corporation. Even so, people often get promoted although they don't deserve it, merely because they have the right relationship with the right person. The Peter Principle thrives, but no one notices. Nonperformers sometimes hang on to important positions because they have conned those in power into thinking they're indispensable. Choices like those are political, based on the acquisition or brokering of influence. It's not fair, but no one said life in a corporation (or anywhere else, for that matter) was fair. Besides, corporations are no different from any other organization—the same principle is alive and well everywhere.

The realm of politics has expanded far beyond the definition of government and the private sector to include associations, clubs, schools, sports and even neighborhoods. Professional football coaches throw tantrums on the field to get calls reversed by officials. That's politics. Little League fathers act like terrorists to get Johnny up at bat. That's politics, too. Empire builders jockey for position to become elected officers of private clubs. Relationships between the faculty and the administration at universities often resemble mud-wrestling matches. All that falls under the category of politics. Today every arena is permeated with manifestations of political behavior. It's all about power. Like it or not, we've all experienced and practiced it.

Scott Adams has made himself enough money to buy a couple of Third World countries by lampooning corporate politics in his comic strip *Dilbert*. Dilbert's world is inhabited by pin-headed bosses, smart-mouthed consultants and long-suffering coworkers, just like in real life. You may feel you're living in a freeze-frame of *Dilbert*. But here's some news: You don't have to let the turkeys get you down. If you're willing to lean on God as your source, the parade of nincompoops around you can't affect your present or your future.

OVERCOMING THE OBVIOUS

The selection from *The Life of Sharks* is vivid in what it leaves to the imagination. The mishap of falling overboard clearly implies the reality of being eaten by sharks even before going down for the third time. You probably think that making a mistake at work would qualify you for the same outcome. You can see visions of ravenous coworkers out to get you, swirling about, eager to take advantage of your weakened condition. And if you aren't sure of your relationship with God, that's probably close to the truth.

But Psalm 97:10 says, "He delivereth them out of the hand of the wicked." And Psalm 145:20 says, "The Lord preserveth all them that love him: but all the wicked will he destroy." Sounds good, right? Well, this isn't idle chat. It's for real.

STORM WARNING

Several years ago I was a board member of a public facility. The manager that had directed the facility for years had not been willing to develop and grow to the point where he could successfully manage the operation any longer. We had to go through the painful process of letting him go and finding a new replacement. Since my two areas of focus as a board member were marketing and human resources, it fell to me to coordinate the process of finding a new director. We followed the process prescribed by the city and county to the letter of the law in searching for a candidate. We posted the job, allowing local candidates to apply; when no one was found who had the necessary experience and competency, we hired a search firm.

So far so good. The search firm sent the three best candidates for final interviews with the board. We ended up hiring someone from out of state with a tremendous amount of experience and a passion for the challenges associated with the venue. It was three weeks after the new director got here when it all hit the fan.

Suddenly, I began to get angry phone calls from a man in town who cried foul, saying I had been unfair. He felt he was qualified for the job (he wasn't), and he thought his elimination in the earlier round of interviews was politically motivated. Before I knew it, he had the newspaper writing stories about me, calling me every name but cool. Headlines used *fix* and *bigot* and other hurtful words to describe both the process and me. It hurt plenty.

One day I got a call from the deejay of a local radio show who began to assault me with names, accusations and threats—on the air! I was appalled and frightened. I was also devastated, because I knew we had followed the legally prescribed process and chosen the best person for the job. Someone who would benefit the fans and the city. But the sharks were circling my carcass.

I had nowhere to go but to God. Of course, that's a pretty good place to go; none of my friends had the power or the wisdom to stop the storm. The High Priestess of Guilt and Condemnation was operating in overdrive, telling me that I had screwed up, that I was a worthless gump, that what I really needed to do was get back at him. It was hard not getting into strife, because my flesh wanted to carpet-bomb his reputation with a few well-placed responses to the press.

A HEART CHANGE

I went to the Lord and said, "Father, I can't deal with this. This is more than I can handle. Your Word says that You're my refuge and my strength—a very present help in trouble [Ps. 46:1]. And I'm in big trouble! I repent for taking offense. I ask You to forgive me, and I ask You to forgive this man who is causing all the media stink. And I pray Your blessings into his life. With Your forgiveness I forgive him, and with Your love I love him. Now I roll the care of this onto You."

The next day there was another blistering article in the newspaper. I didn't read it. It took all I had to keep praying for the guy and confessing that the Lord is "a very present help in trouble" (Ps. 46:1).

The next day nothing. And the next. Quiet on all fronts, as all the criticism stopped. I went on with my life; after a couple of months I forgot all about the incident. In the meantime, the new director took hold and began to do a terrific job. Eighteen months later I got a call from the very man who had trashed me in the press. He wanted to come by my office to talk to me, so I agreed; however, I wasn't prepared for what he had to say.

He began by stating, "I came to apologize for what I did to you over a year ago. My behavior was reprehensible; I misread the facts, and you're not any of those things I accused you of." I was knocked out! But that wasn't the miracle. The miracle was that I had to have help from him reconstructing why I was mad at him in the first place. God had done such a complete job of the forgiveness process that He'd erased the painful facts from my memory. It was as if I were beginning a new relationship with someone I barely knew.

God had produced a heart change in both of us, a change from anger to forgiveness. He had taken my hurt and fear and made me sharkproof by standing on His promises and practicing forgiveness, even though my flesh didn't want to go along with the program. This man and I are very supportive of each other to this day.

God will never let you drown or be eaten by killer fish as long as you know about His protection policy and are willing to follow His directions. He loves you; He wants you safe so He can bless you with all that He has paid the price for you to have.

WHAT TO DO

If you'd like to find out about the protective shield available to you, check out these steps. No, don't just check them out—*do* them. You'll never be sorry.

1. Study the following scriptures: Deuteronomy 33:27; Psalm 5:12; 17:4; 31:19–20; 34:7; 46:1; 91; 97:10; 107:20; 119:116–117; 121:8; 145:18–20; Proverbs 1:33; 2:8; 3:25–26.

2. Now make a list of all the things you're afraid of.

3. Repeat everything you're afraid of, one by one, and follow each one with two or three of these scriptures. For example: "Father, I've always been afraid of being alone at night, but Your Word says that You hold me up, and I shall be safe. Therefore, I cast this fear onto You, and I rest in Your protection."

4. Don't expect overnight change, but change will come. Keep at it and live free.

43

WING TIP TORTE

It was a short run between St. Louis and Memphis, and the flight attendants were trying to serve a hot meal. My friend Donna Kay was serving in the first-class cabin. The hot meal was a bad idea. With not enough time to serve the food, she and the other flight attendants were slinging meals like Frisbees. Donna Kay said they were practically snatching forks out of peoples' mouths to pick up food trays in time for landing.

The plane was in final descent while people were halfway through dinner. In her haste she grabbed trays from two passengers; as she turned, a chocolate tart with whipped cream slid off one of the trays. It, too, went into final descent. The tart flipped over and landed squarely on a first-class passenger's wing tip shoes. Donna Kay stood frozen, wanting to shoot herself for the mistake. "Oh, I'm s-o-o-o sorry," she wailed, trying to scoop it off.

The man looked at her, pointed his finger in her face and growled, "You will not only clean my shoe, but you will personally clean out every hole in my wing tip." (If you're not familiar with wing tips, they feature trim on the toes that's marked with dozens of little holes in the leather.) On a good day it would take several of Santa's helpers, armed with toothpicks, about four hours to hit every hole.

The passenger was so menacing that Donna Kay cringed. There was dead silence in the cabin. From the seat behind the wing tip shoes came a man's loud voice: "Hey, you with the tart on your toe! You're a jerk!" Dead silence. Then the cabin erupted in laughter. Mr. Wing Tip was now so furious that he began wagging his finger at Donna Kay, demanding her name so he could write to the president of the airline. She was laughing so hard she could hardly write her name down. Everyone was craning to look at the chocolate-and-cream-decorated shoe and howling with laughter at the improbable crack from the man behind.

When the plane touched down, laughter was still in the air as the irate passenger stomped off the flight. "Don't you worry," the other passengers kept telling Donna Kay. "You couldn't help it, and you groveled for his forgiveness. If he can't get over it, that's his problem." Easy for them to say.

RADIO WISDOM

How many times have you been involved with someone like Mr. Wing Tip, someone who delights in making you feel small and incompetent? People like him aren't mature enough emotionally to handle life's upsets, so they take their discomfort out on you. They're bullies. But if you fall for it, you're equally in error. Bullies know they can remain in control as long as they can scare those around them into acquiescence. I used to have a boss like that. He'd huff and puff and threaten to blow my house down—and I'd go home with a matched set of knots in my stomach that would haunt me all night. I wasn't emotionally mature enough at the time to realize that his temper tantrums didn't have anything to do with me; they were *his* issues. And here's the key: There was nothing I could do or say to make it right with him, because he wasn't right with himself. Bullies are desperately insecure individuals who don't know how to have relationships. Instead, they take hostages.

One day I was driving around doing errands and listening to Dr. Laura on the radio. A woman called about a moral dilemma she was having with her mother-in-law. "She makes decisions about my children that I don't agree with, but I go along in order to keep peace," the caller said.

"How old are you?" Dr. Laura asked.

"Thirty-seven," replied the caller.

"And how much do you disagree with the decisions she's been making that involve your children?" Dr. Laura asked.

"Emphatically. What she's allowing my children to do when they stay with her is in direct conflict with what they're being taught at home," wailed the caller.

"Why don't you put your foot down?" asked Dr. Laura.

"Because when I make an issue of it, she gets upset and makes my husband unhappy, and I'm caught in the middle."

"And how old are you again?" Dr. Laura asked.

"Thirty-seven," responded the caller.

"Right. Well, you know what? You're a grownup now, and it's time you started acting like a grownup. Adults stand up for principles that are important to them regardless of the consequences. I think that as a thirty-seven-year-old, you should be prepared to act like an adult, do what's right and be prepared to face the discomfort of inappropriate responses from some people."

Dr. Laura said it all. When you're doing the right thing, be prepared to face the discomfort of inappropriate responses from some people. Why is it so hard to do that instead of being taken hostage by someone else's agenda? Mainly, it's because of fear—fear of anger, accusation and criticism from others. The usual response is one of the following:

1. Acquiescence (you go along to get along)
2. Anger at the person who has manipulated you into buying into something you never intended
3. Backing up, shrinking from any activity that could bring on the angry behavior of the bully

HOLY BOLDNESS

Let's look at how Jesus handled disappointment. This was extreme disappointment caused by an industrial-strength bully. His beloved John the Baptist was in prison because he'd had the nerve to tell Herod he couldn't fool around with Herodias, his brother Philip's wife. This didn't go down too well with either Herod or Herodias. When Herod's birthday rolled around, the daughter of Herodias danced before Herod and pleased him. (See Matthew 14:6.) Herod, ever the big shot, pledged to give the young daughter anything she wanted. Being influenced by her mother, the young maid asked for the head of John the Baptist on a platter.

211

King Herod was distressed over the request, but he couldn't take back his oath. He had John the Baptist beheaded, and "his head was brought in a charger, and given to the damsel: and she brought it to her mother" (Matt. 14:11). Verse 12 says, "And his disciples came, and took up the body, and buried it, and went and told Jesus."

Jesus didn't buckle under, get mad or back up. Instead He withdrew to a private place, but the people came in droves to find Him. Though He was grieved, Jesus "went forth, and saw a great multitude, and was moved with compassion toward them, and healed their sick" (v. 14). He went right on doing what was right, including feeding the five thousand through the multiplication of the fishes and the loaves.

Jesus' entire ministry was marked by unswerving obedience to do His Father's will regardless of the constant negative reactions He experienced. Jesus knew what was right, and He never compromised His actions to please anyone. How was He able to do that? He knew who He was and who His Father was. And He knew circumstances couldn't bind Him. Wouldn't you like to operate in the same confidence?

WHAT TO DO

1. Look up the following scriptures: Psalm 34:10; 37:4; Proverbs 10:24; Isaiah 55:11; Matthew 21:22; John 14:13–14; 15:7; 16:24; Romans 4:20–21; 8:32; Ephesians 3:20.

2. These are scriptures for confidence and assurance. Write down all the promises afforded you in these verses.

3. Meditate on them for a week. You'll feel your confidence meter rising.

4. The next time a friend of Mr. Wing Tip gives you trouble, do what's right and follow Jesus' model.

44

WHY GALLUP IS WRONG

I recently saw a political cartoon showing Moses descending from the mountaintop holding the Ten Commandments on tablets. Waiting for him at the bottom of the hill was a crowd of people saying, "Yes...but Moses, what do the opinion polls say?" Imagine what would have happened if God had set up the world based on opinion polls.

Whether we like it or not, there really is right and wrong. There really is truth and error. Let's face it; God did not create the Ten Suggestions. He made them commandments, not because He's a grumpy autocrat, but because He has provided boundaries for acceptable behavior to keep us in position to receive His blessings.

As our nation's founders walked out of Constitution Hall and congregated on the front steps of the building, Ben Franklin was asked the question, "What do we have, a democracy or a republic?"

He said, "A republic...if you can keep it." Some mistake our form of government for a democracy, but it was set up as a republic. There's a big difference.

A republic is ruled by law, not people. Voters elect officials to act on their behalf and vote in the best interests of the country and its citizens. A democracy, on the other hand, is ruled by a majority of people. Decisions are made based on what most of the people think. A purely democratic system can be risky; if the wrong majority of people rule, everyone reaps the consequences.

America was established as a nation governed by law; those who are elected and appointed to positions of authority are expected to follow the law. The law is the Constitution of the United States. What holds it all together is honor. But when the people of a republic stop being people of principle, they cease following the law. That's how a republic can be lost, and that's what Ben Franklin meant in his warning.

FEEL-GOOD DECISIONS

We have become a quick-fix, add-water-and-mix society, obsessed with rights and entitlements and insulated from the responsibilities and consequences that go with those rights. Since 1960 violent crime has increased by 560 percent, illegitimate births have increased by 419 percent, the divorce rate has doubled and the teen suicide rate has tripled. It's a deplorable record, yet in some cases the courts have reinterpreted the Constitution to ease the consequences of bad behavior, which has only added to the statistics. To make matters worse, legislation has been passed based on the whims of special interest groups. After all, it felt good. But we've done a con job on ourselves. The numbers prove it.

The compromising of principle to avoid sacrifice may feel good for now, but it reaps conditions that will hurt far worse in the future.

SURPRISE!

Dudley and his high school friends had an occasional favorite pastime. They'd ride two or three to a car at night and toss cherry bombs into people's yards. They knew it was wrong, but they reasoned no one was actually getting hurt. Besides, it was a hoot to watch quiet houses turn into beehives of activity while occupants tried to figure out what had just exploded out front.

Repeated practice had made Dudley's right arm a pretty accurate instrument; he could land the cherry bomb within a few feet of the front steps. One night, however, he got some ricochet retribution. Dudley's two friends were in the front seat and he was in the back, the lobber-in-charge. As the car slowed in front of a palatial mansion, Dudley aimed his shot for the front sidewalk and fired. Too bad the driver had closed the window. When the lit cherry bomb hit the closed window, it bounced back and landed at Dudley's feet. His life flashed in front of him, and he attempted a half-gainer into the front seat. It was then the cherry bomb went off—blowing the back out of Dudley's pants and burning his backside badly enough to resemble rare hamburger.

"I had a scab on my rear end the size of Minnesota," Dudley said. "I couldn't sit down for two weeks." A few momentary laughs had been traded for an inflatable cushion and decades of teasing from his friends.

It was a painful lesson of right and wrong learned back in the late '50s when there really *was* right and wrong. Today right and wrong have been replaced by situational ethics. People call their own shots about acceptable parameters of behavior. But God's law is still the law, regardless of how many polls show the opposite.

Cesar Rodney's Ride

History books don't often mention his name, nor is his name as recognizable as those of George Washington, Thomas Jefferson or some of the others whose signatures appear on the Declaration of Independence, but Cesar Rodney's demonstration of principle is a lesson in personal accountability.

It was the summer of 1776, and the delegates of the Continental Congress had taken a preliminary vote on a proposed resolution for independence. Twelve of thirteen colonies had either abstained or voted for the resolution. That left only Delaware with its three votes. Delaware's three votes were split, one for and one against. Rodney's was the third vote, and he was sick with a high fever and malignant cancer. The delegates had agreed that in order for the resolution to pass the formal vote, it must be unanimous.

Rodney's vote was needed to break the tie. He rose from a sickbed and rode on horseback eighty miles, arriving at Independence Hall just as the vote was being taken. He was too weak to dismount and had to be carried inside on a stretcher. When Washington put forth the question, Rodney responded, "I vote for independence." The power of a single voice had broken the tie, pushing Delaware into the resolution column, making the vote unanimous among the thirteen colonies.

Cesar Rodney's sense of personal responsibility during this time precluded any possible trip to England for treatment of cancer, yet his legacy is a single vote that echoes through history. Rodney and many of the founding fathers sacrificed their lives, property, fortunes and families for the freedom we enjoy today. They were men of honor and principle.

THE PRIZE

Jesus gave His life for you to enjoy all the freedom provided in His promises. He paid a huge price for you to receive the prize of everlasting life, righteousness, peace and joy in the Holy Ghost (Rom. 14:17). Listen to what the Amplified Bible says is His gift is to you: "And God is able to make all grace (every favor and earthly blessing) come to you in abundance, so that you may always and under all circumstances and whatever the need be self-sufficient [possessing enough to require no aid or support and furnished in abundance for every good work and charitable donation]" (2 Cor. 9:8). Sounds like the mother lode to me.

God is able to provide all that for you. It's already been paid for in the spiritual realm. All you have to do is receive it into your life. You do that by following God's principles.

WHAT TO DO

If you're interested in living beyond Gallup Poll results and building your life on a rock that can't be shaken by people or events, here's a road map to success:

1. Commit to spend thirty minutes a day in the Word, finding out the real truth of acceptable behavior.

2. Make a list of your current character defects that you would like to change.

3. Ask the Lord to reveal any other character flaws you may not be aware of.

4. Read one chapter of the Book of Proverbs every day for a month. There are thirty-one, and they're short. On the first day of the month you can read chapter 1, on the second day chapter 2, on the third day chapter 3 and so forth. It provides wisdom for life. You can't go wrong.

45

THE GREAT RIP-OFF

What is it like in your church on Sunday morning? Does it rock with music that shakes the gates of hell open, or is it quiet and reserved? Is there a joyous atmosphere, or is it polite and restrained? Many churches are so proper that you can hear a pin drop, so structured that the choir doesn't even break a sweat.

Most of my life was spent in congregations where we sang but our lips didn't move, where sermons went out over pews filled with people frozen into position. We didn't interact with each other or the minister; we looked for all the world like statues in a wax museum. No one was excited about God. I guess that's OK if you enjoy going to a funeral every Sunday, but that never did anything for me.

Interestingly, some people who attend quiet, reserved churches can go wild at sporting events. You've seen it and participated in it yourself, I'll bet. You're at the football game, your team is down by six points and there's less than a minute to go. The other team has the ball, the clock is running out, the opponents are down on your twenty-yard line—and suddenly there's a fumble. One of your team picks up the ball, throws off multiple tackles, streaks down the field and scores just as the clock runs out. You go berserk, jumping up and down, screaming at the top of your lungs in utter joy. You even hug those around you—perfect strangers but now bosom buddies in victory.

Now think of this: You got so excited about a football player and the last-minute reversal of fortune that you hollered your head off. You clapped, jumped and cheered like a maniac. But not one on that field died for you. Not one suffered excruciating pain, took all your sins and bore all the horror of the world so you don't have to. Not one loves you unconditionally. But Jesus does. Why can't you get that excited about Him?

PICTURE THIS

You've seen the crowds at basketball games, especially around the time of the NCAA tournament. People with basketballs on their heads, others with half their faces painted blue and the other half silver, fans with tiger tails coming out the backs of jeans, hats with longhorns on them, people sporting red helmets shaped like pigs. We used to have a character called the Medicine Man who showed up at every basketball game. He was always naked to the waist, wearing animal skins, a fur hat with horns and strings of animal teeth around his neck. He'd run around to different sections of the arena eliciting cheers for the team. Like idiots, we'd go right along with the gag. It was all part of the fun.

Why then do most of us become the frozen chosen on Sunday? God is cool, you know. He has a sense of humor (just look at us for starters). Besides, the Bible tells us to "be glad in the Lord and rejoice, shout for joy" (Ps. 32:11). Now, when was the last time you heard someone shout for joy in church? But that's exactly what God's Word tells us to do. Don't believe me? Psalm 5:11 says, "But let all those that put their trust in thee rejoice: let them ever shout for joy, because thou defendest them: let them also that love thy name be joyful in thee."

The Amplified translation says, "Let those also who love Your name be joyful in You and be in high spirits." In 1 Chronicles 15:16 David "told the chief Levites to appoint their brethren the singers with instruments of music—harps, lyres, and cymbals—to play loudly and lift up their voices with joy" (AMP). Nehemiah 8:10 reminds us that "the joy of the Lord is [our] strength." And just in case you thought all that rowdiness went out with the Old Testament, in Matthew 5:11–12 we find Jesus instructing His disciples on how to act when people give them a hard time because of Him. "Blessed (happy, to be envied, and spiritually prosperous—with life-joy and satisfaction in God's favor and salvation, regardless of your outward conditions) are you when people revile you and persecute you and say all kinds of evil things against you falsely on My account. Be glad and supremely joyful, for your reward is heaven is great (strong and intense), for in this same way people persecuted the prophets who were before you" (AMP).

In other words, get excited and jump up and down when critics bum-rap you about Jesus. After all, the prophets were treated with disdain, too. Jude 24–25 says, "Now to Him Who is able to keep you without stumbling or slipping or falling, and to present [you] unblemished (blameless and faultless) before the presence of His glory in triumphant joy and exultation [with unspeakable, ecstatic delight]—to the one only God, our Savior through Jesus Christ our Lord, be glory (splendor), majesty, might and dominion, and power and authority, before all time and now and forever (unto all the ages of eternity). Amen (so be it)" (AMP).

Now, doesn't it sound as if final-minute, football-game behavior is called for in front of the Lord instead of stiff-as-a-poker reverence?

BALLISTIC MISSILES

All through the Bible exuberant praise and worship is used as both offensive and defensive weapons. Let's take a look:

Offensive warfare

In the Book of Joshua the Lord instructed Joshua about how to take the city of Jericho, which was a walled town. The Lord said, "See, I have given Jericho, its king and mighty men of valor, into your hands" (Josh. 6:2, AMP). Then the Lord tells him how to go about it. Joshua is instructed to assemble his men of war and to march around the city once a day for six days in a row. Then on the seventh day "you shall march around the enclosure seven times, and the priests shall blow the trumpets. When they make a long blast with the ram's horn and you hear the sound of the trumpet, all the people shall shout with a great shout; and the wall of the enclosure shall fall down in its place and the people shall go up [over it], every man straight before him" (vv. 4–5).

Of course, it didn't make sense in the natural, but Joshua was obedient, his armies did what was instructed, and the walls fell just as God had promised. They never had to fire a shot.

Defensive warfare

In Acts 16 Paul and Silas had been beaten, thrown into jail in the inner dungeon and put into stocks. They had every reason to gripe and moan about their circumstances. But do you know what they did? They began to sing songs of praise to the Lord so loudly that the other prisoners were listening to them. "Suddenly there was a great earthquake, so that the very foundations of the prison were shaken; and at once all the doors were opened and everyone's shackles were unfastened" (v. 26, AMP).

Paul and Silas had nowhere to turn for help, yet the power of praise had the strength of ballistic missiles to bring God on the scene. Both of these examples demonstrate that outrageous praise, not mealy-mouthed restraint, brings results.

Why haven't we known about this? Because we've been ripped off by the great deceiver (Satan), who knows that as long as he can keep us impotent, we'll never accomplish anything for God's kingdom. His special emissary, the High Priestess of Guilt and Condemnation, makes sure you stay in line with warnings about how stupid you'll look if you participate in exuberant praise. "What will people think?" she intones. "You'll be laughed to scorn." Well, you may be laughed at by some people, but what's more important to you—the acceptance of other people or getting all your problems solved? It's your choice.

AND THAT'S NOT ALL

Besides acting as both offensive and defensive weapons, praise also has other advantages:

- It lifts your spirits (1 Sam. 30:6).
- It frees your mind of the problem so your faith can go to work (Phil. 4:6–7).
- It pleases God (Ps. 69:30).

With a list of benefits like this, why would any of us not want to leap and jump for joy in the presence of the Lord? You may not have ever seen or experienced praise like that called for in the Bible, but that's no excuse. God is no egotist who desires flattery to build up His self-esteem; He knows that praising Him for the answer empowers Him to bring about the results you desire. Here's a way to transition into the state of worship He wants from you.

WHAT TO DO

1. Go to a store that sells Christian tapes and CDs. Listen to samples of music from traditional to contemporary and decide what appeals to you.

2. Buy what you like and take it home. Put in on and turn up the volume.

3. Practice holding up your hands to the Lord and singing to Him (Ps.134:2; 1 Tim. 2:8). OK, I know you feel stupid, but you'll get used to it.

4. Find a church where praise and worship is an important and powerful part of the service. Remember, we don't praise and worship God to gain His approval; we praise and worship Him because we have gained His approval through Christ.

46

NAME TAG ID

Flying back from Nevada one night, I discovered that it's tough to get away from your thoughts during a four-hour flight. Even though the meeting I'd attended went perfectly well, I felt sad and vexed, as if I'd done something wrong. It wasn't long before I began to feel guilty about the quality of the time I'd been spending with the Lord. You know—I'd sort of been "clocking in" but not really there. I was feeling condemned; in fact, I was consumed with condemnation.

How much of my life has been spent this way? I wondered. *Romans 8:1 clearly states that "there is therefore now no condemnation to them which are in Christ Jesus, who walk not after the flesh, but after the Spirit." I'm in Christ Jesus as a born-again child of the living God, so why do I feel this way? I used to feel like this all the time, now only occasionally—but how does it sneak up on me?*

My friend Joanie, who is a spiritual champion, says the enemy has a carpetbag full of tricks at his disposal. Tricks that have worked on us in the past—deceptions, temptations, accusations that we've continually fallen for. As we grow in the Lord we tend to become more immune to the traps that have snared us. First Peter 5:8 says, "Be sober, be vigilant; because your adversary the devil, as a roaring lion, walketh about, seeking whom he may devour." He's not actually a lion—he'd just like you to think he is. And that carpetbag full of stunts is ever ready to test you in an area of your life where you thought you had victory.

Since "What will people think?" had been my mantra for so many years, I'd built my life around trying to be perfect for everyone in the solar system. That's a one-way ticket to condemnation. It was easy, therefore, to transfer that demand for perfection onto God and to assume that receiving from Him was linked to my performance. What a lie that was!

Receiving from the Lord has nothing to do with what I do and everything to do with what He has already done. It's His performance at Calvary that made me who I am, not anything I do or don't do. Yet all those years of feeling unworthy had allowed the enemy to add condemnation to his bag of tricks.

When I got home Joanie reminded me I'd lost sight of my righteousness. Spending some time reading scriptures about righteousness helped reacquaint me with what my name tag reads. It has given me new clarity about acceptability from three vantage points: man's view, the devil's view and God's view.

You won't be surprised to find that God's view offers the only accurate perspective.

CELEBRITY STATUS

A friend of mine frequently visits Montana, where the skies are big, the population sparse and the air clear. He was standing in line one evening at one of the town's only restaurants, waiting for a table. A well-known celebrity couple suddenly appeared and cut to the front of the line. (I'm not saying who, but he's a media mogul and his wife is an actress.) The person handling seating assignments objected to the couple cutting in line. The wife said, "Don't you know who I am?"

The maître d' said, "Yes, but you haven't been waiting in line like the others here."

The wife said, "Call the owner of the restaurant immediately! I insist on talking to him!"

"As you wish," he answered.

About two minutes later the owner came out of the kitchen. "May I help you?" he asked.

The wife bellowed, "Apparently your waiter here doesn't understand who we are. We're here to eat dinner, and we want to be seated now!"

"Not in my restaurant, you won't! I couldn't care less who you are, and your celebrity status doesn't make you any more desirable than anyone else in line. In fact, if I'd known you were coming I'd have told you not to bother. It's my restaurant, and I choose not to serve folks like you! Good evening."

What followed was loud clapping and whistling from everyone in line who was within earshot. The stunned, gaping couple finally stalked off. How typical. Man's idea of identity is based on recognition and status. We've become a nation of people who worship celebrities. We let them tell us how to vote, what products to use and how to live our lives. We measure success by media reports and bank balance statements and judge ourselves unworthy in comparison to them. This is man's view of your acceptability—endorsed by men.

Slug Status

What about the enemy's view of your acceptability? An illustration from my father's side of the family paints a nice word picture. My grandfather was head of the Federal Aviation Administration at one time. Because he had to travel frequently, he sometimes took my father with him. When my dad was in his late teens my grandfather took him on a business trip to Europe. They traveled by ocean liner both ways. Because my grandad was an experienced traveler, he was proud of his ability to pack just what he would need for the trip without being weighed down with extra baggage. He packed three suits for the trip and several white shirts and ties.

The crossing was rough. Most passengers got seasick and had to stay in their rooms. Not Grandad. Day one he strolled out to the deck and seated himself in a deck chair next to an English gentleman. They got involved in an animated conversation when suddenly the Englishman turned green, leaned over and barfed all over Grandad. That was suit number one.

Day two dawned dark and gloomy with continued rough seas. Grandad was walking up the steps to get breakfast when he came face to face with another passenger descending the stairs to his room. The other passenger, who was also green, paused right in front of my grandfather, took a deep breath and barfed all over suit number two. In those days, they didn't have dry-cleaning capability on board, so now the clothing choices were down to one. My dad wasted no time chiding his father about his commando packing and how he had now been reduced to wearing one suit for the rest of the week.

The next day Grandad stood on the promenade deck looking out to sea. It was still rough, but the sun was just beginning to peek through the iron-grey clouds way off in the distance. Another American came up next to him, and the two stood looking out at the horizon talking about how rough the crossing had been. In mid-sentence, the American turned the color of the ocean, opened his mouth and started to throw up. Unfortunately, Grandad was downwind of him, so he got hit in the face with all of it. You guessed it—that was the third and final suit.

The story is a pretty accurate representation of the devil's view of your acceptability. Over and over he reminds you of your slug status by cluttering your head with thoughts of condemnation, of not measuring up. And unless you renew your mind with the Word of God, you live your life in a similar cycle as my grandfather did—suiting up each day, expecting things to be different, and ending up disappointed each night that they're not. The enemy's interpretation of your identity is endorsed by the High Priestess of Guilt and Condemnation, who runs a continuous-loop tape recorder in your head.

REAL STATUS

Neither man's nor the High Priestess's view of who you are is the correct one. God says you are the righteousness of Him in Christ (2 Pet. 1:1). And His version is the only one that counts. Man's idea of validation is based on performance. The devil's idea is based on lack of performance. But God's idea is based on association with Him. And it's endorsed by the Holy Spirit. You see, it's not what you've done—it's what He's done that makes you special.

You have real status. Listen up. Galatians 2:20–21 says:

> I have been crucified with Christ [in Him I have shared His crucifixion]; it is no longer I who live, but Christ (the Messiah) lives in me; and the life I now live in the body I live by faith in (by adherence to and reliance on and complete trust in) the Son of God, Who loved me and gave Himself up for me. [Therefore, I do not treat God's gracious gift as something of minor importance and defeat its very purpose]; I do not set aside and invalidate and frustrate and nullify

the grace (unmerited favor) of God. For if justification (righteousness, acquittal from guilt) comes through [observing the ritual of] the Law, then Christ (the Messiah) died groundlessly and to no purpose and in vain. [His death was then wholly superfluous.]

—AMP

Romans 4:5–6 says, "But to one who, not working [by the Law], trusts (believes fully) in Him Who justifies the ungodly, his faith is credited to him as righteousness (the standing acceptable to God). Thus David congratulates the man and pronounces a blessing on him to whom God credits righteousness apart from the works he does" (AMP). Your faith is what makes you acceptable, not your bank balance or your press clippings. Your acceptability has nothing to do with the works that you do. What a relief!

BETTER THAN A BODYGUARD

When I was a little girl we lived down the street from a real grouch. I used to go down to his house with some of the neighborhood kids and yell, "Hi, Mr. Ware. Can you see us?" Then we'd watch him come roaring out of the house with a broom in his hand to chase us away.

One day another little girl and I stood under his window and chanted, "I see London, I see France, I see Mr. Ware's underpants. Are they pink? Are they blue? Boy, do they stink, P.U." We thought we were so cute. Several seconds later Mr. Ware shot out the front door like a heat-seeking missile, carrying a rifle and screaming, "I'm going to kill you two smart alecks!" He chased us all the way down the block, down my driveway and into the garage. Fortunately, my father was just getting home from work.

My friend and I, shrieking in fear, skittered into the garage and behind my father. He looked up to see Mr. Ware shouting at us, waving the rifle. My dad said, "What's going on here?"

Mr. Ware bellowed, "These brats have been tormenting me."

My father stood up tall and said, "Girls, what have you done?"

We repeated the little ditty we had sung under Mr. Ware's window. My father looked at Mr. Ware and said, "Is that all? You mean, Harold, that two seven-year-olds have gotten you scared? Scared enough to grab a rifle and chase them like dogs?"

"Well, I don't appreciate them coming onto my property," Mr. Ware said. My dad gave him one of those if-looks-could-kill stares and said, "I'll make sure they stay off your property. Now, if you don't get off mine in five seconds, I'm going to call the police and have you arrested for child abuse! Are we clear on this?"

It felt so good to have the protection of my father, who at the time seemed at least fourteen feet tall against our adversary. So it is with God—only He's much bigger. When anyone comes against you, He's always there to plead your case, because you're righteous before Him. You are approved of by God because you are His child. Even if you have screwed up, the Lord will never leave you or forsake you (Heb. 13:5). With a promise like that, why should any of us ever be condemned? We shouldn't, but it takes action to overcome the stunts the enemy keeps in his carpetbag.

WHAT TO DO

1. Study the following scriptures: Romans 3:22; 4:5–6; 5:18–19; 2 Corinthians 5:21; Galatians 2:21; 3:6–10; Philippians 3:9.

2. Meditate on those words until they renew your mind and you can see your heavenly Father standing in front of you like a bodyguard.

3. When the High Priestess of Guilt and Condemnation tries to make you feel like a slug, repeat the scriptures out loud just as Jesus did when the devil came to tempt Him. It worked for Him, and it will work for you.

47

MAKING YOURSELF IMMORTAL

How did we become such a selfish people? Why is it that most of us think the meaning of life is to figure out how to make ourselves happy? Do you think Jesus sat around saying, "Yes, but what about *My* needs?" Do you think Mary spent a lot of time asking Joseph, "Do you think this robe makes me look fat?" Not likely.

We're in danger of becoming a nation of "hollow men"—constantly in search of validation and never finding it. Yet God's plan is for us to be "the salt of the earth" and "the light of the world." (See Matthew 5:13–14.) Why salt? Well, think about what salt does. It's a preservative, and it enhances the flavor of food. Salt adds to the enjoyment of meals. God intended for Christians to add to the quality of life for those around them—to offer them hope and preserve them through prayer, demonstrating a better way of life by walking in love, compassion, right moral standing and courage.

Now think about what light does. It dispels darkness. Light makes choices available by making alternate paths visible. Light eliminates confusion. God intended for Christians to be able to shed the light of the gospel on a lost and hurting world to show a better way. He has given us a huge assignment—one that's impossible as long as we've got our underwear in a knot because we're so needy ourselves.

A New Attitude

In verse 16 of Matthew 5 Jesus instructs His disciples, "Let your light so shine before men that they may see your moral excellence and your praiseworthy, noble, and good deeds and recognize and honor and praise and glorify your Father Who is in heaven" (AMP). As a Christian you're a disciple, too. And if you're walking in the full knowledge of who you are in Christ, your accomplishments will be so noticeable that others will be drawn to you in search of the power that sustains you.

The High Priestess of Guilt and Condemnation has devoted her entire career to making you feel like worthless pond scum, incapable of helping yourself much less anyone else. But here's the truth: You are a gift from God to the world. Just think about that for a minute. You are a gift to be given to others.

Scott Adams, the creator of the *Dilbert* comic strip, tells a story from his life that's instructive in developing a new attitude. The events took place when Adams was a teenager and earned money by shoveling snow in Windham, New York. He had an agreement with a retired Greek couple, Mr. and Mrs. Amanatides, that following a snowfall he would be at their house by six in the morning to shovel the sidewalk before Mr. Amanatides walked to town.

Their house was half a mile away, and often Adams had to crawl through waist-high snowdrifts, arriving exhausted. His job included shoveling a walkway around the house, a patio area and several sets of steps, plus four inches past the edge on each side to allow for drainage when the snow melted. Adams had to shovel "like a crazed beaver" to complete the job in time for school—and then he had to return and do the driveway after school.

At that time, five dollars would have been fair pay, but Mr. Amanatides paid Adams twenty dollars. After a while, Adams tried to convince him to pay less—he felt uncomfortable taking that amount of money from such a nice man.

"Mr. Amanatides did a quick read on the situation and told me to put my shovel down and listen," Adams writes. "He explained his thinking in simple terms, distilled from seventy years of living. He said in his thick Greek accent, 'You're worth it!' I thanked him for the money and never brought up the topic again."

You're worth it. I can remember my boss telling me that in the early part of my career. I would have walked on hot coals for him because he had faith in me.

BAD PRESS

You may not have been fortunate enough to have someone tell you how valuable you are. If not, let me be the first to tell you that you're special, talented and loved by God. He has waited for you expectantly all these years. His greatest desire is for you to fellowship with Him. He is the Father in the story of the prodigal son in Luke 15:11–32. As his wayward son was returning home, the father saw him "a great way off...and had compassion, and ran, and fell on his neck, and kissed him. And the son said unto him, Father, I have sinned against heaven, and in thy sight, and am no more worthy to be called thy son." But the father told his servants to bring the best robe and put it on his son, to put a ring on his hand and to kill the fatted calf to celebrate his homecoming. Instead of being called a dirty dog, the son was welcomed back by his rejoicing father.

That's the way your heavenly Father waits for you to come to Him. God has gotten bad press from those who believe they have to clean themselves up before they come to Him, or that He's an angry God who is disappointed in them for not being perfect. That's simply not true. In Zephaniah 3:17 the Bible says, "The Lord your God is in the midst of you, a Mighty One, a Savior [Who saves]! He will rejoice over you with joy; He will rest [in silent satisfaction] and in His love He will be silent and make no mention [of past sins, or even recall them]; He will exult over you with singing" (AMP).

It doesn't make any difference what you've done in the past or how worthless you feel in the present; you're valuable to Him. He wants to be your father, mother, brother, sister, husband and friend. He doesn't love conditionally like mortals do; He loves boundlessly, extravagantly, uncon-ditionally with *agape* love. *Vine's Complete Expository Dictionary of Old and New Testament Words* defines *agape* love (from the original text) as "totally unselfish and ready to serve." That's how He loves you. That's how worthy you are.

A NEW PICTURE

Now, if this is a new concept for you, begin to get used to it. It should be the foundational truth of your life. If you can begin to grasp how much God loves you, try thinking how you could turn around and show His love to others, bringing blessings into their lives. You can make yourself immortal by sowing into the lives of people who have lost hope.

A word of encouragement, a hot meal, teaching a Bible study, taking someone to church, giving to the poor—there are endless ways for all of us to give. Even a smile can turn someone's day around. A visitor who has come to my church several times recently said she keeps coming back because she's hugged and smiled at as soon as she walks in the door. I had the same impression when I first visited. It was the first time I can ever remember feeling loved without having to perform first.

LOOK OUT

You have an infinite capacity to make a difference. As you concentrate on blessing others, God is on the scene making sure you are being blessed. You know the runaway disasters Job experienced—fires, theft, loss of life, disease, boils and poverty. You also know if you've read the earlier part of this book that God restored double to Job everything that he'd lost. But do you know what the turning point was? Look at Job 42:10 for the answer: "And the Lord turned the captivity of Job, when he prayed for his friends: also the Lord gave Job twice as much as he had before." Even though Job was as low as a human could get, he still was a gift to his friends. He made a decision to pray for them. And look what the Lord did in response.

WHAT TO DO

If you would like to turn the tables on the High Priestess and begin living beyond your natural means, do the following:

1. Read Hebrews 12.

2. Now, read it again and look at Christ as your example. Think about what He did for you and the power He has given you to do for others.

3. Daily look for ways to sow into the lives of those around you.

48

EVERYBODY GETS
AN A

Benjamin Zander, the conductor of the Boston Philharmonic, says his job as leader is to teach musicians to be expressive performers of great music. The problem is that often they are unable to let that music through to the audience. Why? Zander says it's because of what he calls the "conversation in the head."

He says, "In any performance there are always two people onstage: the one trying to play and another one who whispers, 'Do you know how many people play this piece better than you do? Here comes that difficult passage you missed last time–and you're going to miss it again this time!' Sometimes that other voice is so loud that it drowns out the music. As a leader, I'm always looking for ways to silence that voice."

Sounds like the High Priestess of Guilt and Condemnation to me. Zander doesn't give the voice a name, but that's who it is, The taunting voice of failure. Zander is looking for ways to silence that voice. But that voice can only be permanently muzzled by a renewed mind. If you're working the steps at the end of each of these chapters, you're well on your way.

PERFORMANCE ART

According to Zander, the job of a leader is to create new definitions that allow people to move beyond conventional choices and find new possibilities in their work and in their lives. He says, "The leader's role is to create a powerful vision that allows room for things to occur that are as yet undreamed of. The leader must hold the definition of the vision so clearly that all the players involved are able to align with it daily. And that vision leads to great performances."

He teaches students at the New England Conservatory of Music. There he perfected a simple technique of quieting that taunting voice. Every fall, on the first day of class, Zander makes the following announcement: "Everybody gets an A." There is a condition—but only one. Each student must turn in a letter written that first day, but dated the following May, that begins like this: "Dear Mr. Zander: I got my A because..." Students have to tell him at the beginning of the course whom they will become by the end of the course that will justify such a superior grade.

Zander says that transforms his relationship with everyone in the room. How so? He contends that leaders are constantly giving out grades in every encounter with people. As a result, leaders can operate one of two ways: giving out grades as an expectation to live up to, then reassessing "students" according to performance, or offering grades as a possibility to live into.

Zander says the second choice is far more powerful. He's right, because that choice is built upon a biblical principle—calling "those things which be not as though they were" (Rom. 4:17). The Amplified translates it like this: "God in Whom he [Abraham] believed, Who gives life to the dead and speaks of the non-existent things that [He has foretold and promised] as if they [already] existed."

By assigning A's to students and having them call themselves A students, Zander knows they begin to demonstrate the characteristics to support the superior assessment. It worked for Abraham, and it works for performers.

Many misunderstand this concept. It's not about pretending that everybody is the same. The A helps to get at what's unique in people and at individual barriers that must be broken. The letters from the students provide insightful information about how they stack up against their dreams. It's the kind of information that assists Zander in helping students perform their best.

"Yes," you say, "but I don't play music. I wouldn't recognize Beethoven if he fell over me at Walgreens. What does all this have to do with me?"

SUPERCHARGED LIVING

GOD HAS GIVEN YOU AN A

When you asked the Lord Jesus to come into your life and be your Savior, you became a completely new person, a new creature in Christ: "Therefore if any man be in Christ, he is a new creature: old things are passed away; behold, all things are become new" (2 Cor. 5:17). Verse 21 says, "For he hath made him to be sin for us, who knew no sin; that we might be made the righteousness of God in him." You are righteous, according to almighty God. *Righteousness* (according to the Hebrew and Greek original texts of the Bible) means "the character or quality of being right or just; used to describe an attribute of God, which shows that 'the righteousness of God' means essentially the same as His faithfulness, or truthfulness, that which is consistent with His own nature."

God has already given you His nature, His seal of approval, His quality of being right. It's an A to live into. He furthermore has designated you His ambassador as Christ's personal representative to be an example of Him (2 Cor. 5:20–21). That's something to live into!

You see, He gives you an A by declaring you righteous, and then He gives you the vision for what you will become if you'll hearken to His voice and allow His Word to become your handbook for life. He sees you as His completed work. Imagine!

Ben Zander says, "Never doubt the capacity of the people you lead to accomplish whatever you dream for them." It's a principle great leaders—from Ghandi to George Washington, Abraham Lincoln to Margaret Thatcher—have demonstrated. Yet your heavenly Father did even more than that. He loved you so much that He sent His very best—Jesus—to be your substitute for sin and to reconcile you to Him (2 Cor. 5:19). Then He spoke His dream for you when He said through Jesus, "Verily, verily, I say unto you, he that believeth on me, the works that I do shall he do also; and greater works than these shall he do; because I go unto my Father" (John 14:12).

Jesus is saying that if you believe in Him, you'll do even greater works than He does. Is that possible? Of course. The very next verse tells you how: "And whatsoever ye shall ask in my name, I will do." The name of Jesus is powerful. It gives you power of attorney. It's a warranty that if you ask according to God's Word and in the name of Jesus, your request will be answered. Is there a catch? Only one: Faith is the currency that makes it happen. That means you have to know the Word, know the power in the name of Jesus and stand in faith while your answer is being manifested.

So you see, God has dreamed big dreams for you and has given you a way to achieve them. He already knows you're an A performer.

THE TICKET TO THE DANCE

The first and most critical step to your dreams is knowing you're righteous, righteous according to God Himself. I don't care what anyone else says, what your family has said, what the High Priestess of Guilt and Condemnation has said—you're righteous. If you get that down in your spirit, nothing can stop you.

WHAT TO DO

Righteousness is mentioned in forty books of the Bible. God obviously thought the subject was pretty important or it wouldn't play such a prominent role.

1. Get out your concordance and look up *righteousness.*

2. Look up some of the scriptures from both the Old and New Testaments.

3. Write down the ones that really speak to you and memorize them.

4. Meditate on each of them until you get a picture inside your head and heart of yourself in the middle of each verse.

5. When "the other voice" (the High Priestess) comes to taunt you, say, "Oh no, you don't—the Word of God says I'm...(and then quote the scripture)." I promise you, it works.

49

THE GREAT ENABLER

Whatever happened to risk, reward and personal discipline? How did we turn into a nation of whiners that blame others for our own poor decisions? Easy. We've been sold on the idea that we're *entitled* to life, liberty and happiness—not just the opportunity to pursue them. As we've become more and more averse to risk, we've enabled the behavior that drives us nuts!

Enabling means "standing in the way of or softening the natural consequences of a person's behavior." It's easy to do. If your child gets into trouble, your natural impulse is to intervene to minimize the pain. Most of us can't stand to see our children suffer. But we don't learn from our mistakes when someone else pulls our bacon out of the fire. We only learn when we experience the painful consequences of our bad choices.

Enabling has become a national pastime. We enable politicians to skirt the law if we like their policy decisions. We enable high-profile sports heroes to rough up female groupies because they're famous studs and rock stars to trash hotel rooms because they're larger-than-life celebrities. We enable criminals to repeatedly break the law through wimpy judicial rulings that favor criminals at the expense of crime victims. We enable mediocre employee performance through gutless management. And in many of our relationships, we allow destructive behavior to continue because we stand in the way of accountability.

The Great Enabler

CAN YOU SAY STUPID?

I have a friend whose son has been on drugs for more than fifteen years. Time after time the father has been conned into rescuing the addict. He's been bailed out of jail more times than the cast of *Gunsmoke*. He has enrolled in college more times (at his dad's expense) than the Four Freshmen. And he's left enough jobs to personally elevate the national unemployment rate. But according to the addict, it's never his fault. Dad keeps paying for his scrapes, getting him jobs and picking up the pieces after him, always hoping that this time will be different. It never is.

How can his dad be so dense? Well, unknowingly an enabler helps the one he loves to continue his downward spiral of self-destruction. An enabler continues to "help" even though his assistance is being abused. Helpers rescue friends and loved ones from their responsibilities—thus prolonging the problem. Here are some examples:

- *Covering up the behavior of a friend:* "Oh, he really wasn't drunk. He just had a couple of glasses of wine and was in a really good mood."
- *Bailing a friend out of jail:* "I know he probably should have spent the night in the slammer, but he's learned his lesson now."
- *Making excuses for them:* "He's not a bad person; he's just had a lot of bad luck lately. You can't really blame him for blowing off steam."
- *Minimizing your friend or loved one's problem:* "He's not an alcoholic; he just drinks a lot."
- *Blaming yourself:* "It's really not his fault. If I hadn't made him mad, he wouldn't have acted that way. I'm really the one to blame."
- *Giving them "one more chance," over and over again:* "I know he's failed to follow through before, but this time he's really sorry and really serious about changing. He's promised to do the right thing this time."

BIBLICAL EXAMPLES OF ENABLERS

Apparently, we didn't just recently invent enabling. First Kings 21 reveals the same behavior in Jezebel. King Ahab, her husband, blew his top and pouted because Naboth wouldn't sell him his vineyard. When Jezebel came across Ahab and his sullen attitude, she conjured up a devious plan that would result in Ahab getting the vineyard he wanted. Then she could rescue him from his funk.

Eli was also an enabler. First Samuel 3:13 says Eli's sons "were bringing a curse upon themselves [blaspheming God], and he did not restrain them" (AMP).

Contrast these two examples with the father of the prodigal son, who was not an enabler. Although he joyously welcomed his son home, he didn't rescue the son from his responsibilities. In Luke 15:16–17 the son hit bottom, realized he was in deep trouble, broke out of his denial and made a choice to change. His decision to change his life began with his return to his compassionate father. And I mean compassionate—this father loved his son enough to let him fall on his face so he could grow up and become a man.

Compassion doesn't mean bailing out the offender. The well-meaning intentions of the enabler only strengthen the dependent person's denial and delusion. Then enabling behaviors become habit-forming. The dependent person needs the enabler to support his denial and deceit. That's usually accomplished by making the enabler feel guilty by saying or implying, "If you really loved me, you'd..." It's a sucker bet the enabler falls for every time.

GOLDEN OLDIES

You may recognize some of these. They're favorites used by enablers to avoid confronting and dealing with the destructive behavior of loved ones. These defenses help neutralize the anxiety that truth produces.

1. *Denial,* which is a refusal to accept the reality of a situation or condition with salvos. Examples: "This time will be different," or "It's really not so bad."

2. *Delusion,* which uses false beliefs not based in rational objectivity. Examples: "If he would just get a job, he'd feel so much better about himself," or "I'll feel better if I eat (or drink) this," or "Tomorrow I'll stop doing this," or "It's really my fault that my husband loses his temper and abuses me."

3. *Projection,* which blames others for your own feelings, attitudes or thoughts. Example: "It's because of her that I feel so miserable and hopeless. She makes me do things I'd never do if she didn't make me so mad."

4. *Rationalization,* which excuses your own behavior driven by irrational impulses. Example: "I've been on a sugar binge for a week, but I've been under so much stress. You know how difficult it is to live under the same roof with my husband."

5. *Withdrawal,* which removes yourself physically or psychologically from situations. You think this guarantees freedom from having to deal with your own emotions and confronting the destructive person. It only guarantees that you'll have to deal with it later.

6. *Controlling,* which manipulates the thoughts, feelings and actions of others to compensate for your own inadequacy.

7. *Acting out,* which reduces anxiety and tension by negative behaviors that express previously rejected thoughts, impulses and attitudes. Examples: sexual promiscuity, vandalism and abuse.

According to the medical profession, there are others. But these should give you a snapshot of how the mind works to keep you and the aggressor tied up in the pattern of destruction. You see, the real enabler is the High Priestess of Guilt and Condemnation. She enables you through fear to keep yourself locked into using some of the defense mechanisms listed above in order to survive. As long as she can keep you believing you can't confront the self-destructive behavior of your family and loved ones, she knows you'll begin to use self-destructive behavior on yourself.

What's the payoff from her standpoint? When your time and energy is being used up in emotional turmoil, you can't live a victorious life or do anything to serve God. Snappy plan, right? But the problem is that it works.

Pain Meter

OK, now be honest. Have you practiced any of these golden oldies? If the answer is yes, let's examine why. Take the father with the son on drugs. Why doesn't he let his son hit bottom the way the father of the prodigal son did? Probably because he's afraid he may have played a role in his son's mental state, so he's motivated by guilt. And—and this is a big *and*—he's probably afraid that confronting his son will uncover his own not-so-perfect behavior and he'll *also* be forced to change. Therefore, if his son continues to "need" him, the enabling father can protect himself from the need to change. I know it sounds malevolent and irrational, but there's nothing rational about addictive or enabling behavior.

We tend to consider change as loss and not gain, so change only comes when the pain of what we're experiencing is worse than the fear of the unknown. I can relate. I almost dug my grave with my teeth—eating compulsively to dull the pain of unresolved conflict. It was only when I hit sheer desperation on my pain meter that I sought help and welcomed change. It was one of the most liberating decisions of my life.

WHAT TO DO

If you want to unravel your own destructive behavior patterns and put yourself on a level playing field with difficult people, get out that pad of paper.

1. Make a list of the people in your life who continue to get your goat, those who somehow manipulate you into saying *yes* when you really mean *no*.

2. Now pray and ask God to reveal to you how you're compensating for your unwillingness to confront the issues.

3. Once you and the Lord have that figured out, write down what you're really afraid of relative to confrontation—like abandonment, rejection, lack, loneliness, anger and so forth.

4. Read the next chapter for some ways to confront positively.

50

THE RETURN OF THE GREAT ENABLER

Fear is number one on the most wanted list. It is the biggest and most dangerous criminal that needs to be behind bars. Fear is the enemy's most potent weapon against you, and it's the favorite of his enforcer, the High Priestess of Guilt and Condemnation. Why? Because your faith can be neutralized through fear—which, of course, is the drill. As long as your faith is in hibernation, you have no power to transform your circumstances or solve your problems.

For the believing Christian, faith is a critical part of life in God. Think of it this way—without faith, it's impossible to please God (Heb. 11:6). And all things are possible to him who believes (Mark 9:23). Enough proof?

Why, then, do so many of us quake in our loafers when it comes time to tell one of our family members that their behavior is totally unacceptable? Why do we turn into human roadkill rather than face the consequences of confrontational conversations? Because we feel inadequate ourselves. Feeling inadequate leads to a deprivation mentality. When you feel deprived of something, your actions are focused on getting and maintaining the substance you lack. If you're broke and fearful about finances, you tend to hoard what little cash you have. If you don't feel loved, you're prone to accept whatever crumbs of love you can get—regardless of how unauthentic they are.

Confronting an important person in your life carries with it risk—risk of anger, rejection, loss or retaliation. But as long as your fear is the driving

241

force behind your interactions, you'll have to settle for a cheap counterfeit of a real relationship.

ULTIMATE DECEPTION

I came within three weeks of marrying someone whom I suspected was an emotional cripple, but I didn't have the guts to confront him because I didn't want to give him up. He was tall, handsome, bright and popular—and I thought I'd finally hit the big time. There were concerns along the way; we seemed to be on two totally different paths. He wanted to live in a garret and write the great American novel, and I was the ultimate capitalist wanting to achieve fame and fortune in corporate America. I thought love would work it all out. What a doofus I was.

Three weeks before the wedding, with the bridesmaids' dresses hanging in the closet and the wedding gifts pouring in, the relationship began to unravel. I got a long letter from Mr. Wonderful telling me he'd been dishonest for the previous two years, only pretending to be in graduate school. He admitted he never graduated from college in the first place, which according to him was not a big deal since he only wanted to pursue writing.

To show you how unconscious I was, I'd attended the same college he did (he was two years ahead of me) and followed him to California to finish out my last two years while he went to graduate school. And I spent every weekend with him and his parents at their home. Hear no evil, see no evil, speak no evil—that was me!

His letter went on to say he hoped I'd forgive the deception and marry him anyway. Well, that was it! He had made me look stupid—an unforgivable sin at that point in my life. But the signs were there all along if I had chosen to look at them. Instead, I ignored my misgivings, hoping for a change of heart on his part.

Look what happened—I settled for a counterfeit relationship with someone who wasn't trustworthy because of my own fear of loss. Ultimately I had to face the truth of his duplicity and my cowardice; I had to accept loss anyway. Only this time, the loss included getting stuck with six seafoam green chiffon dresses in various sizes and spending two weeks returning silver compotes.

THE TRUTH, THE WHOLE TRUTH AND NOTHING BUT THE TRUTH

You learned in the last chapter what enabling is and what the symptoms (defensive mechanisms) are. Hopefully, you prayerfully made a list of the major underwear twisters in your life and asked the Lord to show you if and how you're compensating by not dealing with them. If you got that far, then you also know what your fears are regarding confrontation. That's a good place to be before taking the next step.

Remember, you're trying to stop falling into the pothole called enabling. Enabling comes from internal fear of inadequacy. Feeling "less than" means you're operating from a mind-set of lack. Yet the opposite of operating in a deficit mentality is operating in abundance. If you're a whole and complete individual because of your relationship with Jesus Christ, you don't need to settle for anything less that what the Lord has paid the price for you to have, part of which is strong relationships built on principle and mutual respect.

If you want relationships built on integrity, start by considering that conflict is neither good nor bad. Conflict is natural between any two people on the planet, and it's something neither to be avoided nor short-circuited. Now consider how you can confront without being judgmental. One of the keys is the use of the word *and* (instead of *but*).

Look at these sentences:

- I care about our relationship, *and* I feel strongly about this issue.
- I want to hear what you think, *and* I want to express my view clearly.
- I want to respect your opinions, *and* I want respect for mine.

The word *and* says that both views are valuable. Using the word *but* would negate the other person's point of view, as in this example: "I've listened to your arguments carefully, but I can't put myself in a position to accept them." See how much more reasonable the statement sounds if you read it substituting the word *and* for the word *but*.

CONFRONTING WITHOUT JUDGING

Concentrate your feedback on the behavior, not the person who practiced it. When you say, "When you yell at me and talk down to me, it hurts my feelings and makes me very angry," you're expressing criticism of the actions, not the person. This way your statement isn't a personal affront and allows leeway for the other person to change his behavior without feeling personal rejection.

Concentrate on your observations, not your suspicions. Forget what you think or imagine. Comment only on what you've seen or heard: "When you didn't show up for the PTA meeting as you promised and came home drunk later, I was very disappointed and let down." Consider the alternative: "I should have known you'd never show up at the PTA meeting. You never follow through on what you promise." The latter statement is guaranteed to evoke immediate defensiveness.

Use clear descriptions in your comments, not judgments. Don't waste your time describing the other person's behavior as wrong or nasty or rude. Those words are all laced with value judgments that will elicit a defensive barrage. Instead, try saying, "I'm aware that when I asked where you were, you didn't answer me. Could you tell me what your silence means?" It's hard to get in a tussle with that kind of clear-headed question.

Forget the name-calling. You'll never get anywhere calling the other person names like loudmouth, whiner, selfish, clinging or whatever. Sticking to nonemotional, clear descriptions of the offensive behavior and how it impacts *you* goes a long way toward opening the door to dialogue.

This just gives you a smattering of suggestions. Self-help books are full of ways to deal with dysfunctional members of your family and "friends" who take advantage of you. But bear in mind you can't fix them. You can only fix you.

If you'd like to permanently release yourself from the grip of the High Priestess, the ball's in your court. It's not easy, but living in fear isn't easy either.

WHAT TO DO

1. Study out and meditate on these scriptures that offer freedom from the fear of others: Psalm 56:11; Proverbs 29:25; Isaiah 51:7; Hebrews 13:6.

2. The sword of the Spirit spoken repeatedly will destroy the stronghold of fear when applied often. Speak these truths and put fear on the run: Deuteronomy 31:8; Psalm 23:4; 27:1; 34:4; 91:5; Proverbs 18:10; Isaiah 41:10; Matthew 28:20; 2 Thessalonians 3:3; 1 John 4:18; Revelation 21:7–8.

51

BOB DYLAN OR RICKY NELSON?

Which is it? Whose philosophy do you endorse? Bob Dylan's song "Gotta Serve Somebody" talks of the reality of serving yourself or serving a higher power—there is no in-between. Ricky Nelson's song "Garden Party," which he recorded in the latter part of his career, says that because you can't please everyone, you do what is necessary to please yourself. Nelson's philosophy seems to be the one embraced in this day and age, but does his philosophy bear fruit?

In John 15:4-5, Jesus says, "Dwell in Me, and I will dwell in you. [Live in Me, and I will live in you.] Just as no branch can bear fruit of itself without abiding in (being vitally united to) the vine, neither can you bear fruit unless you abide in Me. I am the Vine; you are the branches. Whoever lives in Me and I in him bears much (abundant) fruit. However, apart from Me [cut off from vital union with Me] you can do nothing" (AMP).

God is a straight shooter. He tells us not to plan on success without Him—it just won't happen. Serving yourself can only bring momentary pleasure. Replicating that pleasure takes bigger and bigger doses of self-indulgence, until you become a slave to the shopping mall, the refrigerator, the bottle, TV or relationships.

SUPERCHARGED LIVING

MRS. ASTOR

My friend Barbara finally got so desperate she thought she'd try an Alcoholics Anonymous meeting. She'd been on a bender for three weeks. She hadn't bathed, run a brush through her hair or taken off her makeup. She just kept piling on more layers of it. She was still drunk as she pondered what to wear to the meeting.

Convinced she was superior to the lowlifes she'd probably encounter there, she put on her full-length fur coat, fastened her hair on the top of her head with a clip and systematically put on every piece of jewelry in her fairly substantial collection. If Barbara had been sober, she would have known she looked like Halloween waiting to happen. Dressed in her finery, she swept into the AA meeting and sat down next to another woman.

The woman looked up, said hello, looked back down, looked up again and this time said, "Honey, even your *hair's* drunk!"

Barbara was appalled! How dare this woman, this commoner, make such a judgment about her. Besides, she certainly was *not* drunk! She'd had a few cocktails maybe, but she was not drunk. Of course, the woman next to her had about twenty years of sobriety behind her, so she knew a drunk when she saw one—drunk hair too, for that matter.

Barbara now laughs about her attire and attitude at that first meeting. What a pitiful attempt to say she was somebody, by piling on jewelry and mink—as if clothes could count for character. Barbara and I both wish it were that easy. The simple truth is that Barbara was bearing the fruit of choosing to serve herself. A lifetime of unresolved hurt had turned into resentment, fury and a blinding passion to escape through alcohol. She was out of control.

Her story reminds me of one of the first twelve-step meetings I attended. I'd been to enough meetings to feel safe in sharing some of my own experience. As I did, however, I made sure I shared my business background—as if they'd drum me out of the meeting if I didn't make the grade. It was my own pitiful attempt to say, "I am somebody."

Jesus said, "By their fruits ye shall know them" (Matt. 7:20). Neither Barbara nor I had much to speak of. We were walking signboards indicating we had chosen to serve ourselves.

246

DANGEROUS EXCEPTIONS

Most of us haven't developed the habit of accurate self-appraisal. It's a biblical truth that every time you're disturbed—no matter what the cause—there's something wrong with *you*. Even if someone hurts your feelings and you get mad, you're still at fault. "But that's not fair!" you say. "There must be some exceptions to that rule. What about justifiable anger? If someone humiliates me or steals from me, am I not entitled to go ballistic?" Nope.

If you make exceptions, resentments will take you hostage. Resentments turn into big hairy grudges, which spawn revenge, which triggers backlash—all of which make you miserable and ineffective. And the whole time that you're going through the stages of "justifiable anger," whom are you serving? I rest my case.

This stuff is insidious. Once I got all bent out of shape over seeing my ex-husband's picture in the newspaper with some sweet young thing and another couple I've been good friends with for years. It's not the ex-husband and the girl who's young enough to be his daughter that I minded seeing. (OK, just a little sarcasm). The problem was that they were obviously with the other couple at some big event. I suddenly began to feel rejected and abandoned by the other couple. Before long, I was tripping over my lower lip and feeling sorry for myself. I called my friend Barbara and said, "I've gotten my feelings hurt, and I'm starting to get obsessive; I know that's not good for anyone. Help me get my lower lip straightened out."

She said, "I know it hurts, but you're just finding out that as a newly divorced female, you're a disposable product. The perception is you can't do anything socially for anyone. But you know what? Those who really place importance on your social contribution aren't your real friends anyway. Besides, you never know what anyone else's motives really are; you're only responsible for yours." That's when she hit me with the kicker: "You need to examine your own agenda for the friendship and why you're currently upset." Ouch.

THE GREENER GRASS SYNDROME

I'm so grateful that the Lord doesn't think I'm a disposable product. He thinks I'm wonderful no matter what I do. He thinks the same of you. And He's not all eaten up worrying about whether He's seen at all the

247

big-ticket events. When I thought through my motives, I had to admit I'd taken offense over not being included in something that I used to attend all the time and never enjoyed in the first place. What kind of nuts is this? It's the classic by-product of the deception that my value is established by whom I know and what I do. It's also a by-product of my focusing on me instead of serving someone else. Bob Dylan could have read my mail.

You'd think I'd have gotten a clue by this time, but the High Priestess is ever ready to lead me away from the only thing that provides genuine inner peace—resting on the promises of God.

In all of life's valleys and mountaintop experiences we need restraint, an honest analysis of what's going on, the willingness to admit when we've screwed up and just as much willingness to forgive when someone else does. It takes practice, and you won't get it right overnight, but my favorite saying from twelve-step programs is, "We look for progress, not perfection." Whew—that means I don't have to be perfect!

I'm working on developing self-restraint. I know that when I respond out of my emotions instead of the Word, I'm quick to criticize and act rashly. That means my tolerance and ability to see things clearly evaporates. That is quickly followed by self-pity and sulking. These are all traps. They're baited by pride, and they produce splintered relationships and bad fruit.

THE NARROW GATE

In Matthew 7:12–13 Jesus says, "So then, whatever you desire that others would do to and for you, even so do also to and for them, for this is (sums up) the Law and the Prophets. Enter through the narrow gate; for wide is the gate and spacious and broad is the way that leads away to destruction, and many are those who are entering through it" (AMP). Jesus isn't talking about getting into heaven. The gate He's talking about is a way of life, the same way that's revealed in Deuteronomy 30:19 (blessings or cursings) and Jeremiah 21:8 (the way of life or the way of death). His hint: Choose life! That includes hearing and doing His sayings, which bear fruit.

The fruit of the Spirit is love, joy, peace, patience, kindness, goodness, meekness, faithfulness and self-control (Gal. 5:22–23). That's a pretty tidy list—one I'd like to walk in every day of my life. Notice that self-control is the caboose after all the others. I can't get there without first walking in love and all the others.

So here's what I've learned. Bearing fruit takes the following:

- Being willing to be led by God's Word, not my emotions
- Being willing to think through my motives
- Knowing that the opposite of self-pity is gratitude (as my friend Gillian keeps reminding me)
- Practicing forgiveness for others and myself

God wants you to know you are somebody. Not because of your business résumé, your wardrobe or whom you know, but because you're His child, a child of the King. He wants you to choose the path through the narrow gate so He can pour out His blessings on you. He wants you to choose life so you won't be deceived into worshiping false gods and get distracted from being His hands and feet on the earth. He wants you to serve Him with all your heart so you'll be filled with joy every day of your life. If that sounds good to you, read on.

WHAT TO DO

1. Read Isaiah 30:15–18. The solution to all your problems is found in Him.

2. Study Psalm 121. You'll see how God is your helper and keeper.

3. Look up Isaiah 61:6–8. You'll understand how God rewards and recompenses you.

4. Now write down Hebrews 11:6: "He is a rewarder of those who diligently seek him."

Make a decision each day to serve Him, not your flesh. You'll never regret it.

52

IS IT SOUP YET?

So you've gotten this far. You want to know what you've accomplished, if you've won, whether you've made any *real* progress. We Americans always want to know the score to see how we're doing. So here's the score:

If you've flipped around in this book, reading some of it, and now you're peeking at the last chapter to see what happens in the end, you're a curious thrill-seeker—not a real seeker. Give yourself a D.

If you read all the way through this book, but didn't do any of the steps, you've probably gotten some insight into your relationship with God and with others. If you're lucky, you'll remember about 10 percent of what you read, but your life won't change much for the better. Give yourself a C.

If you've read all this book and done some of the steps, you've experienced some change in your attitude and your relationship with the Lord. Congratulations on a good start. Give yourself a B. Now, go back and take your time re-reading the chapters and doing *all* the steps this time.

If you've read all the way through this book and done all the steps, you're already experiencing major change. You're being rewarded for the diligence of your efforts. You're also reaping the benefits of breaking out of your comfort zone because you're beginning to walk in the promises of God. Give yourself an A.

THE REAL GRADE

This book is merely a resource to provide structure for a closer walk with God. It only consists of stories, concepts and words on paper. Its purpose is to introduce you to a deeper understanding of how much God loves you and how abundantly He has provided for you. Some may read this book and scoff. That's OK. Don't take my word for what you've read here. Study it for yourself and ask God to reveal Himself to you through the steps. He's up for the challenge.

Don't expect instant change in the resolution of your problems or the manifestation of your dreams. One thing of which you can be confident, though, is that your problems will unravel and your dreams will be made manifest if you keep your relationship with Jesus on the front burner of your life. He's promised to show you the truth and change your heart if you hang out with Him. From that point on, it's the truth that you *know* and the truth that you *do* that will set you free.

This is truly a process without grades. Improvement (whether in your business or our personal life) involves having a strategy to exceed expectations and to increase output. Your walking with the Lord is the way of continuous improvement. It's not an event—it's a process.

Your relationship with your heavenly Father is strictly between you and Him. It's special, unique and based on your own study. How you proceed from this point will determine the quality of the victory in your life.

STATE-OF-THE-ART NAGGING

For best results, go back over this book again and again. Why? Because as human beings we leak. We forget things, fall into deceptions, interpret things incorrectly—and we need to get back on the path of truth to get our heads straightened out. After all, we live in a world that's much like the Mad Hatter's tea party, where fiction is represented as truth and truth is discounted as fiction. Constant reinforcement of the real facts of life helps stop the leaks.

Here are some reminders to help you reinforce what you've learned:

1. Don't ever forget that God is a loving God. He's not mad at you. He loves your socks off.

2. You can't outgive God. Whatever time you spend with Him will be multiplied back to you a hundredfold.

3. There's more to God than any of us have experienced. Don't be tempted to put restrictions on Him by thinking He can't perform beyond the parameters of what your mind can envision. If God isn't smarter than what your mind can dream up, we're all in trouble. Besides, if He couldn't perform beyond the capacity of the human mind, then we wouldn't need Him; we'd have all the answers ourselves. One look at the world around us is all the proof we need that we lack answers.

4. Retire the High Priestess of Guilt and Condemnation from her post in your head. You now have the tools to shut her up and build patterns that replicate success in every area of your life. When she comes calling with her continuous-loop recording of taunts, respond with the Word the way Jesus did, and you'll see her pack up her tent and leave.

5. You can only keep what you have by giving it away. What you've learned is what hurting people need to hear. Share the love of God with others. It doesn't matter how much or how little you know—if you have a day's study under your belt, that's a day more than many others around you have. As you give away what you've learned, you'll guarantee your possession of it in greater measure then you ever imagined.

Now, if you want a real lift, go back to the test you took at the beginning of this book and take it again. You'll get different answers. Progress comes at different speeds, but progress comes if you don't give up.

Remember—you're special. No one else has ever been created just exactly like you, and no one ever will be. You're God's unique workmanship, His individual snowflake to be used to bring hope and answers into a lost and dying world. Don't squander a minute listening to any voice—inside or outside your head—that doesn't line up with His love letter to you, His Word.

Now take this message and pass it on. You'll never be sorry.

NOTES

CHAPTER 18
A BACKWARD KINGDOM

1. John Avanzini, *30, 60, Hundredfold: Your Financial Harvest Released* (Tulsa, OK: Harrison House, 1971), 9, 23, 35, 45, 53, 69, 81, 93, 105, 117, 125, 135, 147, 157, 169.

CHAPTER 25
WHAT, ME WORRY?

1. This section on the five strategies of fear is taken from "The Five Lying Personalities" by John Avanzini. Used by permission.

CHAPTER 35
ROOM TEMPERATURE IQ

1. *Harvard Business Review,* November/December, 1998, "What Makes A Leader?" by Daniel Goleman, p. 9-102.

CHAPTER 42
SHARKPROOF

1. Paul Budker, *The Life of Sharks* (New York: Columbia University Press, 1971), 109.